AF791617

0 8 MAR 2023

Nottingham Trent University
BOOTS LIBRARY
www.ntu.ac.uk/llr

Enquiries: 0115 848 2175

50 0056414 3

Palgrave Studies in Risk, Crime and Society

Series Editors
Kieran McCartan
Department of Criminology
University of the West of England
Bristol, UK

Beth Weaver
School of Social Work and Social Policy
University of Strathclyde
Glasgow, Lanarkshire, UK

Risk is a major contemporary issue which has widespread implications for theory, policy, governance, public protection, professional practice and societal understandings of crime and criminal justice. The potential harm associated with risk can lead to uncertainty, fear and conflict as well as disproportionate, ineffective and ill-judged state responses to perceived risk and risky groups. Risk, Crime and Society is a series featuring monographs and edited collections which examine the notion of risk, the risky behaviour of individuals and groups, as well as state responses to risk and its consequences in contemporary society. The series will include critical examinations of the notion of risk and the problematic nature of state responses to perceived risk. While Risk, Crime and Society will consider the problems associated with 'mainstream' risky groups including sex offenders, terrorists and white collar criminals, it welcomes scholarly analysis which broadens our understanding of how risk is defined, interpreted and managed. Risk, Crime and Society examines risk in contemporary society through the multi-disciplinary perspectives of law, criminology and socio-legal studies and will feature work that is theoretical as well as empirical in nature.

More information about this series at
http://www.palgrave.com/gp/series/14593

Kasia Uzieblo • Wineke J. Smid
Kieran McCartan
Editors

Challenges in the Management of People Convicted of a Sexual Offence

A Way Forward

palgrave
macmillan

Editors
Kasia Uzieblo
Van der Hoeven Kliniek
Utrecht, The Netherlands

Free University of Brussels
Brussels, Belgium

Kieran McCartan
Department of Criminology
University of the West of England
Bristol, UK

Wineke J. Smid
The Forensic Care Specialists
Utrecht, The Netherlands

Palgrave Studies in Risk, Crime and Society
ISBN 978-3-030-80211-0 ISBN 978-3-030-80212-7 (eBook)
https://doi.org/10.1007/978-3-030-80212-7

© The Editor(s) (if applicable) and The Author(s), under exclusive licence to Springer Nature Switzerland AG 2022
This work is subject to copyright. All rights are solely and exclusively licensed by the Publisher, whether the whole or part of the material is concerned, specifically the rights of translation, reprinting, reuse of illustrations, recitation, broadcasting, reproduction on microfilms or in any other physical way, and transmission or information storage and retrieval, electronic adaptation, computer software, or by similar or dissimilar methodology now known or hereafter developed.
The use of general descriptive names, registered names, trademarks, service marks, etc. in this publication does not imply, even in the absence of a specific statement, that such names are exempt from the relevant protective laws and regulations and therefore free for general use.
The publisher, the authors and the editors are safe to assume that the advice and information in this book are believed to be true and accurate at the date of publication. Neither the publisher nor the authors or the editors give a warranty, expressed or implied, with respect to the material contained herein or for any errors or omissions that may have been made. The publisher remains neutral with regard to jurisdictional claims in published maps and institutional affiliations.

Cover illustration: Graphic designer Rik Staesens from RikGrafiek

This Palgrave Macmillan imprint is published by the registered company Springer Nature Switzerland AG.
The registered company address is: Gewerbestrasse 11, 6330 Cham, Switzerland

Dedicated to our children.
Let us meet the challenges now so that future generations can reap the benefits.

Preface

The core of understanding how we effectively prevent and respond to sexual abuse is communication. Communication is the lynchpin that holds together effective risk management and allows individuals, communities, and professionals to work together. But communication is not easy, and it has many challenges. This edited collection started life as a product of communication and conversation, and will hopefully promote the continuation of it.

This edited collection started life as a conversation as part of the planning and development of the "At the Crossroads (ATC) 2.0: Future directions in sex offender treatment and assessment" conference in Belgium in 2020. The conference, with a first edition that took place in 2016 (see, Uzieblo et al., 2016), was organised by the Dutch/Flemish Association of the International Association for the Treatment of Sexual Abusers (NL-ATSA), the University Forensic Centre (UFC, Antwerp, Belgium), and the University of Antwerp (Belgium) and took place on 4 and 5 February 2020 in Antwerp, just before the world got hit by the COVID-19 pandemic, and, thus, this was for many the last offline conference for a long time. From the observation that still too little research finds its way into practice, the ATC-conferences focus mainly on the question of how scientific findings on topics of primary concern to practitioners and academics can be translated into practice. During the ATC 2.0 conference,

17 internationally renowned speakers made this translation exercise for more than 270 practitioners from the criminal justice and mental health sector, policy officers, and researchers. No fewer than nine different countries were represented: Belgium, Canada, Germany, Iceland, the Netherlands, Slovenia, Spain, the United Kingdom, and the United States. The lectures mainly dealt with the underlying mechanisms of sexual violence, specific sexual violent behaviours, and the management of people who have committed sexual offences (for a longer account of the conference, see De Boeck & Uzieblo, 2020).

The conference taught us, more than anything about sexual offending, that communication is key; whether it is about communication between professionals, the public, politicians, and/or the media does not matter, it is more the fact that we were talking about the reality of sexual abuse that matters. After the conference, we were left with the question of how do we continue the conversation and communicate the insights that we developed in Antwerp. The answer, an edited collection!

In developing this edited collection, we revisited the conference content and speakers, thinking about what important debates and challenges in the field of sexual abuse are. The aim of this book was not to merely copy the conference content but rather to expand upon and develop it. The idea was to give a rounded review of the field of sexual abuse and the challenges that exist within for professionals; therefore, we needed to make sure that the content of the book reflected these and took a deep dive into the full breath of the conference content including keynotes, workshops, poster presentations, and conversations that arose during networking events. Therefore, decisions about the selection of content for the book was based upon significant and emerging issues in the field of sexual abuse discussed at the conference. The book is rooted in the considerations, concerns, debates, and challenges that frontline staff and academics face in respect to preventing as well as responding to sexual abuse. This reflection of the lived experience of working in the field of sexual abuse gained from the conference gives the book a contemporize flavour, and has allowed new topics and topics that have been occupying the field for some time to be included. As the conference content was in the main based around adult males who committed sexual abuse, this too means that the edited collection will be so focused, not because we believe that this is the only group of sexual abuse perpetrators that matter but rather because this is the largest group of people who commit sexual abuse, and, consequently, this is the group most research, treatment, and rehabilitation fields focus on. This begs the question of how we continue the conversation started in this edited collection with other sexually offending demographics.

One of the major strengths of the conference, and therefore this edited collection, is that all authors included are drawn from an international base (with countries including Belgium, Canada, Germany, Italy, the Netherlands, the United Kingdom, the United States, to name a few) and a range of disciplines (e.g., psychology and criminology), and they span a range of professions (e.g., academic, criminal justice, mental health, and the third sector), all of which highlights that sexual abuse is an international issue that must be tackled interdisciplinary on the primary, secondary, tertiary, and quaternary levels. This book highlights that there are more aspects of sexual abuse that are similar internationally than are different, which means that we need to look to each more often to check our poor practice as well as share our good practice. We are all having the same conversation, albeit at different stages and in different ways, and therefore we need to collaborate so that we can share good practice and go forward in unison. We wanted as much material from the conference to be in the book as possible; therefore, we needed the chapters to be structured, concise, and accessible. Each author was given the same remit in writing their chapters, to consider the main issues and evidence base in their topic area currently, what the main challenges are over the next five years and how the field might move towards resolving them. Hopefully, what you see in this edited collection is a detailed snapshot of various important issues and debates that professionals across the field of sexual abuse are facing and consideration on how to best respond to them.

The way that this edited collection is constructed leads the reader through the following important areas that form the basis of many professional and practical conversations about sexual abuse:

(1) The first section *on sexual offending behaviours* has five chapters that cover the aetiology and/or characteristics of behaviours involved in sexually offending across a range of topics and subgroups, including

grooming behaviours (Winters, Spriggs, and Jeglic), *sexual fantasies* (Bartels), *sexual homicide* (Beauregard), and *sibling sexual abuse* (Yates and Allardyce).

(2) The second section on *assessment of people who have committed a sexual offence* has chapters on the *indirect measurement of sexual interests* (Schmidt and Banse), on working with *individuals who have accessed Child Sexual Exploitation Material* (Merdian and Perkins), *risk assessment* (Uzieblo, de Beuf, De Boeck, and Smid), and *case formulation* (Craig and Rettenberger).

(3) The third section on *treatment of people exhibiting deviant sexual interests and/or behaviours* includes five chapters which focus on *sexual self-regulation problems* (Smid), *Risk Need Responsivity* (Jung), *rehabilitative prison climates* (Blagden), facilitating *help-seeking behaviour in minor-attracted persons* (Uzieblo and De Boeck), and *how to thrive in treatment as a professional* (Clarke).

(4) The penultimate section of the book focuses on *community engagement and integration of people exhibiting deviant sexual interests and/or behaviours*; in this section, there are three chapters which include one on *Circles Europe* (McCartan, Höing, and Taylor), one on *desistance narratives* (de Kruijff and Blokland), and *Stop it now!* (De Boeck, Coleman, Van Dijk, and Findlater).

(5) The final section focuses on *future directions for the field of sexual abuse*, mainly addressing the need for *international professional, collaboration, and networking* (Keulen-de Vos, Uzieblo, De Boeck, Brown, and Xella) and resolving *the challenges of coordinating evidence, policy, and practice* (McCartan).

The book highlights and expands upon existing debates offering new insights (e.g., Risk Need Responsivity, grooming, desistance, and risk assessment) as well as brings new debates into the conversation (e.g., sexual fantasies, sibling sexual abuse, and help-seeking behaviour), therefore indicating the current state of the field and asking us what direction next from the crossroads?

In closing, the core of this text, as well as the conference that it is based on, is about communication, debate, and sharing insights. We heard the voice of attendees and produced a fit for purpose collection that addressed their needs and concerns, an edited collection to aid frontline policy and practice. Sexual abuse is a personal, community, national, and international issue, and the only way that we can look to respond to it and prevent it in the future is through having frank conversations about it and facing new as well as existing challenges head on. Thus, let us not remain at this crossroads, but let us embrace the numerous valuable insights and get to work with them.

Utrecht, Netherlands — Kasia Uzieblo
Brussels, Belgium — Wineke J. Smid
Bristol, UK — Kieran McCartan
09/03/2021

References

De Boeck, M., & Uzieblo, K. (2020). At the crossroads 2.0: recente ontwikkelingen in de behandeling van seksuele delinquenten. Een congresverslag. *Tijdschrift Klinische Psychologie, 50*(3), 212–221. https://vvkp.be/crossroads-20-recente-ontwikkelingen-de-behandeling-van-seksuele-delinquenten

Uzieblo, K., Vertommen, T., De Boeck, M., Lemlijn, L., Smid, W., & Goethals, K. (2016). Quo vadis? Een verkenning van recente ontwikkelingen in de behandeling van zedendelinquenten. *Tijdschrift Klinische Psychologie, 46*(4), 263–270. https://vvkp.be/quo-vadis-een-verkenning-van-recente-ontwikkelingen-de-behandeling-van-zedendelinquenten

Acknowledgements

The editors would like to thank NL-ATSA and the University Forensic Centre (UFC) for their support and contribution.

Contents

Notes on Contributors

Stuart Allardyce is a director of the UK Child Protection Charity, the Lucy Faithfull Foundation. He has worked for 20 years in the child sexual abuse prevention field, and is the co-author of 'Working With Children and Young People Who Have Displayed Harmful Sexual Behaviour' (Dunedin Press, 2018).

Rainer Banse is Professor of Social and Legal Psychology at the University of Bonn. His main research interest lies in indirect measures in psychology. In legal psychology, the focus of his work is on offender rehabilitation, the quality of legal psychology expert opinions, and the diagnosis and aetiology of paedophilia.

Ross M. Bartels, PhD is a senior lecturer in Forensic Psychology at the University of Lincoln, UK, where he leads the 'Forensic and Clinical Research Group'. His research and published work focus on understanding atypical sexual interests, fantasies, and cognitions. He has also co-edited two books on sexual deviance.

Eric Beauregard is a professor in the School of Criminology at Simon Fraser University. Dr Beauregard has published over 100 peer-reviewed journal articles on the topic of sexual violence, more specifically on sexual homicide, the crime-commission process, decision-making, and the criminal investigation.

Nicholas Blagden is Associate Professor in Forensic Psychology at Nottingham Trent University, where he is the head of the Sexual Offences, Crime and Misconduct Research Unit (SOCAMRU). He is a co-founder and trustee of the Safer Living Foundation and a Chartered Psychologist.

Arjan Blokland is senior-researcher at the NSCR, Amsterdam, professor of Criminology and Criminal Justice, Leiden University, and Obel visiting professor at Aalborg University, Denmark. His research interests include criminal careers, life-course criminology, sexual offending, and criminal networks.

Sarah Brown is the chair of NOTA, a fellow of ATSA, a forensic psychologist, a chartered psychologist, and associate fellow of the British Psychological Society. She has conducted research into sexual violence for over 25 years, and is an adjunct professor at USC, Australia, and visiting fellow at UWE, UK.

Joanna Clarke is Director of Petros Ltd. She has a 23-year career in criminal justice, initially working with those convicted of sexual offences; her interest then focused on how to enable staff undertaking this work to thrive. She is a sought-after trainer, consultant, and public speaker, both nationally and internationally.

Jenny Coleman, MA, LMHC joined Stop It Now! as their helpline director in 2011, and now serves as Now!'s Director, overseeing a national child sexual abuse prevention programme. She has written on Stop it Now!, Title IX, Abuse in Faith-Based Institutions, and other prevention topics.

Leam A. Craig, PhD is a consultant clinical and forensic psychologist, and partner at Forensic Psychology Practice Ltd. He works as an expert witness in the civil and criminal courts. He is affiliated to the University of Lincoln, Birmingham City University, and University of Birmingham. He has over 120 publications.

Tamara De Beuf, MSc is a PhD student at the Faculty of Psychology and Neuroscience of Maastricht University. Her research focuses on the evaluation of adolescent risk assessment. As project coordinator within a

Dutch youth care service, she leads a risk assessment implementation and monitoring project.

Minne De Boeck, MSc works as a criminologist at the University Forensic Centre, an outpatient treatment centre for patients with paraphilia and/or sex offenders. She also coordinates Stop it Now! Flanders and is the current president of the Dutch chapter of the Association for the Treatment of Sexual Abusers.

Lucile de Kruijff studied Victimology (Tilburg University), and was a junior-researcher at the NSCR, Amsterdam. She specializes in qualitative research on forensic populations, including survivors of domestic violence, people convicted of sexual or capital offenses. At present, she works as coordinator judicial support Program Human Trafficking, Red Cross, the Hague.

Donald Findlater set up the Wolvercote Clinic, a residential programme for men with allegations of or convictions for sexual offences against children. He is the founder and current director of Stop It Now! UK and Ireland as well as founder of CoSA UK and Ireland.

Mechtild Höing, PhD is a senior researcher at the Avans Center of Public Safety and Criminal Justice. She has been involved in the development and evaluation of COSA projects in the Netherlands and other European Countries, and has (co-)authored a series of research papers, articles, and book chapters on COSA.

Elizabeth L. Jeglic, PhD is a professor of Psychology at the John Jay College of Criminal Justice in New York. Her research focuses on sexual violence prevention and evidence-based public policy.

Sandy Jung, PhD, RPsych is a professor of Psychology at MacEwan University in Edmonton, Canada, and a forensic psychologist who practises in the province of Alberta. Her area of expertise focuses on the risk assessment, treatment, and management of individuals who have committed sexual violence, intimate partner violence, and homicide.

Kieran McCartan (University of the West of England, Bristol) researches sexual offending, risk management, trauma informed practice, and developmental criminology. He is an executive board member of ATSA and NOTA, the chair of the Confederation of European Probation working group on sexual offenses, and advises the Council of Europe.

Hannah L. Merdian, PhD She is Associate Professor, School of Psychology, University of Lincoln, UK. She is Co-Director of the online-PROTECT research group and a founding member of the International Working Group for the Prevention of Online Sex Offending (IWG_OSO). Previously, she was a board member of IATSO.

Derek E. Perkins, PhD He is Professor of Forensic Psychology, School of Law, Royal Holloway University of London. He is a chartered clinical and forensic psychologist and co-director of the onlineProtect research group. He was chief psychologist at Broadmoor Hospital, previously working in the UK Prison Service and Midland Centre for Forensic Psychiatry.

Martin Rettenberger is the director of the Centre for Criminology in Wiesbaden, and is Professor at the Department of Psychology at the Johannes Gutenberg University of Mainz, Germany. He is the secretary general of the International Association for the Treatment of Sexual Offenders and editor-in-chief of the IATSO open access e-journal.

Alexander F. Schmidt is Senior Lecturer in Social and Legal Psychology at the Johannes Gutenberg University of Mainz. His main research focus is the link between paraphilic interests and sexual offending utilizing indirect measures. He is also working on offender rehabilitation, the stigmatization of paraphilias, and legal psychological expert assessments.

Wineke J. Smid is Head of the Research Department at Forensic Care Specialists in Utrecht, Netherlands. She conducts empirical research (e.g., the etiology of sexual deviance), carries out individual (risk) assessments of residential high-risk sex offenders, and is European master trainer for the risk assessment instruments Static-99R, Stable-2007, and Acute-2007.

Sharron Spriggs is a clinical psychology PhD student at Fairleigh Dickinson University. Her research interests focus on the impact of viewing police brutality videos on social media.

Riana Taylor held senior roles in criminal justice and worked in South Africa, the UK, China, and Vietnam. She became Circles UK's CEO in 2016. She finds tremendous fulfilment in this role as she believes that people can change, and has a deep commitment to social inclusion and restorative work.

Kasia Uzieblo, PhD is a senior researcher at the Research Department at Forensic Care Specialists in Utrecht, the Netherlands, and is Associate Professor at the Department of Criminology of the Free University Brussels, Belgium. Her main research interests are psychopathy, sexual/family violence, and forensic psychological assessment, including risk assessment.

Jill van Dijk, Msc operated the Dutch Stop it Now! helpline, provided workshops and lectures, and co-developed various information material to stop (online) sexual child abuse. She currently works as a psychologist at the Waag, a centre for outpatient forensic psychiatry, providing treatment for clients that exhibit sexually transgressive and/or criminal behaviour.

Marije Keulen-de Vos, PhD is a senior researcher at Forensic Psychiatric Center de Rooyse Wissel in Venray, and the Radboud University Nijmegen, the Netherlands. Her research interests are sexual violence, emotional states, intellectual disabilities, and forensic treatment.

Georgia M. Winters, PhD is an Assistant Professor and deputy director of the Forensic Psychology master's programme at Fairleigh Dickinson University. Her research interests include sexual grooming behaviours, paraphilic interests and disorders, and sexual violence prevention.

Carla Maria Xella (CIPM-Lazio) is a psychotherapist, the president of CoNTRAS-Ti Scientific Committee, and a member of the ATSA Adult Clinical and International Committees and of the CIFAS Permanent Organizing Committee. She is the author of several books and articles and acts as a consultant.

Peter Yates is Programme Lead for Social Work at Edinburgh Napier University. He has undertaken commissioned work on sibling sexual abuse for the Scottish Government and the Centre of Expertise on Child Sexual Abuse. He co-authored the book *Working with children and young people who have displayed harmful sexual behaviour*.

List of Figures

List of Tables

Part I

Sexual Offending Behaviours

1

The Complexities of Understanding Sexual Grooming Behaviours

Georgia M. Winters, Sharron Spriggs, and Elizabeth L. Jeglic

Sexual grooming involves a multitude of tactics and strategies used by persons who seek to commit a sexual offense against a minor to prepare the child for the impending abuse and prevent detection (van Dam, 2001; Winters, & Jeglic, 2017; Wyre, 2000). Despite sexual grooming being used by a large portion of perpetrators in child sexual abuse (CSA) cases (Canter et al., 1998; Groth & Birnbaum, 1978), there remains a

We have no known conflict of interest to disclose.

G. M. Winters (✉) • S. Spriggs
Fairleigh Dickinson University, Teaneck, NJ, USA

E. L. Jeglic
John Jay College of Criminal Justice, New York, NY, USA

© The Author(s), under exclusive license to Springer Nature Switzerland AG 2022

K. Uzieblo et al. (eds.), *Challenges in the Management of People Convicted of a Sexual Offence*, Palgrave Studies in Risk, Crime and Society,
https://doi.org/10.1007/978-3-030-80212-7_1

dearth of empirical literature and universal consensus in the field about what constitutes sexual grooming. To highlight this issue, the present chapter will provide an overview of the sexual grooming literature, and then identify the challenges to understanding sexual grooming and recommended future directions in the field. It should be noted that sexual grooming may not be limited to in-person contact, as some people with sex offense histories may engage in online grooming (Kloess et al., 2019); however, the present chapter will focus on in-person grooming behaviours as it has been suggested that online grooming may differ in significant ways (Davidson & Gottschalk, 2011). While it is important to investigate the impact of online sexual grooming as it has increased tremendously (Kloess et al., 2014), online grooming is beyond the scope of the present chapter.

Overview of Sexual Grooming

In the past several decades, the term 'sexual grooming' has become strongly associated with CSA (McAlinden, 2013), particularly following highly publicized cases such as that of Pennsylvania State University football coach Jerry Sandusky and the Catholic Church CSA scandal. Indeed, research suggests that sexual grooming is utilized in approximately one-third to one-half of CSA cases (Canter et al., 1998; Groth & Birnbaum, 1978; Spraitz et al., 2018; Tallon & Terry, 2008). Grooming behaviours are considered to be a deliberate process that is complex and nuanced (McAlinden, 2013). These deceptive behaviours are intended to develop initial trust with the victim, decrease the likelihood of disclosure or discovery, and facilitate future sexual contact (Lanning & Dietz, 2014).

One of the complexities of identifying and assessing sexual grooming behaviours is the fact that these acts may differ based on the person seeking to commit the offense, the targeted victim, and the context in which the sexual grooming occurs. Differences in sexual grooming may be due to the age or gender of the adult and victim (e.g., Kaufman et al., 2006). Moreover, numerous contextual factors might impact the type and frequency of sexual grooming behaviours, including the 'effectiveness' of the tactics, the fear of disclosure, the relationship between the adult and child, and cultural factors (e.g., socio-economic status, religious beliefs, and practices). Also, there is variability in the time used to sexually groom a victim; the in-person sexual grooming process can take place over a short time (i.e., days or weeks), but may also occur over a long period (i.e., years; Craven et al., 2007; McAlinden, 2006). Lastly, research shows that individuals who sexually abuse children may not just groom their potential victim, but often themselves (i.e., "personal grooming" including justification, minimization, and denial of their behaviours; Craven et al., 2006; McAlinden, 2006) or other people (i.e., familial and institutional/community grooming; McAlinden, 2006; van Dam, 2001).

Sexual Grooming Behaviours

Broadly speaking, sexual grooming behaviours are utilized by an individual to select a vulnerable child. Then, they seek to develop trust, gain access, and isolate the child from others, which ultimately leads to desensitizing the child to sexual advances (Winters et al., 2020). Following the initial abuse, the individual may continue to sexually groom the child to prevent disclosure and/or facilitate future abuse of the child. Potential behaviours identified in the literature that may be utilized throughout the process are outlined below.

People who sexually groom children typically select a vulnerable victim as the initial step in the sexual grooming process (Harms & van Dam, 1992; Lanning, 2010), or may target numerous children to identify those who may be most susceptible to these manipulative tactics. Evidence suggests that a vulnerable child may be identified based on physical characteristics (e.g., a child who is perceived as young or small; Conte et al., 1989; Elliott et al., 1995), or emotionally or psychologically vulnerable (e.g., the child who is perceived as trusting, lacking self-esteem, isolative, neglected, troubled, or in need of affection; Elliott et al., 1995; Kaufman et al., 2006). Additionally, a person may look to the child's family circumstances (e.g., single-parent home, a lack of parental supervision, parental discord, and mental health/substance use issues; Craven et al., 2006; Jackson et al., 2015; Kaufman et al., 2006).

Once a vulnerable victim is identified, behaviours and/or tactics are used to gain access and isolate the targeted child from others (Craven et al., 2006; Lanning, 2010; Leclerc et al., 2005; Olson et al., 2007; Winters & Jeglic, 2017). This could include gaining access by manipulating family members, working in a child-serving organization, or providing the child with voided emotional needs. The adult seeking to commit a sexual offense will then work to isolate the child physically and emotionally from their family and peers (Craven et al., 2006).

After gaining access and isolating the targeted child, the person engaging in grooming behaviours may seek to develop trust and cooperation with the child (Craven et al., 2006; Leclerc et al., 2005; Olson et al., 2007). People who sexually abuse children may present as pleasant and charming, which may be part of their tactics to eventually earn 'insider' status within the community (Lanning & Dietz, 2014). They will likely aim to develop a close relationship with the child through making the child feel loved, using bribes or inducements, exploiting his/her vulnerabilities, engaging in peer-like activities, befriending them, or providing them with drugs or alcohol (Bennett & O'Donohue, 2014; Berliner & Conte, 1990; Harms & van Dam, 1992; Leclerc et al., 2005).

Once a trusting relationship is developed, the individual often begins to gradually introduce sexual conversation and physical touch to desensitize the child to the impending sexual abuse (Berliner & Conte, 1990; Harms & van Dam, 1992; McAlinden, 2006; Olson et al., 2007). The perpetrators may tell inappropriate jokes related to sex, provide sexual education, show child sexual exploitation material (CSEM), or engage in other sexual conversations. Physical contact may be gradually escalated, such as hugging, kissing, or touching the child excessively or inappropriately (McAlinden, 2006; Olson et al., 2007; Wyre, 2000).

To be able to continue the abuse and prevent detection, those who engage in sexual grooming may use maintenance behaviours, including encouraging the child to maintain secrets about the abuse (Craven et al., 2006; Harms & van Dam, 1992), stating that the sexually abusive behaviour is acceptable (Jackson et al., 2015), misrepresenting standards for appropriate touching (Bennett & O'Donohue, 2014), making the child feel responsible for the abuse (Harms & van Dam, 1992), or using threats (Bennett & O'Donohue, 2014).

Global Research on Sexual Grooming

The majority of the sexual grooming literature has come out of the United Kingdom (e.g., Craven et al., 2006; McAlinden, 2006) and the United States (e.g., Elliott, 2017; Winters & Jeglic, 2017) and, thus, relatively little is known about how sexual grooming behaviours may be manifested cross-culturally in other parts of the world. There is evidence that CSA rates and methods vary globally. Assessment of the prevalence of CSA varies widely over the globe between 14 and 50 percent of all children experiencing sexual abuse (Carson et al., 2013; Collings, 1997; Ji et al., 2013; Madu, 2001). None of these studies from other countries have examined sexual grooming, and a recent review highlighted differences in methodology and cross-cultural issues in disclosure as limiting factors in international CSA research (Barth et al., 2013). As social and cultural issues vary by region, it is imperative to: (a) assess sexual grooming rates internationally and by region, (b) identify whether there are cultural and racial/ethnic differences in the behaviours and tactics employed by those who engage in sexual grooming in different parts of the world, and (c) work globally to use this information to engage in prevention initiatives.

Challenges to Understanding Sexual Grooming

While there has been a rise in attention to grooming in recent decades (Winters & Jeglic, 2017), much of this literature has focused on examining the phenomenon of online sexual grooming. Previous literature on in-person sexual grooming typically includes theoretical reviews (e.g., Bennett & O'Donohue, 2014; Craven et al., 2006). There are very few empirical studies of in-person sexual grooming, including research on persons who committed CSA (e.g., Conte et al., 1989; Elliott et al., 1995) and victims of CSA (e.g., Berliner & Conte, 1990). Moreover, of the studies that have been conducted, most were conducted in the 1980s and 1990s, with more recent literature being more theoretical. The lack of *recent* empirical research on in-person sexual grooming is troubling and may be attributable to the inherent difficulties in studying this subject, including the following: (1) sexual grooming behaviours are not unlike normal adult/child interactions, (2) there is no universal definition of sexual grooming, and (3) there is a lack of consensus on the stages involved in the process.

The Behaviours Are Not Unlike Normal Adult/ Child Interactions

Howitt (1995) described the grooming process by indicating it "is in some way analogous to adult courtship" (p. 176), although inadequately (and illegally) directed at children. Additionally, the individual sexual grooming behaviours often mirror normal adult/child interactions, although the underlying intention is deviant. Thus, it is unlikely that law enforcement would detect sexual grooming behaviours before the commission of sexual abuse, especially in intrafamilial and institutional cases (Gillespie, 2002). Indeed, recognizing sexual grooming behaviours following the disclosure of the sexual offense is likely much easier than prospective identification (Craven et al., 2006). Empirical research has supported this notion, finding that there is a hindsight bias associated with the sexual grooming of children, in which individuals tend to overestimate the likelihood that they could have predicted these behaviours were taking place after they learn an individual has committed a sexual offense (Winters & Jeglic, 2016). In a follow-up study, Winters and Jeglic (2017) found that individuals in the sample were unable to recognize sexual grooming behaviours, as would be expected given the seemingly innocent appearance of such acts. Ultimately, the inability to effectively differentiate sexual grooming behaviours versus normal adult/child interactions poses a significant barrier to understanding and researching the topic.

There Are Multiple Definitions of Sexual Grooming

There has yet to be a consensus on how to define sexual grooming. In fact, in the literature, there have been over 13 proposed definitions (Winters et al., 2020). These definitions vary in terms of the language used to describe the process and specific behaviours that are indicative of grooming. Some notable limitations of prior definitions include the following: identifying a narrow category of adults who may engage in grooming (e.g., "paedophile"; Howitt, 1995) or type of victim (e.g., "boy"; Spiegel, 2003); including specific behaviours rather than describing the general process (e.g., showing affection, using inducements, and befriending the child; Gillespie, 2002; Salter, 1995); and omitting the steps of the process addressing victim selection and post-abuse maintenance behaviours, as this has been indicated in the literature to be an important aspect of grooming (e.g., Brakenridge, 2001; Craven et al., 2006; Sheldon & Howitt, 2007). McAlinden (2013) argued that "grooming" is a term that deserves a place in the lexicon of CSA but strongly cautioned against the term becoming a "catch-all" category that undermines the complex nature of sexual grooming. Ultimately, with so many proposed definitions, it reflects a lack of agreement across various fields regarding the construct.

There Are Numerous Proposed Models of Sexual Grooming

Similar to the lack of a universal definition of grooming, there has been a lack of consensus on what steps or stages are involved in the process. There have been at least 17 prior models of sexual grooming that have been proposed (see Winters et al., 2020). While there is overlap in themes and behaviours among these models, they lack unanimity in terms of defining specific stages, behaviours, and outcomes of the sexual grooming process. Despite these numerous prior attempts, none of the published models had been empirically validated, until recently.

To address some of the limitations of previous models, Winters and Jeglic (2017) reviewed the extant grooming literature and developed a model of sexual grooming comprised of behaviours that could be observable to others and measurable. This five-stage model, called the Sexual Grooming Model (SGM), drew upon the commonalities identified in several of the previously proposed models, as well as identified gaps of information. Winters and Jeglic's (2017) model of grooming behaviour proposes five overarching stages including (1) selecting a vulnerable victim, (2) gaining access and isolating/creating alone time with the victim, (3) developing trust with the child and others (e.g., caretakers and community members), (4) desensitizing the child to sexual content and physical touch, and (5) maintenance behaviours following the commission of the abuse (Fig. 1.1). Winters et al. (2020) were the first to subsequently establish content validity for the SGM of adult males who seek to commit a sexual offense against a child. First, a thorough review of the literature was conducted to identify a comprehensive list of sexual grooming behaviours (n = 77). Second, 18 experts in the field (i.e., individuals who had published literature on sexual grooming or had clinical expertise with this population) completed a survey which asked them to rate the extent to which each of the five stages and potential sexual grooming behaviours was relevant to the process. Results provided support for the SGM and produced 42 behaviours that were considered to be sexual grooming tactics within these stages. The behaviours included tactics used in the five

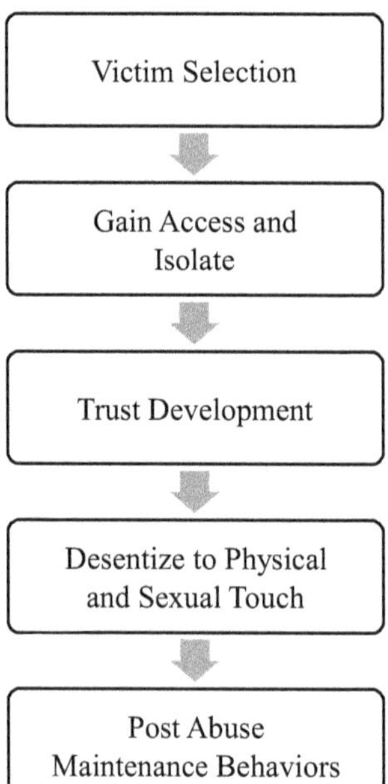

Fig. 1.1 Stages of the sexual grooming model

stages of victim selection (e.g., selecting children who are compliant and trusting of adults, or considered 'needy'), gaining access and isolation (e.g., involvement in youth-serving organizations and taking the child on overnight outings), trust development (e.g., gaining 'insider' status, engaging in childlike activities, and showing the child favouritism), desensitization to physical content and contact (e.g., asking questions about the child's sexual experience and relationships and gradually increasingly physical contact), and post-abuse maintenance (e.g., telling the child not to tell what happened and encouraging secrets). As elaborated on below, while this advancement has significant immediate implications for the field, there remains much research to be done to further validate this model.

Future Directions

In light of the aforementioned limitations of the field of sexual grooming, there are numerous future directions for research and important implications for the topic as it relates to clinical evaluation and treatment, investigation and prosecution of CSA cases, primary prevention, and policy.

Research

As noted above, recently, Winters et al. (2020) established content validity for the SGM—a step towards better understanding the construct of sexual grooming. This model has the potential to shed light on many of the aforementioned challenges, including facilitating the creation of an empirically informed definition, providing support for the stages and behaviours involved in the process, allowing for the investigation of differences between normal adult/child interactions and grooming, and establishing updated prevalence rates. The next step is to further examine the proposed conceptualization, through rigorous examination to ensure the stages accurately represent the complex process of sexual grooming. This can be accomplished by applying the model to actual cases of CSA, such as victim's experiences of the grooming process or reports of these pre-offense behaviours as documented in official CSA records (e.g., court documents and police records). For example, this research could shed light on how children understand grooming, observable warning signs, and beneficial interventions. One strategy that would help validate the model is to develop a standardized assessment measure. The measure should be created to gather information about an individual's offense process regarding sexually grooming their victim for the abuse. The development and validation of a standardized measure of the sexual grooming process is a necessary future direction in the literature given that a reliable and valid measure would allow researchers *and* clinicians a means of quantifying these behaviours. Of note, additional research could be conducted to establish models of grooming in other populations, such as females and juveniles who have groomed child victims, as there is a dearth of literature on these topics.

Clinical Evaluation and Treatment

Importantly, while there is much research to be conducted on in-person sexual grooming, there are implications that the current literature and theory can have on clinical practice. Clinicians can utilize the SGM in gathering information about an individual's offense both in evaluation and treatment. The grooming behaviours and stages described in the model can potentially shed light on an individual's risk factors for reoffending and recommendations for prevention (e.g., relapse prevention plans detailing the people, places, and situations that may lead to future offending). Importantly, people who sexually groom and commit an offense against a minor may not always follow the same behavioural patterns in the future; however, it is nevertheless important to understand prior offense cycles to shed light on possible reoffending patterns. Moreover, as those who abuse children may have cognitive distortions about their behaviour and its impact on victims (also sometimes referred to as self-grooming), understanding how these behaviours led to abuse can potentially facilitate changes in the individual's thoughts, beliefs, and behaviours in treatment and provide them the tools to avoid old sexual grooming tactics (Salter, 1995). The SGM can also be used in treating victims of CSA, such as providing psychoeducation about the offense process. Often victims experience guilt and blame following sexual abuse (Batool & Abtahi, 2017), and, thus, informing victims about the manipulative behaviours the person may have used could reduce this self-blame.

Investigation, Prosecution, and Policy

While countries will differ in terms of how CSA cases are investigated and prosecuted, those involved in the process could all benefit from increased education about sexual grooming, although the empirical foundation for the construct first needs to be further developed and validated. If that can be achieved, law enforcement may benefit from understanding these types of behaviours that could potentially be used to identify suspects (e.g., if a child reports abuse and there were adults in the child victim's life that employed such tactics) or additional victims (e.g., reviewing the individual's current or past relationships with other children). Those prosecuting cases of CSA could use the SGM framework to help form arguments in the case (e.g., if the defendant had repeated, close contact with the child before the alleged abuse). Importantly, as noted above, there remain gaps in the literature before these steps can be taken by law enforcement and lawyers (e.g., which behaviours or constellation of behaviours can help distinguish between those grooming and not). Down the road, once more empirical research has been gathered, there are opportunities for the subject of sexual grooming to inform important decisions in cases, such as investigations, prosecution, conviction, sentencing, and post-release guidelines.

Lastly, countries can work towards establishing improved legislation related to in-person sexual grooming. Currently, legal definitions of sexual grooming tend to focus solely on the online solicitation of minors (International Centre for Missing and Exploited Children, 2017), although some countries have developed legislation that could be applied both to online and in-person sexual grooming cases. Notably, it is important to have a legal definition of sexual grooming for the prosecution of these crimes; however, legal definitions typically lack specificity (e.g., what behaviours would be indicative of grooming). It is vital to improve our research on sexual grooming so we can begin informing the laws that can be implemented to combat the issue.

Primary Prevention

One especially impactful implication of better understanding sexual grooming is its application to primary prevention. Given that only 5 percent of sex crimes are committed by those on the sex offender registry, preventing sexual abuse from happening can have wide-reaching societal benefits (Sandler et al., 2008). If future research shows that the SGM can be validated, then its list of specific, observable acts can potentially assist the community in better recognizing worrisome (constellations of) behaviours and enhance the likelihood that suspicion and concern will be raised before the abuse occurs. While it remains unclear to date if specific sexual grooming and normal/adult–child interactions can be distinguished, we hypothesize that future research may show that we especially need to be attentive to *clusters*, or *high frequency of use*, of these possible predatory behaviours in adults spending time with children, while each behaviour in and of itself may not be indicative of sexual grooming. If the empirical evidence allows, a checklist of behaviours could be developed and disseminated to inform individuals who work with children, such as teachers or coaches, about (constellations of) behaviours that indicate a risk of grooming so they can possibly monitor for these behaviours and notify parents or authorities if there are concerns for further investigation. For example, O'Leary et al. (2017) suggested that sexual grooming can be used to inform screening and recruitment, policies and training, and reporting breaches of conduct for various institutional settings as these can help to establish guidelines for appropriate adult/child interactions that if violated can result in retraining or termination. Ultimately, knowledge of sexual grooming can increase vigilance and awareness in the community which can possibly stop abuse before it even occurs.

Conclusion

It is important to gain an understanding of how victims are sexually groomed by those who commit CSA. However, given the complexity of sexual grooming behaviour, distinguishing these behaviours has proved to be arduous. The future of the sexual grooming field should be directed towards research that validates the newly proposed model of sexual grooming, to provide evidence for its use in both academic and clinical settings. Further, more global studies are needed to understand how this phenomenon manifests cross-culturally. Ultimately, this research must transcend the academic world to the real-world application in various settings.

References

Barth, J., Bermetz, L., Heim, E., Trelle, S., & Tonia, T. (2013). The current prevalence of child sexual abuse worldwide: A systematic review and meta-analysis. *International Journal of Public Health, 58*(3), 469–483. https://doi.org/10.1007/s00038-012-0426-1

Batool, S. S., & Abtahi, A. (2017). Psychosocial impact of childhood sexual abuse: Perspective of victims. *Journal of Arts and Social Sciences, 4*(2), 36–48.

Bennett, N., & O'Donohue, W. (2014). The construct of grooming in child sexual abuse: Conceptual and measurement issues. *Journal of Child Sexual Abuse: Research, Treatment, & Program Innovations for Victims, Survivors, & Offenders, 23*(8), 957–976. https://doi.org/10.1080/10538712.2014.960632

Berliner, L., & Conte, J. R. (1990). The process of victimization: The victims' perspective. *Child Abuse & Neglect, 14*(1), 29–40. https://doi.org/10.1016/0145-2134(90)90078-8

Brakenridge, C. H. (2001). *Spoilsports: Understanding and preventing sexual exploitation in sport.* Routledge.

Canter, D., Hughes, D., & Kirby, S. (1998). Paedophilia: Pathology, criminality, or both? The development of a multivariate model of offence behaviour in child sexual abuse. *Journal of Forensic Psychiatry, 9*(3), 532–555. https://doi.org/10.1080/09585189808405372

Carson, D. K., Foster, J. M., & Tripathi, N. (2013). Child sexual abuse in India: Current issues and research. *Psychological Studies, 58*(3), 318–325. https://doi.org/10.1007/s12646-013-0198-6

Collings, S. J. (1997). Child sexual abuse in a sample of South African women students: Prevalence, characteristics, and long-term effects. *South African Journal of Psychology, 27*(1), 37–42.

Conte, J. R., Wolf, S., & Smith, T. (1989). What sexual offenders tell us about prevention strategies. *Child Abuse & Neglect, 13*(2), 293–301. https://doi.org/10.1016/0145-2134(89)90016-1

Craven, S., Brown, S., & Gilchrist, E. (2006). Sexual grooming of children: Review of literature and theoretical considerations. *Journal of Sexual Aggression, 12*(3), 287–299. https://doi.org/10.1080/13552600601069414

Craven, S., Brown, S., & Gilchrist, E. (2007). Current responses to sexual grooming: Implication for prevention. *Howard Journal of Criminal Justice, 46*(1), 60–71. https://doi.org/10.1111/j.1468-2311.2007.00454.x

Davidson, J., & Gottschalk, P. (2011). Characteristics of the Internet for criminal child sexual abuse by online groomers. *Criminal Justice Studies: A Critical Journal of Crime, Law & Society, 24*(1), 23–36. https://doi.org.ez.lib.jjay.cuny.edu/10.1080/1478601X.2011.544188

Elliott, I. A. (2017). A self-regulation model of sexual grooming. *Trauma, Violence, & Abuse, 18*(1), 83–97. https://doi.org/10.1177/1524838015591573

Elliott, M., Browne, K., & Kilcoyne, J. (1995). Child sexual abuse prevention—What offenders tell us. *Child Abuse & Neglect, 19*(5), 579–594. https://doi.org/10.1016/01452134(95)00017-3

Gillespie, A. A. (2002). Child protection on the internet-challenges for criminal law. *Child & Family Law Quarterly, 14*, 411.

Groth, A. N., & Birnbaum, H. J. (1978). Adult sexual orientation and attraction to underage persons. *Archives of Sexual Behavior, 7*(3), 175–181. https://doi.org/10.1007/BF01542377

Harms, R., & van Dam, C. (1992). *Child abuse prevention: What the educator needs to know*. Office of the Superintendent of Public Instruction.

Howitt, D. (1995). *Paedophiles and sexual offences against children*. John Wiley and Sons.

International Centre for Missing and Exploited Children. (2017). *Online grooming of children for sexual purposes: Model legislation & global review*. https://www.icmec.org/wp-content/uploads/2017/09/Online-Grooming-of-Children_FINAL_9-18-17.pdf

Jackson, S., Newall, E., & Backett-Milburn, K. (2015). Children's narratives of sexual abuse. *Child & Family Social Work, 20*(3), 322–332. https://doi.org/10.1111/cfs.12080

Ji, K., Finkelhor, D., & Dunne, M. (2013). Child sexual abuse in China: A meta-analysis of studies. *Child Abuse & Neglect, 37*(9), 613–622. https://doi.org.ez.lib.jjay.cuny.edu/10.1016/j.chiabu.2013.03.008

Kaufman, K. L., Mosher, H., Carter, M., & Estes, L. (2006). An empirically based situational prevention model for child sexual abuse. In R. Wortley & S. Smallbone (Eds.), *Crime prevention studies: Vol. 19. Situational prevention of child sexual abuse* (pp. 101–144). Criminal Justice Press.
Kloess, J. A., Beech, A. R., & Harkins, L. (2014). Online child sexual exploitation: Prevalence, process, and offender characteristics. *Trauma, Violence, & Abuse, 15*(2), 126–139. https://doi.org/10.1177/1524838013511543
Kloess, J. A., Hamilton-Giachritsis, C. E., & Beech, A. R. (2019). Offense processes of online sexual grooming and abuse of children via internet communication platforms. *Sexual Abuse, 31*(1), 73–96. https://doi.org/10.1177/1079063217720927
Lanning, K. V. (2010). *Child molesters: A behavioural analysis* (5th ed.). National Center for Missing & Exploited Children.
Lanning, K. V., & Dietz, P. (2014). Acquaintance molestation and youth-serving organizations. *Journal of Interpersonal Violence, 29*(15), 2815–2838. https://doi.org/10.1177/0886260514532360
Leclerc, B., Proulx, J., & McKibben, A. (2005). Modus operandi of sexual offenders working or doing voluntary work with children and adolescents. *Journal of Sexual Aggression, 11*(2), 187–195. https://doi.org/10.1080/13552600412331321314
Madu, S. N. (2001). The prevalence and patterns of childhood sexual abuse and victim perpetrator relationship among a sample of university students. *South African Journal of Psychology, 31*(4), 32–37. https://doi.org/10.1177/008124630103100404
McAlinden, A. M. (2006). Setting 'em up': Personal, familial and institutional grooming in the sexual abuse of children. *Social & Legal Studies, 15*(3), 339–362. https://doi.org/10.1177/0964663906066613
McAlinden, A. M. (2013). 'Grooming' and the sexual abuse of children. http://blog.oup.com/2013/01/grooming-child-abuse/
O'Leary, P., Koh, E., & Dare, A. (2017). *Grooming and child sexual abuse in institutional contexts.* Royal Commission into Institutional Responses to Child Sexual Abuse, Sydney, Australia.
Olson, L. N., Daggs, J. L., Ellevold, B. L., & Rogers, T. K. K. (2007). Entrapping the innocent: Toward a theory of child sexual predators' luring communication. *Communication Theory, 17*(3), 231–251. https://doi.org/10.1111/1j.1468-2885.2007.00294.x
Salter, A. C. (1995). *Transforming trauma: A guide to understanding and treating adult survivors of child sexual abuse.* Sage Publications, Inc.

Sandler, J. C., Freeman, N. J., & Socia, K. M. (2008). Does a watched pot boil? A time-series analysis of New York State's sex offender registration and notification law. *Psychology, Public Policy, and Law, 14*, 284–302. https://doi.org/10.1037/a0013881
Sheldon, K., & Howitt, D. (2007). *Sex offenders and the Internet*. John Wiley & Sons Ltd..
Spiegel, J. (2003). *Sexual abuse of males: The SAM model of theory and practice*. Brunner-Routledge.
Spraitz, J., Bowen, K. N., & Strange, L. (2018). Proposing a behavioural taxonomy of priest sexual grooming. *International Journal for Crime, Justice and Social Democracy, 7*(1), 30–43. https://doi.org/10.5204/ijcjsd.v7i1.387
Tallon, J. A., & Terry, K. J. (2008). Analyzing paraphilic activity, specialization, and generalization in priests who sexually abused minors. *Criminal Justice and Behavior, 35*(5), 615–628. https://doi.org/10.1177/0093854808314374
van Dam, C. (2001). *Identifying child molesters: Preventing child sexual abuse by recognizing the patterns of the offenders*. Haworth Maltreatment and Trauma Press/The Haworth Press.
Winters, G. M., & Jeglic, E. L. (2016). I knew it all along: The sexual grooming behaviours of child molesters and the hindsight bias. *Journal of Child Sexual Abuse: Research, Treatment, & Program Innovations for Victims, Survivors, & Offenders, 25*(1), 20–36. https://doi.org/10.1080/10538712.2015.1108945
Winters, G. M., & Jeglic, E. L. (2017). Stages of sexual grooming: Recognizing potentially predatory behaviours of child molesters. *Deviant Behavior, 38*(6), 724–733. https://doi.org/10.1080/01639625.2016.1197656
Winters, G. M., Jeglic, E. L., & Kaylor, L. E. (2020). Validation of the sexual grooming model of child sexual abusers. *Journal of Child Sexual Abuse: Research, Treatment, & Program Innovations for Victims, Survivors, & Offenders*. https://doi.org.ez.lib.jjay.cuny.edu/10.1080/10538712.2020.1801935
Wyre, R. (2000). Paedophile characteristics and patterns of behaviour. In C. Itzin (Ed.), *Home truths about sexual abuse influencing policy and practice: A reader* (pp. 49–69). Routledge.

2

Understanding Sexual Fantasising: Implications for Forensic Practice and Research

Ross M. Bartels

Sexual offending is the result of a complex and varying interplay of factors. The accurate assessment and treatment of sexual offending behaviour, therefore, requires a good understanding of these various factors. One key variable in most sex offending theories is 'sexual fantasy' (Marshall & Barbaree, 1990; Ward & Beech, 2006). This is understandable since sexual offending is a type of sexual behaviour (Smid & Wever, 2019) and sexual fantasies are a key component for understanding sexual behaviour (Leitenberg & Henning, 1995). Furthermore, sexual fantasies are commonly defined as any *mental imagery* that is sexually arousing

I have no known conflict of interest to disclose.

R. M. Bartels (✉)
School of Psychology, University of Lincoln, Lincoln, UK
e-mail: rbartels@lincoln.ac.uk

© The Author(s), under exclusive license to Springer Nature Switzerland AG 2022

K. Uzieblo et al. (eds.), *Challenges in the Management of People Convicted of a Sexual Offence*, Palgrave Studies in Risk, Crime and Society,
https://doi.org/10.1007/978-3-030-80212-7_2

(Leitenberg & Henning, 1995). This emphasis on mental imagery is important. Mental imagery is defined as a perceptual experience in the absence of sensory input (Kosslyn et al., 2001) and is argued to have a core function, that is, to enable the mental simulation or 'pre-experience' of future behaviour (Moulton & Kosslyn, 2009). Similarly, Renner et al. (2019) describe mental imagery as a "motivational amplifier" that promotes engagement in an overt behaviour. This is based on numerous studies showing that mental imagery can have a causal influence on corresponding behaviour (Baumeister et al., 2011), including sport performance, academic performance, food consumption, and gambling behaviour. Thus, as a form of mental imagery, it is theoretically sound to assume that sexual fantasy can also influence (sexual) behaviour.

In line with this view, the use of offence-related sexual fantasies tends to correlate with the corresponding behaviour (Noorishad et al., 2019; Williams et al., 2009). Noorishad et al. (2019) found these correlations ranged from weak (r = 0.22) to strong (r = 0.74), as did Williams et al. (2009) in relation to paraphilic and offence-related themes (*r's* ranged from 0.26 to 0.79). Greater sexual fantasy use has also been found to be predictive of both past sexually offensive behaviour (Bondü & Birke, 2020; Klein et al., 2015) and sexual recidivism (Hudson et al., 2002; Kenny et al., 2001). Of course, these data are correlational and so do not tell us whether sexual fantasising causes sexual behaviour. It is possible that a sexual behaviour is experienced first and then subsequently sexually fantasised about (or both). Nevertheless, a relationship exists between sexual fantasising and behaviour that warrants further examination and understanding.

Most studies examining sexual fantasies have focused on content, prevalence, and various correlates, such as sexual arousal, personality, and emotions (Bartels & Gannon, 2011). While this research has been instrumental in providing a foundation for understanding sexual fantasies, we need to start focusing on the processes that underpin sexual fantasising. This will offer a deeper insight into its functions and effects, which is crucial if we wish to form a solid understanding of how sexual fantasising influences sexual offending. The present chapter aims to inspire this shift in focus. First, a recent theory of sexual fantasising will be outlined. Then, a discussion on how this theory (along with other relevant research findings) can be used to guide forensic practice, specifically how to (1) effectively approach the subject of sexual fantasising, (2) efficiently assess sexual fantasising, and (3) help clients reduce and manage their sexual fantasising.

Understanding Sexual Fantasising

Historically, our understanding of how sexual fantasies operate has been limited. Existing theoretical accounts have focused on how sexual interests and fantasy content arise (Laws & Marshall, 1990; MacCulloch et al., 2000), rather than the processes underpinning the act of sexual fantasising. In response to this, Bartels and colleagues developed the *Dual-Process Model of Sexual Thinking* (DPM-ST; Bartels & Beech, 2016; Bartels et al., 2021). This theory is based on the idea that 'sexual fantasy' is distinct from 'sexual fantasising'. The former is a noun that refers to a knowledge *construct* containing information about the behaviours, targets, and contexts that one finds sexually interesting. Sexual fantasising, however, is a verb that refers to a cognitive *process*, a mental activity that takes place in the mind's eye. Drawing upon the wider cognitive literature (e.g., Christoff et al., 2016; Kavanagh et al., 2005; Mildner & Tamir, 2019), Bartels et al. (2021) make a further distinction between fleeting sexual thoughts and prolonged sexual fantasising. They define a 'fleeting sexual thought' as a passing internal mental event, involving visual and/or verbal sexual content, that arises spontaneously during the dynamic flow of thought. This is distinguishable from 'sexual fantasising', which we defined as the prolonged act of mentally simulating a sexual scenario. The key difference is that sexual fantasising involves envisioning content that is elaborated and directed in either an active or passive manner. Most thoughts are fleeting, with a median duration of five seconds (Klinger, 1978). Thus, fleeting *sexual* thoughts are likely to have a similar short duration, while sexual fantasising will have a longer duration (e.g., many minutes or longer) given its directed and elaborative nature.

According to the DPM-ST (Bartels et al., 2021), these two types of sexual thought are underpinned by distinct cognitive processes. Fleeting sexual thoughts are underpinned by associative processes. They arise when external or internal cues activate sex-related information in long-term memory, or a sex-related propositional thought related to the cue (e.g., spontaneously imagining a stranger naked, or verbally thinking "I wonder what they look like naked"). Sexual fantasising, however, is underpinned by more elaborative processes. This includes searching for and recalling a prior sexual experience, imagining and/or planning a future experience, or simply constructing and imagining a fanciful sexual idea. These processes can unfold in a passive manner (e.g., due to the sexual saliency of the imagery) or an active manner (e.g., to achieve a specific goal). Either way, the envisioned imagery is afforded more attention and directed by the thinker, leading the imagery to become prolonged.

Although both forms of sexual thinking are distinct, they are not unrelated. For example, a sexual thought that pops into mind may not always be fleeting. If one's attention is drawn towards the sexual thought (e.g., because it is highly arousing), it will enter an appraisal process, whereby it is evaluated on the basis of one's beliefs and attitudes about the content. If it does not match their beliefs or attitudes (e.g., "Sex with children is harmful"), the person will attempt to suppress or expel the sexual thought from their mind. If, however, the sexual thought *does* match their beliefs (e.g., "Children enjoy sex with adults"), it will be appraised as 'valid'. In turn, the sexual thought may be elaborated upon within the person's mind in the form of a prolonged sexual scenario. This is the act of sexual fantasising, which, as mentioned, can involve reliving a prior experience, planning a future experience, or imagining a fanciful idea (Bartels et al., 2021; Gee et al., 2003). Some people may, however, find it difficult to expel an incongruent thought from their mind if it is particularly sexually arousing (which, for some, may be due to the fact that sexual thought reflects a taboo, illegal, immoral, or risky behaviour). In these instances, the sexual thought will be experienced as unwanted or negative, potentially causing feelings of shame or guilt for having elaborated upon it. In sum, the DPM-ST offers a contemporary and nuanced account of sexual thinking, providing useful implications for forensic practice. These implications will now be discussed.

Approaching the Topic in Practice

Based on the DPM-ST, clinicians should be mindful of the distinction between content and process when approaching the topic of sexual mental imagery in practice. Both are important and so both should be considered. Specifically, clinicians should distinguish sexual fantasy (content) from the process by which the content is envisioned (i.e., fleeting sexual thought versus prolonged sexual fantasising). This will enable a clearer formulation to be developed regarding the role that sexual fantasising plays in a client's life. For example, establishing that a client has a sexual fantasy about children (content) may help establish that they have a sexual attraction to children. However, this may be all that it indicates, as 'sexual fantasy' is not the same as sexual fantasising. In other words, the individual may refrain from sexually fantasising about their interest in children. Alternatively, they may experience unintentional, fleeting sexual thoughts about children but control themselves from envisioning prolonged sexual scenarios involving children. Thus, it would need to be established whether the client actually thinks about their sexual interest, as well as how often and in what form(s) the thought is experienced (i.e., fleetingly vs prolonged). Figure 2.1 provides an overview of the distinctions between sexual content and sexual processes, the different forms of sexual thinking, and their progression (according to the DPM-ST).

In addition, it is important to establish whether the content is based on a prior experience or purely imagined. If it is the former, it would indicate that they have engaged in the behaviour before and, thus, may be enjoying the experience of mentally reliving the event (Gee et al., 2003). Moreover, it will provide further useful process-related information, as memory-related factors affect the fantasising experience. For example, sexual fantasies based on prior experience tend to be more vivid than those based purely on imagination (Bartels et al., 2018).

This increased vividness may lead to a more frequent sexual fantasising as it would be more arousing and rewarding. This may then increase the likelihood to re-engage in the behaviour. On the other hand, if one's sexual mental imagery is based purely on imagination, the clinician should establish whether the content is future-oriented or purely fanciful. Episodic

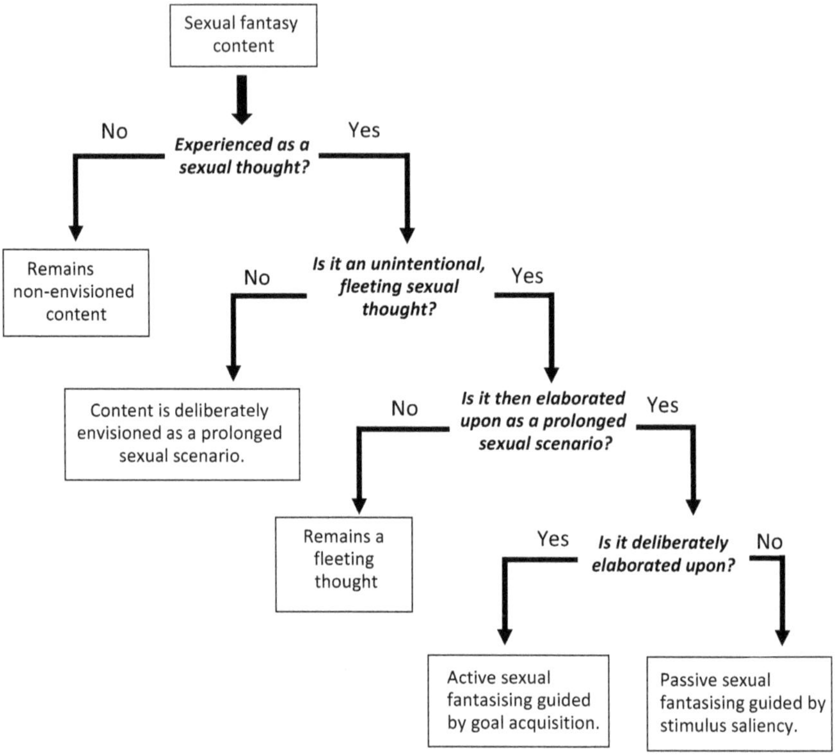

Fig. 2.1 Flowchart depicting the different sexual thoughts and their progression

future thinking involves drawing upon prior memories and recombining them to form a novel future scenario (Schacter et al., 2008). This has links to planning or modelling, which is a function of sexual fantasising (Gee et al., 2003), and may indicate a desire to enact the behaviour. However, if the imagination-based scenario is a purely fanciful idea, then there may be no intention to act it out. Instead, its use will be confined to a non-behavioural function, such as inducing sexual arousal or alleviating a negative mood (Gee et al., 2003). It may also offer a means to mentally experience an improbable scenario (e.g., sex with a celebrity), or a behaviour that one cannot do it in real life because it is physically impossible (e.g., vorarephilia), a cause of embarrassment, or socially unacceptable to enact. In my view, sexual mental imagery that is purely imagined and fanciful in nature is the 'true' meaning of the term 'sexual *fantasy*', as it refers to non-realistic content (i.e., a fantasy world). This is not to say that the content can never become realistic in the mind of an individual. Thus, if a client envisions content that is offence related but purely fanciful, it should still be given consideration like any other offence-related imagery.

Another reason to distinguish content and process pertains to offending behaviour. Intrusive fleeting sexual thoughts of a deviant nature may impact subsequent sexual behaviour, although there is little research on this. However, given their brevity, it is reasonable to propose that fleeting sexual thoughts are less likely to incite high levels of sexual arousal or create a detailed fantasy script/scenario (Bartels & Gannon, 2011). Sexual fantasising, on the other hand, has the capability to do all of the above due to its prolonged nature. Moreover, the controllability of the imagery means that an individual can guide the course of the scenario so that it reflects what they wish to do in real life (Leitenberg & Henning, 1995). Also, given its prolonged and more controlled nature, the client would have the time to masturbate to the imagery (in the right context), further entrenching the rewarding effect of the imagery via conditioning processes (Laws & Marshall, 1990). Based on all this, sexual fantasising is likely to have a stronger causal effect on offending behaviour compared to fleeting sexual thoughts. This reinforces my recommendation to distinguish and address both content and process (and their interrelationship) when focusing on sexual fantasy in practice. I would also recommend refraining from using the term 'sexual fantasy' with a client and instead use more descriptive terminology. For example, one could ask a client about "any sexual thoughts/scenarios that you deliberately envision for a prolonged amount of time". This approach helps to clearly convey what we mean, while also reducing any misunderstanding, concern, or embarrassment associated with the term 'fantasy'. Having covered the above points, I will now discuss how they can be applied and incorporated into assessment and treatment.

Assessing Sexual Fantasising

Sexual fantasies are primarily assessed using self-report measures. One specific approach is to thematically code the content of a written sexual fantasy scenario (e.g., Zurbriggen & Yost, 2004). This approach can provide rich detail about the fantasy content (e.g., who is involved and where it takes place). It can also be combined with the use of a 'fantasy logbook' (Vanhoeck et al., 2011) so that other accompanying factors can be documented (e.g., associated emotions and triggers). However, this approach does have its limitations. For example, analysing written fantasy scripts does not provide any indication for how often the content is fantasied about (if at all). As a result, clinically useful information is potentially missed. For example, in a treatment group, every individual may write out an offence-related sexual fantasy. However, the clinician will not know who envisions the content rarely and who envisions it on a regular basis. In addition, the clinician would not know whether the content is typically experienced fleetingly or for a longer duration. Thus, by focusing solely on content, process-related information goes undetected. This can be avoided by including questions about frequency of use, as well as by providing a clear definition of sexual fantasising (e.g., using the descriptive phrasing mentioned earlier). This will allow both content- and process-related information to be ascertained.

Another method of measurement is to use a fantasy questionnaire. Most comprise a list of sexual fantasy themes (items) that are rated in terms of how often they are used, typically using a Likert scale. Examples include the Wilson Sex Fantasy Questionnaire (Wilson, 1978) and the Sexual Fantasy Questionnaire (Gray et al., 2003). These questionnaires are useful as, in addition to covering a range of sexual fantasy themes (content), they provide an indication of how frequently the content is used. Studies using these questionnaires have provided insights regarding prevalence rates and associated factors (Bartels et al., 2020; Noorishad et al., 2019; Williams et al., 2009).

Despite this, sexual fantasy questionnaires also suffer from some key issues. First, most do not provide a definition of sexual fantasy, or they define it as *any* thought that is sexually arousing (e.g., O'Donohue et al., 1997, p. 170). As a result, a response made by someone who frequently experiences unintentional, fleeting sexual thoughts about a certain behaviour will be indistinguishable from a response given by someone who frequently envisions the same behaviour in a deliberate and prolonged manner. Second, frequency is confounded with duration (Purdon, 2004). This means that someone who experiences many fleeting sexual thoughts will score higher than someone who engages in fewer but much longer periods of sexual fantasising. Indeed, Cameron and Biber (1973) found that fleeting ('in-passing') sexual thoughts occur more frequently than longer ('focal') sexual thoughts. This is important to consider because, if an individual reports a low score on a frequency-based questionnaire, they may be seen to have no problems with their use of deviant sexual fantasies. However, this may not be the case. The person may, instead, sexually fantasise for very long periods of time, but at a relatively low frequency. This issue of duration should also be measured because a longer episode of sexual fantasising is likely to induce greater levels of sexual arousal, which is a motivating factor for sexual offending (Smid & Wever, 2019)

Based on the above, a few recommendations can be put forward. First, clinicians should establish a good level of rapport with their client given that disclosing offence-related sexual thoughts can be embarrassing and associated with a fear of negative repercussions. As mentioned, clinicians should also clearly define what is meant by sexual fantasising, preferably avoiding the term 'sexual fantasy'. Following this, clinicians can then enquire about the client's *current* sexual fantasising experiences (Akerman et al., 2020). This should include asking whether the client deliberately envisions offence-related sexual behaviours (content) and how often (frequency), as well as how long, a fantasising episode typically lasts (duration). Other useful information should also be collected. This includes asking about what triggers the client to sexually fantasise, as well as whether the content is based on a prior experience, an imagined future scenario, or a purely fanciful idea. Ideally, this should be followed by an inquiry into the purpose/function of the imagery. Clinicians would need to create a questionnaire or adapt an existing questionnaire to assess these other important facets, as existing questionnaires are primarily confined to assessing frequency of use. Alternatively, clinicians can assess sexual fantasising via an interview (perhaps in conjunction with a logbook). This would allow for rapport to be built and for all of the above facets to be more easily assessed and explored depth (if required). Collectively, the information gathered during the assessment session will help formulate an effective plan for helping a client manage their sexual fantasising, which will now be discussed.

Managing and Treating Sexual Fantasising

Sexual fantasising has the potential to affect actual behaviour, by increasing the incentive value of the behaviour (Smid & Wever, 2019), by enabling one to rehearse the behaviour via mental simulation (Gee et al., 2003; Ward & Hudson, 2000), and/or by desensitising one to the offensive behaviour (Gee et al., 2004). Each of these mechanisms will be intensified if a person regularly engages in prolonged periods of sexual fantasising. The aim of fantasy management, therefore, should be to reduce the frequency and duration of sexual fantasising about illegal sexual activities (Dwyer & Myers, 1990). This can be done by lessening the sexual appeal of the content and/or by targeting the processes that underpin sexual fantasising. The DPM-ST offers some guidance for how these aims can be achieved.

One route is to prevent sexual fantasising from occurring. Once a client's triggers have been assessed, clinicians could help them to disassociate the trigger from the response (e.g., via reconditioning techniques) so that it no longer cues fleeting sexual thoughts or prolonged fantasising. Alongside this, clients can be taught (1) to accept that such thoughts may occur and (2) that they do *not* need to engage with a sexual thought, whether that be evaluating it, fighting it, or acting upon it. Indeed, Dwyer and Myers (1990) found that 88.5% of men completing a community-based sexual offending treatment programme rated these two techniques as being helpful aspects of 'fantasy work'. Thus, rather than engaging with a sexual thought, clients should allow it to simply pass by, like a 'cloud' drifting in and out of consciousness (Singh et al., 2011). By doing so, the likelihood of the thought being elaborated upon (in the form of prolonged sexual fantasising) will be reduced. This will also steer the client away from trying to suppress their sexual thoughts, as this causes 'rebound' effects (Shingler, 2009).

Of course, a triggered sexual thought may elicit strong sexual arousal, making it more difficult to not engage with. Thus, the above techniques would be best used (where possible) in conjunction with reconditioning techniques that reduce the sexual attractiveness of the content (e.g., satiation) and increase the attractiveness of alternative (non-offence related) content (e.g., directed masturbation). These techniques can also help reduce the frequency of prolonged sexual fantasising, as the client will be less interested in or aroused by the offence-related sexual content. The efficacy of these techniques is supported by a few studies using forensic samples (Allen et al., 2020).

When directly treating prolonged sexual fantasising, clinicians should also consider targeting the underlying cognitive mechanisms. One approach is to use an imagery-competing task. According to the DPM-ST, sexual fantasising requires the resources of working memory. Therefore, if someone sexually fantasises while simultaneously performing another task that requires working memory resources, the experience of the sexual imagery would be impaired. This is because the mental imagery and imagery-competing task compete for the same working memory resources. An effective imagery-competing task is 'bilateral eye-movements', such as those used in Eye Movement Desensitisation Reprocessing (EMDR). Using a non-forensic sample, Bartels et al. (2018) found that bilateral eye movements reduced the subjective sexual arousal, vividness, and appraisal of memory and imagination-based sexual fantasies, compared to a 'no eye-movement' condition. In a forthcoming publication, the author found the same effects in relation to negatively appraised sexual fantasy content (including paraphilic and offence-related content). These results suggest that bilateral movements are a promising treatment strategy for treating offence-related sexual mental imagery. They also suggest that EMDR (traditionally confined to treating trauma) may be a viable form of therapy (ten Hoor, 2019).

One final and crucial point. In addition to reducing the use of offence-related sexual imagery, clinicians should help their clients identify and rehearse sexually arousing imagery that is not offence related (Dwyer, 1990). That way, in the likely event that a client wants to sexually fantasise in the future (e.g., to induce/facilitate physiological sexual pleasure), they will have an alternative (offence-free) scenario to recall and envision, rather than returning to old, offence-related imagery.

Conclusion

The DPM-ST offers an updated and nuanced account of sexual fantasising, opening up new insights and avenues for future research. Moreover, when combined with other relevant sexual fantasy literature, the DPM-ST also offers useful implications for forensic practice. This chapter has provided an overview of these implications, alongside theory-led and evidence-based guidance for how to best assess and treat offence-related prolonged sexual thoughts. Further research is needed to corroborate some of the more preliminary suggestions. However, it is hoped that this chapter will inspire the development and testing of new assessment and treatment strategies in both research and practice.

References

Akerman, G., Hardy, J., & Hamilton, P. (2020). Exploring and assessing the current sexual interest of men who have committed sexual and non-sexual violent offences. In G. Akerman, D. Perkins, & R. M. Bartels (Eds.), *Assessing and managing problematic sexual interests* (pp. 23–39). Routledge.

Allen, A., Katsikitis, M., Millear, P., & McKillop, N. (2020). Psychological interventions for sexual fantasies and implications for sexual violence: A systematic review. *Aggression and Violent Behavior, 55*. https://doi.org/10.1016/j.avb.2020.101465

Bartels, R. M., & Beech, A. (2016). Theories of deviant sexual fantasy. In A. R. Beech & T. Ward (Eds.), *The Wiley handbook on the theories, assessment, and treatment of sexual offending* (pp. 165–186). Wiley Blackwell.

Bartels, R. M., Beech, A. R., & Harkins, L. (2021). Understanding sexual thoughts and sexual fantasising: The dual-process model of sexual thinking. In L. Craig & R. M. Bartels (Eds.), *Sexual deviance: Understanding and managing deviant sexual interests and paraphilic disorders*. Wiley Blackwell.

Bartels, R. M., & Gannon, T. A. (2011). Understanding the sexual fantasies of sex offenders and their correlates. *Aggression and Violent Behavior, 16*(6), 551–561. https://doi.org/10.1016/j.avb.2011.08.002

Bartels, R. M., Harkins, L., & Beech, A. R. (2020). The influence of fantasy proneness, dissociation, and vividness of mental imagery on male's aggressive sexual fantasies. *Journal of Interpersonal Violence, 35*(3–4), 964–987. https://doi.org/10.1177/0886260517691523

Bartels, R. M., Harkins, L., Harrison, S. C., Beard, N., & Beech, A. R. (2018). The effect of bilateral eye-movements versus no eye-movements on sexual fantasies. *Journal of Behavior Therapy and Experimental Psychiatry, 59*, 107–114. https://doi.org/10.1016/j.jbtep.2018.01.001

Baumeister, R. F., Masicampo, E. J., & Vohs, K. D. (2011). Do conscious thoughts cause behavior? *Annual Review of Psychology, 62*, 331–361. https://doi.org/10.1146/annurev.psych.093008.131126

Bondü, R., & Birke, J. (2020). Links between aggressive sexual fantasies and presumably non-consensual aggressive sexual behavior when controlling for BDSM identity. *International Journal of Conflict and Violence, 14*(1), 1–18. https://doi.org/10.4119/ijcv-3777

Cameron, P., & Biber, H. (1973). Sexual thought throughout the lifespan. *The Gerontologist, 13*(2), 144–147. https://doi.org/10.1093/geront/13.2.144

Christoff, K., Irving, Z. C., Fox, K. C., Spreng, R. N., & Andrews-Hanna, J. R. (2016). Mind- wandering as spontaneous thought: a dynamic framework. *Nature Reviews Neuroscience, 17*, 718–731. https://doi.org/10.1038/nrn.2016.113

Dwyer, S. M. (1990). Reduction of sex offender paraphilic fantasies. *Journal of Psychology & Human Sexuality, 3*(1), 57–65. https://doi.org/10.1300/J056v03n01_04

Dwyer, S. M., & Myers, S. (1990). Sex offender treatment: A six-month to ten-year follow-up study. *Annals of Sex Research, 3*, 305–318. https://doi.org/10.1007/BF00849185

Gee, D., Ward, T., & Eccleston, L. (2003). The function of sexual fantasies for sexual offenders: A preliminary model. *Behaviour Change, 20*(1), 44–60. https://doi.org/10.1375/bech.20.1.44.24846

Gee, D. G., Devilly, G. J., & Ward, T. (2004). The content of sexual fantasies for sexual offenders. *Sexual Abuse, 16*(4), 315–331. https://doi.org/10.1023/B:SEBU.0000043326.30841.74

Gray, N. S., Watt, A., Hassan, S., & MacCulloch, M. J. (2003). Behavioral indicators of sadistic sexual murder predict the presence of sadistic sexual fantasy in a normative sample. *Journal of Interpersonal Violence, 18*(9), 1018–1034. https://doi.org/10.1177/0886260503254462

Hudson, S. M., Wales, D. S., Bakker, L., & Ward, T. (2002). Dynamic risk factors: The Kia Marama evaluation. *Sexual Abuse, 14*(2), 103–119. https://doi.org/10.1023/A:1014616113997

Kavanagh, D. J., Andrade, J., & May, J. (2005). Imaginary relish and exquisite torture: The elaborated intrusion theory of desire. *Psychological Review, 112*, 446–467. https://doi.org/10.1037/0033-295X.112.2.446

Kenny, D. T., Keogh, T., & Seidler, K. (2001). Predictors of recidivism in Australian juvenile sex offenders: Implications for treatment. *Sexual Abuse, 13*(2), 131–148. https://doi.org/10.1023/A:1026604405398

Klein, V., Schmidt, A. F., Turner, D., & Briken, P. (2015). Are sex drive and hypersexuality associated with pedophilic interest and child sexual abuse in a male community sample? *PloS One, 10*(7), Article e0129730. https://doi.org/10.1371/journal.pone.0129730

Klinger, E. (1978). Modes of normal conscious flow. In K. S. Pope & J. L. Singer (Eds.), *The stream of consciousness: Scientific investigations into the flow of human experience* (pp. 225–258). Plenum.

Kosslyn, S. M., Ganis, G., & Thompson, W. L. (2001). Neural foundations of imagery. *Nature Reviews Neuroscience, 2*(9), 635–642. https://doi.org/10.1038/35090055

Laws, D. R., & Marshall, W. L. (1990). A conditioning theory of the etiology and Maintenance of deviant sexual preferences and behaviour. In W. L. Marshall, D. R. Laws, & H. E. Barbaree (Eds.), *Handbook of sexual assault: Issues, theories, and treatment of the offender* (pp. 209–230). Plenum Press.

Leitenberg, H., & Henning, K. (1995). Sexual fantasy. *Psychological Bulletin, 117*(3), 469–496. https://doi.org/10.1037/0033-2909.117.3.469

MacCulloch, M., Gray, N., & Watt, A. (2000). Brittain's sadistic murderer syndrome reconsidered: An associative account of the aetiology of sadistic sexual fantasy. *The Journal of Forensic Psychiatry, 11*(2), 401–418. https://doi.org/10.1080/09585180050142606

Marshall, W. L., & Barbaree, H. E. (1990). An integrated theory of the etiology of sexual offending. In W. L. Marshall, D. R. Laws, & H. E. Barbaree (Eds.), *Handbook of sexual assault: Issues, theories, and treatment of the offender* (pp. 257–275). Plenum.

Mildner, J. N., & Tamir, D. I. (2019). Spontaneous thought as an unconstrained memory process. *Trends in Neurosciences, 42*, 763–777. https://doi.org/10.1016/j.tins.2019.09.001

Moulton, S. T., & Kosslyn, S. M. (2009). Imagining predictions: Mental imagery as mental emulation. *Philosophical Transactions of the Royal Society, B: Biological Sciences, 364*(3521), 1273–1280. https://doi.org/10.1098/rstb.2008.0314

Noorishad, P. G., Levaque, E., Byers, E. S., & Shaughnessy, K. (2019). More than one flavour: University students' specific sexual fantasies, interests, and experiences. *Canadian Journal of Human Sexuality, 28*(2), 143–158. https://doi.org/10.3138/cjhs.2019-0024

O'Donohue, W., Letourneau, E. J., & Dowling, H. (1997). Development and preliminary validation of a paraphilic sexual fantasy questionnaire. *Sexual Abuse, 9*(3), 167–178. https://doi.org/10.1007/BF02675062

Purdon, C. (2004). Empirical investigations of thought suppression in OCD. *Journal of Behavior Therapy and Experimental Psychiatry, 35*(2), 121–136. https://doi.org/10.1016/j.jbtep.2004.04.004

Renner, F., Murphy, F. C., Ji, J. L., Manly, T., & Holmes, E. A. (2019). Mental imagery as a "motivational amplifier" to promote activities. *Behaviour Research and Therapy, 114*(February), 51–59. https://doi.org/10.1016/j.brat.2019.02.002

Schacter, D. L., Addis, D. R., & Buckner, R. L. (2008). Episodic simulation of future events. *Annals of the New York Academy of Sciences, 1124*, 39–60. https://doi.org/10.1196/annals.1440.001

Shingler, J. (2009). Managing intrusive risky thoughts: What works? *Journal of Sexual Aggression, 15*(1), 39–53. https://doi.org/10.1080/13552600802542011

Singh, N. N., Lancioni, G. E., Winton, A. S., Singh, A. N., Adkins, A. D., & Singh, J. (2011). Can adult offenders with intellectual disabilities use mindfulness-based procedures to control their deviant sexual arousal? *Psychology. Crime & Law, 17*(2), 165–179. https://doi.org/10.1080/10683160903392731

Smid, W. J., & Wever, E. C. (2019). Mixed emotions: An incentive motivational model of sexual deviance. *Sexual Abuse, 31*(7), 731–764. https://doi.org/10.1177/1079063218775972

ten Hoor, N. (2019). *EMDR Treatment of Deviant Arousal: A Randomized Controlled Trial and a Case Study*. Paper presented at the Association for the Treatment of Sexual Abusers' 38th annual conference, Atlanta, Georgia, USA.

Vanhoeck, K., Van Daele, E., & Gykiere, C. (2011). Fantasy management in sex offender treatment. *Sexual Offender Treatment, 6*(1), 1–15. http://www.sexual-offendertreatment.org/94.html

Ward, T., & Beech, A. (2006). An integrated theory of sexual offending. *Aggression and Violent Behavior, 11*(1), 44–63. https://doi.org/10.1016/j.avb.2005.05.002

Ward, T., & Hudson, S. M. (2000). Sexual offenders' implicit planning: A conceptual model. *Sexual Abuse, 12*(3), 189–202. https://doi.org/10.1023/A:1009534109157

Williams, K. M., Cooper, B. S., Howell, T. M., Yuille, J. C., & Paulhus, D. L. (2009). Inferring sexually deviant behavior from corresponding fantasies: The role of personality and pornography consumption. *Criminal Justice and Behavior, 36*(2), 198–222. https://doi.org/10.1177/0093854808327277

Wilson, G. D. (1978). *The secrets of sexual fantasy*. J.M. Dent.

Zurbriggen, E. L., & Yost, M. R. (2004). Power, desire, and pleasure in sexual fantasies. *Journal of Sex Research, 41*(3), 288–300. https://doi.org/10.1080/00224490409552236

3

Lethal Outcome in Sexual Assaults: Predicting the Unpredictable?

Eric Beauregard

One of the most important concerns for the various actors of the criminal justice system working with people convicted of sexual offenses (PCSO) is to predict their risk of recidivism. To help in this complex task, several tools have been developed over the years. On the one hand, we have the actuarial assessment methods (e.g., RM2000, RRASOR, and Static-99(R), STABLE-2007) and, on the other hand, we have the non-actuarial assessment methods, often designated as 'structured professional judgement' (SPJ; for instance, SVR-20, RSVP). Prediction of recidivism has been greatly improved with the use of these tools; however, estimating the

I have no known conflict of interest to disclose.

E. Beauregard (✉)
School of Criminology, Simon Fraser University, Burnaby, BC, Canada
e-mail: ebeaureg@sfu.ca

© The Author(s), under exclusive license to Springer Nature Switzerland AG 2022

K. Uzieblo et al. (eds.), *Challenges in the Management of People Convicted of a Sexual Offence*, Palgrave Studies in Risk, Crime and Society,
https://doi.org/10.1007/978-3-030-80212-7_3

likelihood that an individual will sexually assault another victim in some cases is not enough. In more extreme cases, there are individuals who will kill their victims before, during, or after having committed a sexual assault. Although sexual assaults with a lethal outcome—also referred to as sexual homicides—are relatively rare (James & Proulx, 2014), there is a pressing need to examine whether it is possible to identify earlier on which individuals are more likely to commit these acts (see also, Chap. 7). Not only do these sexual homicides tend to receive the greatest news media coverage, but some monetization studies estimated the cost of sexual homicide of nearly $20 million per incident (DeLisi et al., 2010). Probably even more important is the fact that because of the low base rate of sexual homicide, gaining valuable and reliable knowledge about these crimes and offenders has proven to be exceedingly difficult.

As highlighted by Mossman (2008), it is impossible to accurately predict rare and extreme outcomes using actuarial approaches. Therefore, studies looking specifically at sexual assaults ending with a lethal outcome become of the utmost importance to prevent these crimes from happening. Moreover, these studies are not only important for clinicians who work with these offenders, but also for investigators facing these crimes. This chapter presents the existing knowledge on sexual assaults with a lethal outcome as well as the various challenges involved in this extreme form of sexual violence. Finally, the chapter concludes with some recommendations for practitioners as well as for future research.

What Is a Sexual Homicide?

Contrary to most sexual crimes, there is no legal definition for sexual homicide (Roberts & Grossman, 1993). Sexual homicide has been defined by many as the intentional killing of a person where there is evidence of a sexual element to the murder (e.g., Beech et al., 2005; Douglas et al., 1992; Folino, 2000; Ressler et al., 1988). However, others have emphasized that sexual activity was not necessary for the murder to be sexual as the act of killing itself may be sexually gratifying for the offender (Money, 1990; Schlesinger, 2004). Finally, some attempts were made to capture a broader conceptualization of this type of homicide, suggesting that sexual homicides "result from one person killing another in the context of power, control, sexuality, and aggressive brutality" (Burgess et al., 1986, p. 252).

All these definitions present several limitations. For instance, they are of little pragmatic value when attempting to identify and classify cases of sexual homicide as most of these definitions rely on information known only to the offender and do not provide operationalized criteria that may be used in the classification process. Therefore, cases of sexual homicide may go undetected, which will affect the estimation of the number of cases.

In order to limit these issues, the FBI (see Ressler et al., 1988) suggested a practical definition of sexual homicide, which states that to be considered sexual a homicide has to present at least one of the following: (a) victim's attire or lack of attire; (b) exposure of the sexual parts of the victim's body; (c) sexual positioning of the victim's body; (d) insertion of foreign objects into the victim's body cavities; (e) evidence of sexual intercourse; or (f) evidence of substitute sexual activity, interest, or sadistic fantasy. Instead of relying on the offenders, this definition allows for the identification of sexual homicide cases directly from the crime scene behaviours. However, this definition has been criticized in the past for its potential room for error (e.g., Kerr et al., 2013). Despite these limitations, the FBI definition is still the most efficient to identify and classify cases of sexual homicide (Beauregard & Martineau, 2016). However, to overcome some of its limitations, it has been proposed to demand at least two criteria, instead of only one as suggested by the original definition (see Chopin & Beauregard, 2019).

First Generation: Descriptive Studies

Von Krafft-Ebing presented a comprehensive collection of case studies to gain insight into the phenomenon of lust murder (Von Krafft-Ebing, 1886). Although similar descriptive and case studies followed, they all assumed that individuals committing a sexual homicide should be considered a distinct type of offender. For instance, Brittain (1970) offered a description of the psychosocial profile of individuals who had killed their victims following a sexual assault and were characterized by sadistic acts.

According to his description, these individuals presented a narcissistic and egocentric personality with some obsessive traits, which were typically reflected at the crime scene. These individuals also tended to present more than one paraphilia (e.g., cross-dressing, fetishism, and masochism) and cruelty against animals was also observed. Finally, the killing—which was planned and against a victim who was chosen randomly or for reasons unknown to others—usually happened following a threat to his self-esteem. Although informative, Brittain's (1970) study was mainly based on his clinical experience, and no information was provided regarding the number of cases he had encountered to come up with this portrait.

In order to overcome some of the issues with these case studies, an extensive study was undertaken by the FBI Behavioural Science Unit, in large part through the work of Ressler and his colleagues (e.g., Ressler et al., 1988). These researchers interviewed 36 individuals who had been convicted of a total of 118 sexual homicides to learn about modus operandi, crime scene characteristics, methods employed to escape detection, and criminal profiles. Instead of simply presenting a description of these 36 cases, they proposed a typology with two main profiles: organized and disorganized. The *organized* offender is intelligent and socially and sexually competent. This offender is more likely to show a controlled mood during crime, to use alcohol, and to live with a partner. The *organized* offender is mobile, possessing a car in good condition, follows the crime in news media, and may change jobs or leave town after the murder. His crime is planned, he is likely to target a stranger, and the crime scene reflects an offender who has control over his offense. This offender uses restraints, will exhibit aggressive acts prior to death, and may transport and hide the victim's body after the murder. Usually the weapon or evidence will be absent from the crime scene. As to the *disorganized* offender, he is of average intelligence, socially immature, presents a poor work history, and is sexually incompetent. This offender shows an anxious mood during the crime, is not likely to use alcohol, lives alone, and usually lives and/or works near the crime scene. He has minimal interest in news media coverage of his crime and is not likely to change his lifestyle. The crime of the *disorganized* offender is usually spontaneous, on a known victim, and the crime scene is random and sloppy. He is not likely to use restraints, but sexual acts are committed after death. The body is normally left in view, at the death scene, and the murder weapon and evidence are often present.

The FBI study along with other descriptive studies (e.g., Brown, 1991) enabled the identification of several characteristics that appeared to be associated with sexual assaults ending with a lethal outcome. However, concerns were raised about the validity of these findings as previous studies did not include a control group. Thus, it was impossible to know whether these characteristics identified were truly associated to a specific type of offender or if it was in fact common to most individuals committing sexual assaults.

Second Generation: Comparing Sexual Assaults to Sexual Homicides

To better understand the potential differences between individuals who kill their victims following a sexual assault and those who did not, researchers started to compare the two groups. Early attempts examined the sociodemographic/developmental, psychological, and pre-crime factors (Grubin, 1994; Langevin et al., 1988; Milsom et al., 2003). Findings showed that sexual assaults with a lethal outcome were more likely to be committed by individuals who were older, socially isolated, reported more runaways as a child, and with less prior convictions for sexual crimes. Moreover, these individuals showed more overcontrolled anger, voyeurism, transvestism, and sadism compared to individuals who did not kill their victims during a sexual assault. Finally, these studies showed that sexual assaults ending with a lethal outcome were more likely to be committed by individuals who were socially isolated prior to the crime, lived alone, and had no sexual partner and almost no sexual experience. Although interesting, the studies suffered from several limitations, such as the use of small—sometimes even biased—samples and, more importantly, a limited number of variables examined.

Proulx et al. (2007) attempted to remedy this situation by examining an extensive list of factors using a representative sample including 40 individuals involved in a sexual assault with a lethal outcome and 101 individuals who had committed a sexual assault. Their findings showed that individuals who had killed their victims during a sexual assault were more likely to report being victim of incest, disciplinary problems in school, social isolation, and deviant sexual fantasies in childhood. Although no significant differences were observed between the two groups as to personality, the study showed that individuals who had committed a sexual homicide were more likely to exhibit anger prior to crime, use of alcohol, as well as use of a weapon. More recently, a systematic review by Stefanska et al. (2016) examined ten published studies comparing the same two groups of offenders. In addition to those differences already discussed above, the findings revealed that individuals involved in a sexual assault with a lethal outcome were less likely to have committed vaginal penetration, to plan the crime (see Higgs et al., 2015; Salfati & Taylor, 2006; Vettor & Beech, 2014), and to humiliate the victim (Healey et al., 2013; Higgs et al., 2015). Moreover, the findings were inconclusive as to whether the victim was restrained as well as if they differed in physical victimization, relationship status at the time of the crime, low self-esteem, and age at the time of crime (Stefanska et al., 2016).

Overall, the conclusions of these studies were that individuals who have committed a sexual assault ending with and without a lethal outcome presented more similarities than differences. It was suggested that offenders should not be distinguished based on the outcome of the crime (i.e., lethal or not), and, therefore, individuals killing their victim during the course of a sexual assault did not represent a distinct type of offender.

Third Generation: Comparing Violent Sexual Assaults, Non-Violent Sexual Assaults, and Sexual Homicides

It was assumed that we could compare sexual homicides to sexual assaults that included both violent and non-violent sexual assaults. The inclusion of both violent and non-violent sexual assaults in the same group may have introduced some noise in previous findings. To shed some light on possible differences that may have been missed between these two types of offenders, a new generation of studies compared sexual homicide cases to cases of both violent and non-violent sexual assaults.

Beauregard and Martineau (2016) have examined differences among these three types of sexual assaults on several characteristics. Among the factors investigated, they have looked specifically at the differences related to paraphilias. Results showed that perpetrators of sexual homicide (N = 85) were significantly more likely to have engaged in paraphilic behaviour both as a juvenile and as an adult. Although individuals who have perpetrated sexual homicides were significantly more likely to have engaged in a lifetime of paraphilic behaviour, they were significantly less likely than the two other groups who had committed violent and non-violent sexual assaults to have engaged in the paraphilias involving non-consenting adult and child partners (i.e., rape and paedophilia). Interestingly, the individuals who engaged in non-violent sexual assaults (N = 387) were the most likely to have priorly engaged in child sexual abuse, whereas individuals who had committed violent sexual assaults (N = 144) were most likely to have engaged priorly in rape.

Beauregard and Martineau (2016) also examined developmental factors among the three types of sexual crimes. Offenders who had committed a non-violent sexual assault were more likely than the two other groups to report having been the victim of sexual abuse during childhood. As for individuals who committed violent sexual assaults, these offenders were more likely to report having been the victim of parental abandonment, were younger when they had their first sexual intercourse, and were more likely to come from families with prior suicide attempts/completion as well as families with prior convictions for sexual crimes. The individuals involved in sexual assaults ending with a lethal outcome were characterized by many problems in their childhood, such as having been the victim of sexual (e.g., victim of incest) and physical violence, as well as a number of attitude (e.g., rebellious, anger, and poor self-image) and behavioural problems (e.g., cruelty against animals, prostitution, and reckless behaviours).

As can be seen, individuals who have killed their victims following a sexual assault present a background characterized by abuse and a variety of problematic behaviours. These findings suggest that offenders committing sexual homicide learn specific sexual behaviours early in childhood that suggest a strong need for sexual gratification, and they also may not adequately address their sexual needs, which potentially contributes to the seriousness of their sexual offending. Beauregard and DeLisi (2018a) hypothesized that this investment in solitary, illegal, or obsessive sexual behaviours is the result of their need to regain some control over their lives, as suggested by several of the theoretical models of sexual homicide.

Beauregard and DeLisi (2018b) further investigated the issue of personality in perpetrators of sexual homicide by comparing the same three groups of the same sample as Beauregard and Martineau (2016). They found that the personality profile of the perpetrators of sexual homicide is comprised primarily of comorbid Schizoid and Borderline Personality Disorders. These offenders were also significantly more likely to select a victim, use a weapon, and use drugs and alcohol before their offenses, but less likely to force their victim to engage in sexual acts or humiliate them. Beauregard and DeLisi (2018b) argued that the comorbidity of Schizoid, Borderline, and Antisocial Personality Disorder features presented a unique personality dysfunction that facilitates the lethal sexual violence relative to the non-lethal sexual violence.

In a different study but using the same data, Beauregard et al. (2017) have examined differences among the three groups of offenders on their criminal career. Even though all three groups had extensive and serious offending records, some important distinctions were found. Individuals who had committed non-violent sexual assaults had more convictions for rape/sexual abuse and other sexual offenses relating to exhibitionism as well as more specialization in their offending repertoires compared to the other two groups. Individuals who had committed violent sexual assaults were more versatile in their offending patterns and had more assaults, homicides, kidnappings, and aggravated sexual assaults. Offenders who had committed sexual homicides were similarly versatile and had extensive histories of armed robbery, kidnapping, and homicide, more than the two other groups.

Whereas most studies compare offenders who have committed sexual homicide to other offenders who have committed non-homicidal sexual assaults, the findings presented above show there is important heterogeneity that is lost when offenders are not separated based on additional violence inherent to their index offense. These differences could explain why some offenders, when involved in a sexual crime, are more likely to kill the victim than other offenders who do not present these characteristics.

Implications for Assessment and Treatment

As the third generation of studies seems to suggest, sexual assaults ending with a lethal outcome seem to be committed by different individuals than sexual assaults where the victims survive. This is important as it carries implications for the various actors of the criminal justice system. In terms of risk assessment, most actuarial tools and structured professional judgement methods have not been conceived with this goal in mind. Although these instruments have shown their usefulness in predicting recidivism, they do not inform clinicians and decision-makers on the risk that an individual will kill his victim during a sexual assault. The research discussed in this chapter has allowed to highlight some factors—red flags—associated to sexual homicide and that could be something to look for in the previous crimes committed by an offender. For instance, prior robbery convictions have been associated with the commission of sexual homicide. Although this does not mean that individuals who present robbery antecedents will all commit sexual homicides in the future, for those convicted of sexual crimes, it might constitute a risk factor to engaging in lethal sexual violence. Results of these studies are also important for a better understanding of the offending process of these offenders. The examination of the offense chain of individuals who kill their victims following a sexual assault allows for a more comprehensive understanding of what drives these offenders to sexually assault and kill their victim. As suggested by Darjee and Baron (2018), identifying the pathway to, and motivation for, sexual homicide is crucial for case formulation and effective community management, because there are significant differences in triggers, motivation, personality traits, and risk factors between the various types of offenders.

Identifying the risk factors for sexual homicide as well as the type of offender involved may provide a useful structure to help guide case management. According to Darjee and Baron (2018), treatment programmes should address the relevant needs of the offenders, particularly the sadistic sexual fantasies and sexual preoccupation in sadistic killers; anger, hostility, emotional instability, and attitudes towards women in angry killers; and attitudes, sexual regulation, general self-regulation, attitudes, emotional functioning, and relationships in incidental killers. Moreover, the findings reviewed suggest that the identification of early trauma among these individuals may be a promising avenue for treatment. Considering that individuals involved in sexual assaults with a lethal outcome present a childhood characterized with abuse and problematic behaviours, interventions with these individuals should not only focus on the criminogenic needs but also address these early traumas.

What Is Next?

Research on sexual assaults with lethal outcome suggests that individuals involved in these crimes are different from other offenders who have committed sexual crimes. When examining their offending processes as well as some of their characteristics, these offenders are distinct and need to be treated as such. Considering the research undertaken thus far, as well as the various needs for the actors of the criminal justice system, we have identified some areas where additional work could be done.

The first area is the role of developmental factors in the risk of committing a sexual homicide. Research has already identified that individuals involved in sexual homicides were more likely to present severely disturbed childhoods characterized by diverse adverse childhood experiences (ACE) in a way that was different from other offenders involved in sexual crimes (e.g., Beauregard & DeLisi, 2018a). For instance, DeLisi and Beauregard (2017) showed evidence of a positive trend between the number of ACE and the likelihood of sexual homicide. In other words, offenders who had the most exposure to violence, the most victimization, and the most overall ACE were exponentially more likely to perpetrate sexual homicide. This indicates that simply looking for the presence or absence of ACE is not enough. It is of the utmost importance to consider the frequency and diversity of ACE. Moreover, as suggested by the FBI motivational model (Ressler et al., 1988), to fully understand the role of

ACE on sexual homicide, we will need to investigate the underlying mechanisms between the effect of ACE and the likelihood of committing a sexual homicide.

Although related to the first area, the second area that requires further investigation is the examination of risk factors in combination. Previous studies have identified some risk factors—*red flags*—associated to sexual homicide in individuals who have committed (sexual) violent or non-violent offences. This is important to think of in terms of prediction; however, some studies have also shown that by considering risk factors in combination it is possible to identify "high risk" situation more precisely for individuals committing sexual crimes. For instance, using conjunctive analysis, Mieczkowski and Beauregard (2010) found that a specific combination of criminal event factors—namely the use of a weapon during the crime, the absence of sexual contacts either from the offender or the victim, and a criminal event lasting more than 30 minutes—presented the highest risk of a lethal outcome in a sexual crime. Going back to the ACE previously mentioned, the same logic could be applied to better understand the underlying processes leading an individual to commit a sexual homicide as opposed to letting the victim survive. For instance, it would be very interesting and useful to see whether a specific combination of static and/or dynamic risk factors might be (more) predictive of sexual homicide? This would be very useful for practitioners that assess and treat these offenders. In order to be able to better identify at-risk individuals, we believe that we will need to look beyond the "checklist" approach and start looking at the various interactions between known psychosocial risk factors and offence characteristics.

Finally, future work should focus on identifying a scale that measures the risk of a lethal outcome in sexual crimes. As mentioned at the beginning of this chapter, predicting extreme and rare events can prove difficult. However, given all the existing findings—as well as those that will come, taking into consideration of the ideas suggested above—we believe we are at a point where such a tool can be elaborated and tested. It is important that clinicians and practitioners managing cases of sexual homicides be equipped with a tool that could help them to "flag" individuals more at risk of being involved in a sexual assault ending with a lethal outcome. Such tools exist for individuals involved in domestic violence (e.g., Rettenberger & Eher, 2013). It is time that an instrument predicting the risk of lethal outcome in sexual crimes be developed.

Despite sexual assaults with lethal outcome being a rare and extreme form of crime, attention should be devoted to this specific and distinct type of sexual crime. The relatively rare occurrence of this crime makes it difficult for practitioners having to manage these crimes to develop a form of expertise. However, we believe that it also represents a unique opportunity for clinicians and the police to join forces so that the knowledge on these offenders and these crimes be shared between these two fields. Building a bridge between these two fields should be emphasized and very much encouraged. Finally, through better research on this form of sexual crime will we be able to develop tools and instruments that can be used in the prevention of sexual assaults with lethal outcome.

References

Beauregard, E., & DeLisi, M. (2018a). Stepping stones to sexual murder: The role of developmental factors in the etiology of sexual homicide. *Journal of Criminal Psychology, 8*(3), 199–214. https://doi.org/10.1108/JCP-02-2018-0010

Beauregard, E., & DeLisi, M. (2018b). Unraveling the personality profile of the sexual murderer. *Journal of Interpersonal Violence*, 0886260518777012. https://doi.org/10.1177/0886260518777012

Beauregard, E., DeLisi, M., & Hewitt, A. N. (2017). Sexual murderers: Sex offender, murderer, or both? *Sexual Abuse, 30*(8), 932–950. https://doi.org/10.1177/1079063217711446

Beauregard, E., & Martineau, M. (2016). *The sexual murderer: Offender behaviour and implications for practice*. Routledge.

Beech, A. R., Fisher, D., & Ward, T. (2005). Sexual murderers' implicit theories. *Journal of Interpersonal Violence, 20*, 1336–1389. https://doi.org/10.1177/0886260505278712

Brittain, R. P. (1970). The sadistic murderer. *Medicine, Science, and the Law, 10*(4), 198–207. https://doi.org/10.1177/002580247001000402

Brown, J. S. (1991). The psychopathology of serial sexual homicide: A review of the possibilities. *American Journal of Forensic Psychiatry, 12*, 13–21.

Burgess, A. W., Hartman, C. R., Ressler, R. K., Douglas, J. E., & McCormack, A. (1986). Sexual homicide: A motivational model. *Journal of Interpersonal Violence, 1*, 251–272. https://doi.org/10.1177/088626086001003001

Chopin, J., & Beauregard, E. (2019). Is the sexual murderer a unique or hybrid type of offender? *International Journal of Offender Therapy and Comparative Criminology, 63*, 1597–1620.

Darjee, R., & Baron, E. (2018). Recent research on sexual homicide in Scotland: Characteristics, crime scene themes and comparison with non-homicidal sexual aggressors. In J. Proulx, E. Beauregard, A. Carter, A. Mokros, R. Darjee, & J. James (Eds.), *Routledge International Handbook of Sexual Homicide Studies* (pp. 196–218). Routledge.

DeLisi, M., & Beauregard, E. (2017). Adverse childhood experiences and criminal extremity: New Evidence for Sexual Homicide. *Journal of Forensic Sciences, 63*, 484–489. https://doi.org/10.1111/1556-4029.13584

DeLisi, M., Kosloski, A., Sween, M., Hachmeister, E., Moore, M., & Drury, A. (2010). Murder by numbers: Monetary costs imposed by a sample of homicide offenders. *The Journal of Forensic Psychiatry & Psychology, 21*, 501–513. https://doi.org/10.1080/14789940903564388

Douglas, J. E., Burgess, A. W., Burgess, A. C., & Ressler, R. (1992). *Crime classification manual.* Lexington Books.

Folino, J. O. (2000). Sexual homicides and their classification according to motivation: A report from Argentina. *International Journal of Offender Therapy and Comparative Criminology, 44*, 740–750. https://doi.org/10.1177/0306624X00446009

Grubin, D. (1994). Sexual murder. *British Journal of Psychiatry, 165*, 624–629. https://doi.org/10.1192/bjp.165.5.624

Healey, J., Lussier, P., & Beauregard, E. (2013). Sexual sadism in the context of rape and sexual homicide: An examination of crime scene indicators. *International Journal of Offender Therapy and Comparative Criminology, 57*(4), 402–424. https://doi.org/10.1177/0306624X12437536

Higgs, T., Carter, A. J., & Stefanska, E. B. (2015). Toward identification of the sexual killer: A comparison of sexual killers engaging in post-mortem sexual interference and non-homicide sexual aggressors. *Sexual Abuse, 29*(5), 479–499. https://doi.org/10.1177/1079063215609935

James, J., & Proulx, J. (2014). A psychological and developmental profile of sexual murderers: A systematic review. *Aggression and Violent Behavior, 19*, 592–607. https://doi.org/10.1016/j.avb.2014.08.003

Kerr, K. J., Beech, A. R., & Murphy, D. (2013). Sexual homicide: Definition, motivation and comparison with other forms of sexual offending. *Aggression and Violent Behavior, 18*, 1–10. https://doi.org/10.1016/j.avb.2012.05.006

Kraft-Ebing, R. Von (1886). *Psychopathia sexualis.* (C. G. Chaddock, Trans.). F. A. Davis.

Langevin, R., Ben-Aron, M. H., Wright, P., Marchese, V., & Handy, L. (1988). The sex killer. *Annals of Sex Research, 1*(2), 263–301. https://doi.org/10.1007/BF00852801

Mieczkowski, T., & Beauregard, E. (2010). Lethal outcome in sexual assault events: A conjunctive analysis. *Justice Quarterly, 27*(332–361) https://doi.org/10.1080/07418820902960105

Milsom, J., Beech, A. R., & Webster, S. D. (2003). Emotional loneliness in sexual murderers: A qualitative analysis. *Sexual Abuse: A Journal of Research and Treatment, 15*, 285–296. https://doi.org/10.1177/107906320301500405

Money, J. (1990). Forensic sexology: Paraphilic serial rape (biastophilia) and lust murder (erotophonophilia). *American Journal of Psychotherapy, 44*, 26–36. https://doi.org/10.1176/appi.psychotherapy.1990.44.1.26

Mossman, D. (2008). Analyzing the performance of risk assessment instruments: A response to Vrieze and Grove (2007). *Law and Human Behavior, 32*, 279–291. https://doi.org/10.1007/s10979-007-9123-7

Proulx, J., Beauregard, E., Cusson, M., & Nicole, A. (2007). *Sexual murder: A comparative analysis and new perspectives.* Wiley.

Ressler, R. K., Burgess, A. W., & Douglas, J. E. (1988). *Sexual homicide: Patterns and motives.* Lexington.

Rettenberger, M., & Eher, R. (2013). Actuarial risk assessment in sexually motivated intimate-partner violence. *Law and Human Behavior, 37*(2), 75–86. https://doi.org/10.1037/b0000001

Roberts, J. V., & Grossman, M. G. (1993). Sexual homicide in Canada: A descriptive analysis. *Annals of Sex Research, 6*, 5–25. https://doi.org/10.1007/BF00849743

Salfati, G., & Taylor, P. (2006). Differentiating sexual violence: A comparison of sexual homicide and rape. *Psychology, Crime and Law, 12*(2), 107–125. https://doi.org/10.1080/10683160500036871

Schlesinger, L. B. (2004). *Sexual murder: Catathymic and compulsive homicides.* CRC Press.

Stefanska, E. B., Beech, A., & Carter, A. J. (2016). A systematic review of the literature comparing male non-serial sexual killers and sexual aggressors: Examining homogeneous and heterogeneous characteristics of these groups.

Journal of Sexual Aggression, 22(3), 323–341. https://doi.org/10.1080/13552600.2015.1126657

Vettor, S., & Beech, A. (2014). Rapists and sexual murderers: Combined pathways to offending. In J. Proulx (Ed.), *Pathways to sexual offending* (pp. 285–315). Routledge.

4

Abuse at the Heart of the Family: The Challenges and Complexities of Sibling Sexual Abuse

Peter Yates and Stuart Allardyce

The international media tends to represent child sexual abuse as a problem of 'stranger danger', focusing on the individualistic nature of sensational cases (Weatherred, 2015). The reality is rather different: most child sexual abuse is carried out by people well known to the child and often by other family members. Moreover, it is rarely reported that these other family members may themselves be children; indeed, it is likely that sibling sexual abuse—the sexual abuse of children by their brothers or sisters—is the most common form of intra-familial sexual abuse, estimated

I have no known conflict of interest to disclose.

P. Yates (✉)
Edinburgh Napier University, Edinburgh, UK
e-mail: p.yates@napier.ac.uk

S. Allardyce
Stop-it-Now! Scotland / Lucy Faithfull Foundation, Haslemere, UK

© The Author(s), under exclusive license to Springer Nature Switzerland AG 2022

K. Uzieblo et al. (eds.), *Challenges in the Management of People Convicted of a Sexual Offence*, Palgrave Studies in Risk, Crime and Society,
https://doi.org/10.1007/978-3-030-80212-7_4

to be up to three times as common as sexual abuse by a parent (Krienert & Walsh, 2011; Stroebel et al., 2013). Nonetheless, it remains under-researched and is the least studied form of intra-familial child sexual abuse (Tener et al., 2020).

Children can be sexually abused by adult siblings, but the focus of this chapter is abuse of a child by their child sibling. Such sibling sexual abuse is potentially devastating for families and is a challenging issue for practitioners. Difficult decisions need to be made with respect to risk assessment and the siblings' living and contact arrangements, and the needs of the children may conflict with each other. We often see confused responses by the professionals involved, binary thinking, minimisation of the abuse, or responses derived from adult sex offending. In particular, the significance of the children being siblings is often overlooked.

In this chapter, we provide a brief overview of current research and an exploration of the challenges raised by this form of abuse, before going on to outline future directions for research and practice. The chapter acts as a companion piece to a much longer overview of knowledge and practice in this field (see http://www.csacentre.org.uk/knowledge-in-practice/practice-improvement/sibling-sexual-abuse/).

A Brief Overview of Current Research

While some large studies exist, most research in this area entails small clinical samples, usually from Anglophone countries such as the North America, the UK, Australia, and New Zealand. It is often necessary to draw upon research that is now at least 30 years old. As with child sexual abuse generally, it is difficult to establish with confidence the prevalence of sibling sexual abuse because of its hidden nature (Kelly & Karsna, 2018). Various studies, however, indicate that around 5% of children may be involved in abusive sibling sexual behaviour (e.g., Atwood, 2007; Finkelhor, 1980; Hardy, 2001; Relva et al., 2017).

The most common reported pattern involves an older brother abusing a younger sister, and most of what we know from research relates to this pairing. All combinations of siblings are possible, however, including same-sex abuse, sisters abusing brothers, younger siblings abusing older siblings, and multiple siblings being abused (Adler & Schutz, 1995; Caffaro & Conn-Caffaro, 1998; Carlson et al., 2006; Digiorgio-Miller, 1998; O'Keefe et al., 2014; Stroebel et al., 2013). There is no evidence or theoretical reason to believe that there are differences in the degree of harm caused by abuse involving different sibling sex combinations, and sibling sexual abuse has the potential to be every bit as harmful as sexual abuse by parents (Yates, 2017).

As summarised in Yates (2017), the short-term consequences may include pregnancy, sexually transmitted infections, physical injury, symptoms of post-traumatic stress disorder, and emotional and behavioural problems. The longer-term consequences may include depression or suicidal thoughts, dissociation, flashbacks, nightmares and intrusive thoughts, low self-esteem, alcohol, and other substance misuse problems, eating disorders, and ongoing feelings of guilt and shame. Relationship difficulties throughout life, such as forming or maintaining meaningful or healthy sexual and partner relationships, experiencing physical violence within relationships, or having difficulty trusting other people are reported in many studies. It is also noteworthy that both those harmed and those who harm are likely to be adversely affected, with depression and hyper-eroticisation identified as consequences for all children involved (Stroebel et al., 2013).

Children are not all affected equally or in the same way. The impact of the abuse on a particular child will be mediated through the nature, duration, and context of the abuse, the experiences of other forms of abuse, the meaning of the abuse for the child, and other protective and vulnerability factors. The impact of sibling sexual abuse may be exacerbated or ameliorated by the responses of family members and professionals. Families who do not acknowledge the abuse or misplace responsibility can amplify its impact.

Sibling sexual abuse typically entails a greater number of sexual acts over a longer period than harmful sexual behaviour within the community (Latzman et al., 2011; O'Brien, 1991; Tidefors et al., 2010). This is likely to be due to the level and nature of contact between children within the same family. Sibling sexual abuse is also thought to be less disclosed than other forms of abuse (Carlson et al., 2006). Sexual acts may include a range of behaviours such as touching of genitals, masturbation, oral sex, penetration with fingers and objects, anal and vaginal rape, and sexual behaviours mediated by technology.

Most studies of sibling sexual abuse focus on the characteristics of the child who has harmed or those of their family to the detriment of exploring the sibling relationship. Children who sexually harm siblings typically have fewer antisocial tendencies (e.g., criminal history, juvenile delinquency, impulsivity, substance use, and psychopathy) and atypical sexual interests (e.g., paedophilia, other paraphilias, and excessive sexual preoccupation) than children who sexually abuse outside the family (Martijn et al., 2020). They also typically score lower on offense-supportive attitudes, emotional congruence with children, and interpersonal deficits. Contextual family factors may include domestic abuse, extra-marital affairs, physical discipline, poor sexual boundaries within the family home (such as witnessing sexual activity between parents), parent–child sexual abuse, and a lack of supervision (e.g., Adler & Schutz, 1995; Hardy, 2001; Latzman et al., 2011; Loredo, 1982; Smith & Israel, 1987; Worling, 1995). Environmental factors may also contribute, such as siblings sharing bedrooms and having large amounts of unstructured and unsupervised time (Griffee et al., 2016). Children who have sexually abused a sibling may therefore often be vulnerable and will have experienced abuse and trauma themselves. Because of this, sibling sexual abuse needs to be understood as a problem of, and for, the family as a whole, not just in relation to the psychology of an individual child independent of context. However, the significance of the sibling relationship itself remains under-explored, in terms of both understanding the aetiology of the abuse and helping the siblings to recover and restore a healthier relationship in the future.

Sibling sexual abuse potentially situates at the intersection of a number of different bodies of knowledge and practice: child development and child protection, youth and criminal justice, sex offending, trauma, sibling relationships, and family relationships. Often, however, this complexity of understanding is not maintained. This chapter will go on to explore some of the current challenges in this area of practice, and will focus in particular on the importance of practitioners maintaining a whole family approach, a child developmental and trauma informed perspective, and an understanding of the significance of siblings relationships.

Differentiating Normative from Abusive Sibling Sexual Behaviour

The need to understand sibling relationships becomes apparent when first trying to determine the nature of the sibling sexual behaviour. Not all sibling sexual interactions are harmful and abusive, and it is relatively common for young children, including siblings, to engage in exploratory sexual interactions and sexual play with each other. This is typically harmless and serves a developmental function, helping children to learn about their own bodies and the bodies of those around them (Johnson, 2015).

Inappropriate or problematic sexual behaviours between older siblings, while harmful (Stroebel et al., 2013), may not necessarily involve one sibling abusing another. Mutually initiated sexual behaviour between siblings may emerge from sexual games that go unchecked through a lack of appropriate supervision (Tener, 2019), and some siblings may be drawn together for nurturance and support that later becomes sexualised within the context of other abuse and stresses within the family (Bank & Kahn, 1982). The extent to which both sibling children equally want the sexual behaviour may vary on different occasions, however, and may change over time (Tener et al., 2017). Sexual behaviour starting out as mutually initiated may become coercive. It is not always straightforward to identify one child clearly as the 'victim' and the other as 'perpetrator'. Professional responses that assume there is a clear distinction may force families to label the children in this way, but this may not reflect the nature of the sibling sexual behaviour in specific instances and may hinder the family's attempts to remain unified and move on from the harm that has been caused. Furthermore, while the use of coercion, a large age gap or other obvious power differential between the siblings are common indicators of sibling sexual behaviour being abusive, a significant minority of sexual abuse occurs between siblings close in age or without overt coercion (e.g.,

Cyr et al., 2002; Krienert & Walsh, 2011; Pierce & Pierce, 1990; Russell, 1986). An absence of these factors should not be taken to indicate that the behaviour was necessarily mutually initiated.

All of this means that a research-informed understanding of the complex dynamics of the particular sibling relationship should inform an assessment of the nature of the sibling sexual behaviour (Allardyce & Yates, 2013). Such an understanding would need particular focus upon the dynamics of power, influenced by factors such as birth order, age, gender, cognitive ability, personality traits, and the immediate family and wider culture within which the sibling relationship operates. Gender may confer considerable power differences, particularly in the context of family, ethnic, or religious cultures, which may amplify or sanction women and girls as occupying lower status than men and boys.

Risk Assessment

Understanding family and sibling relationship dynamics is also required to inform risk assessment, both in terms of whether a child may pose an ongoing risk to their siblings and in terms of possible risks to other children in the community. The use of a harmful sexual behaviour risk assessment tool (such as J-SOAP II, PROFESOR) may provide a general indication of the level of risk a young person may present to others in the community, but it does not consider the possible risks to specific children in certain settings (Allardyce & Yates, 2013), notably siblings. In a small study of 34 boys, Yates et al. (2012) found that boys who had abused only siblings were no more likely to have experienced sexual abuse than boys who had abused only in the community. But boys who had abused in both settings were more likely to have experienced multiple forms of trauma, including sexual abuse, and to have begun their sexually abusive behaviour in preadolescence. Boys in the sibling-only group were more likely to have been motivated to abuse by intense feelings of jealous anger, and to have begun abusing during adolescence. While opportunity and access will be factors, this suggests that there may be a trauma-related early-onset route to sibling sexual abuse (where boys may be more likely to abuse both siblings and children in the community) and a later-onset route related to power dynamics and sibling jealousy (where boys may be more likely to abuse only siblings).

Understanding sibling dynamics will therefore have clear implications for risk assessment and therapeutic responses in relation to both the child who has harmed and the child who has been harmed. Accordingly, any use of a structured risk assessment tool needs to be contextualised within a broader family formulation, which considers the dynamics of the abuse, why a particular child was the subject of the abuse, and the nature of the relationship between the child who abused and the child who was harmed.

Decision-Making regarding Sibling Living and Contact Arrangements

Yates and Allardyce (2021) conclude that the following considerations should be explored to inform decisions about sibling living and contact arrangements following abuse becoming known:

- The likely impact, including the emotional impact, of the behaviour upon the child who has been harmed
- The views of the child who has been harmed, however expressed
- The quality and value of the sibling relationship
- An evidence-based assessment of the risks of future sibling sexual behaviour taking place
- The protective abilities and capacities of the parents
- The age and developmental stages of the respective children
- The level to which the family's physical environment is conducive to safety

It is of concern, then, that the impact upon and responses of siblings seem largely to have been overlooked by professionals working with families in which sibling sexual abuse has taken place (Hackett et al., 2014; Yates, 2018). Indeed, there is considerable evidence internationally that the seriousness of sibling sexual abuse is often minimised or goes unrecognised altogether (e.g., Khan & Rogers, 2015; Meyers, 2015; Tener et al., 2018). Yates (2018, 2020) found in particular that social workers rarely considered the possibility that the quality of the sibling relationship might be a causal factor in sibling sexual abuse or that it might suffer as a consequence of the abuse. Decisions relating to sibling contact and living arrangements following the abuse were often made without considering the emotional impact upon either child that such living arrangements and contact might have.

Child sexual abuse is often defined as perpetrated by an adult, so when another child is responsible for the abuse, there may be a tendency to regard the behaviour as somehow less harmful or abusive. These issues become even more acute in the context of sibling sexual abuse. There may be several explanations, but Yates (2020) argues that it may be due to a framing by professionals and parents of sibling relationships as inherently non-abusive. While we accept that siblings may argue and fight, the language of brotherhood and sisterhood suggests equality and alliance (Calvi & Blutrach-Jelin, 2010). Sibling sexual abuse challenges simultaneously our expectations of both childhood and siblinghood, and it may be difficult to contemplate an abusive relationship at the very heart of the family.

Additionally, victims and survivors of sibling sexual abuse may not display trauma symptoms at the time, and, as with child sexual abuse more generally, as children they may regard their sibling sexual experiences as positive or 'normal' and be affected in ways that they do not realise or understand. For many, the impact may not become apparent until adulthood. It is important not to assume that because a child is showing no outward signs of harm that they have not been harmed. Children may miss their siblings or seem happy to see them, but this does not necessarily mean that they have not been harmed or that time spent with their sibling does not compound or perpetuate harm caused. Sibling relationships are complex, and the impact of sibling sexual abuse is likely also to be complex.

That having been said, Allardyce and Yates (2018) note that professionals may alternatively be influenced by heightened public concern about sexual abuse and stereotypical media depictions of adults who commit sexual offences. When children display abusive sexual behaviours, it may challenge our conception of childhood as a period of sexual innocence and may elicit powerful emotions including fear, moral outrage, and disgust. Professionals lacking knowledge or experience may have rather panicky reactions even to situations of quite developmentally normal and exploratory sexual behaviour. The incest taboo may then evoke even greater disgust and therefore exacerbate these anxieties. Such reactions can lead to multi-agency disagreements about risk that result in disproportionate and risk-averse, single-agency responses.

Future Directions for Research and Practice

There is clearly scope for further research in this area. Population studies to establish prevalence could strengthen arguments for the value of such research, as well as highlight the lack of policy and guidance for practitioners. Research to investigate different patterns of sibling sexual behaviour as well as sibling sexual abuse within different types of sibling relationships—step-siblings, adoptive siblings, social siblings—would help develop our theoretical and practical understanding of this issue. Likewise, as most of our current knowledge derives from studies of boys abusing sisters, investigating different pairings and patterns of sibling sexual abuse is essential. Further research and evaluation is required in order to understand what works in family interventions. Existing models of family rehabilitation and reunification may now be outdated and fail to acknowledge fully the developmental status of the child who has harmed and the context of their abuse, setting unrealistic and ultimately unachievable objectives. An additional unexplored area is the ways in which sibling sexual abuse and abusive dynamics are played out online through social media as well as offline in person. Allardyce and Yates (2018) highlight the intertwined nature of children's online and offline worlds and the importance of assessments and interventions incorporating both.

In practice, sibling sexual abuse may require a response from youth justice services, child protection services, trauma services, and family intervention services. By acknowledging the needs of the child who has harmed as well as those of the child who has been harmed, it is also clear that these services cannot be delivered in silos, and the children concerned do not always fit neat categories of 'victim' and 'perpetrator'. Many who cause harm have also experienced harm. In short, more complexity of thinking in research and practice is required rather than simplistic or binary ways of conceptualising this issue.

We need to understand the complex nature of sibling relationships and the particular and ambiguous dynamics of a specific sibling relationship in order to be able to determine the nature of the sibling sexual behaviour, why it has occurred, and its impact, as well as any ongoing risks to the siblings or other children. We also need to make informed decisions regarding sibling living and contact arrangements and the therapeutic work that will be needed to support the siblings and their family to move on from harm. This understanding of sibling relationships needs to be set within a context of the wider family relationships and culture.

Understanding sibling sexual abuse within different cultural contexts represents a considerable gap in knowledge and practice. Caffaro (2020) argues that sibling relationships are influenced significantly by family and wider cultural expectations, which vary across nations but also along economic, occupational, educational, religious, and generational lines. To be effective, family interventions need to take account of these expectations and the strengths and resources different cultures provide, not just as add-ons but as intrinsic to individual and family identities.

Concluding Thoughts

There is clearly a need for further research to inform effective interventions after sibling sexual abuse is identified. Better still would be the prevention of abuse in the first place. Our understanding of the contextual factors that underpin sibling sexual abuse are not yet sophisticated enough to inform research-evidenced targeted prevention measures. However, we know that sibling sexual abuse often emerges within a context of wider family stress and abuse, a lack of parental supervision, and environmental factors that provide opportunity for abuse to occur. Where such issues are present in families known to services, helping those families alleviate current stresses may help to prevent other forms of harm emerging, including sibling sexual abuse. Secondary prevention may also involve targeted advice and support about developmentally healthy social and sexual child development, particularly where non-abusive but problematic sibling sexual behaviour is identified.

However, most sibling sexual abuse occurs in families unknown to services. Greater public recognition of this form of abuse must drive universal prevention. We need to move away from sensationalised and stereotyped representations of child sexual abuse in the media and popular drama, towards wider social recognition that child sexual abuse most often takes place within the ordinary and mundane contexts of family life. That recognition needs to be grounded upon the empirical fact that sibling sexual abuse, like child sexual abuse more generally, exists within a pervasive culture of gendered power imbalances and the condoning of more everyday forms of violence. Changes in wider culture are likely to hold the key to sustainable prevention, and we can all play a part in this tide of change through our everyday social interactions, as professionals, and as members of the society in which we live.

References

Adler, N., & Schutz, J. (1995). Sibling incest offenders. *Child Abuse and Neglect, 19*(7), 811–819.

Allardyce, S., & Yates, P. (2013). Assessing risk of victim crossover in children and young people who display harmful sexual behaviours. *Child Abuse Review, 22*(4), 255–267. https://doi.org/10.1002/car.2277

Allardyce, S., & Yates, P. (2018). *Working with children and young people who have displayed harmful sexual behaviour*. Dunedin.

Atwood, J. D. (2007). When love hurts: Preadolescent girls' reports of incest [Report]. *The American Journal of Family Therapy, 4*, 287–313. http://ezproxy.lib.ed.ac.uk/login?url=https://search.ebscohost.com/login.aspx?direct=true&db=edsggo&AN=edsgcl.167305911&site=eds-live

Bank, S. P., & Kahn, M. D. (1982). *The sibling bond*. Basic Books.

Caffaro, J. (2020). Sibling abuse of other children. In R. Geffner, V. Vieth, V. Vaughan-Eden, A. Rosenbaum, L. Hamberger, & J. White (Eds.), *Handbook of interpersonal violence across the lifespan*. Springer. https://doi.org/10.1007/978-3-319-62122-7_11-1

Caffaro, J. V., & Conn-Caffaro, A. (1998). *Sibling abuse trauma: Assessment and intervention strategies for children, families and adults*. Routledge.

Calvi, G., & Blutrach-Jelin, C. (2010). Sibling relations in family history: Conflicts, co-operation and gender roles in the sixteenth to nineteenth centuries. An introduction. *European Review of History, 17*(5), 695–704. https://doi.org/10.1080/13507486.2010.513120

Carlson, B. E., Maciol, K., & Schneider, J. (2006). Sibling incest: Reports from forty-one survivors. *Journal of Child Sexual Abuse, 15*(4), 19–34. https://doi.org/10.1300/j070v15n04_02

Cyr, M., Wright, J., McDuff, P., & Perron, A. (2002). Intrafamilial sexual abuse: Brother-sister incest does not differ from father-daughter and stepfather-stepdaughter incest. *Child Abuse and Neglect, 26*, 957-973. https://doi.org/10.1016/s0145-2134(02)00365-4

Digiorgio-Miller, J. (1998). Sibling incest: Treatment of the family and the offender. *Child Welfare, 77*(3), 335–346.

Finkelhor, D. (1980). Sex among siblings: A survey on prevalence, variety and effects. *Archives of Sexual Behaviour, 9*(3), 171–194. https://doi.org/10.1007/bf01542244

Griffee, K., Swindell, S., O'Keefe, S. L., Stroebel, S. S., Beard, K. W., Kuo, S.-Y., & Stroupe, W. (2016). Etiological risk factors for sibling incest: Data from an anonymous computer-assisted self-interview. *Sexual Abuse: Journal of Research and Treatment, 28*(7), 620–659. https://doi.org/10.1177/1079063214558941

Hackett, S., Balfe, M., Masson, H., & Phillips, J. (2014). Family responses to young people who have sexually abused: Anger, ambivalence and acceptance. *Children & Society, 28*(2), 128–139. https://doi.org/10.1111/j.1099-0860.2012.00471.x

Hardy, M. S. (2001). Physical aggression and sexual behaviour among siblings: A retrospective study. *Journal of Family Violence, 16*(3), 255–268.

Johnson, T. (2015). *Understanding Children's Sexual Behaviors – What's Natural and Healthy* (Expanded 2015). Holyoke, Massachusetts: Neari Press.

Kelly, L., & Karsna, K. (2018). *Measuring the scale and changing nature of child sexual abuse and child sexual exploitation: Scoping report*. Centre of Expertise on Child Sexual Abuse.

Khan, R., & Rogers, P. (2015). The normalization of sibling violence: Does gender and personal experience of violence influence perceptions of physical assault against siblings? *Journal of Interpersonal Violence, 30*(3), 437–458. https://doi.org/10.1177/0886260514535095

Krienert, J. L., & Walsh, J. A. (2011). Sibling sexual abuse: An empirical analysis of offender, victim, and event characteristics in national incident-based reporting system (NIBRS) data, 2000–2007. *Journal of Child Sexual Abuse, 20*, 353–372. https://doi.org/10.1080/10538712.2011.588190

Latzman, N. E., Viljoen, J. L., Scalora, M. J., & Ullman, D. (2011). Sexual offending in adolescence: A comparison of sibling offenders and nonsibling offenders across domains of risk and treatment need. *Journal of Child Sexual Abuse, 20*(3), 245–263.

Loredo, C. M. (1982). Sibling incest. In S. M. Sgroi (Ed.), *Handbook of clinical intervention in child sexual abuse* (pp. 177–188). Lexington Books.

Martijn, F. M., Leroux, E. J., Babchishin, K. M., & Seto, M. C. (2020). Meta-analysis comparing male adolescents who have sexually offended against intrafamilial versus extrafamilial victims. *Clinical Child and Family Psychology Review*. https://doi.org/10.1007/s10567-020-00320-6A

Meyers, A. (2015). Lifting the veil: The lived experience of sibling abuse. *Qualitative Social Work, 0*(0), 1–18. https://doi.org/10.1177/1473325015612143

O'Brien, M. J. (1991). Taking sibling incest seriously. In M. Q. Patton (Ed.), *Family sexual abuse: Frontline research and evaluation* (pp. 75–92). Sage publications.

O'Keefe, S. L., Beard, K. W., Swindell, S., Stroebel, S. S., Griffee, K., & Young, D. H. (2014). Sister-brother incest: Data from anonymous computer assisted self interviews. *Sexual Addiction and Compulsivity: The Journal of Treatment and Prevention, 21*(1), 1–38. https://doi.org/10.1080/10720162.2013.877410

Pierce, L. H., & Pierce, R. L. (1990). Adolescent / sibling incest perpetrators. In A. L. Holborn, B. L. Johnson, L. M. Roundy, & D. Williams (Eds.), *The incest perpetrator: A family member no one wants to treat* (pp. 99–107). Sage.

Relva, I. C., Fernandes, O. M., & Alarcao, M. (2017). Dyadic types of sibling sexual coercion. *Journal of Family Violence, 32*, 577–583. https://doi.org/10.1007/s10896-017-9918-3

Russell, D. E. H. (1986). *The secret trauma: Incest in the lives of girls and women*. Basic Books.

Smith, H., & Israel, E. (1987). Sibling incest: A study of the dynamics of 25 cases. *Child Abuse and Neglect, 11*, 101–108. https://doi.org/10.1016/0145-2134(87)90038-x

Stroebel, S. S., O'Keefe, S. L., Beard, K. W., Kuo, S.-Y., Swindell, S., & Stroupe, W. (2013). Brother–sister incest: Data from anonymous computer-assisted self interviews. *Journal of Child Sexual Abuse, 22*(3), 255–276. https://doi.org/10.1080/10538712.2013.743952

Tener, D. (2019). "I Love and Hate Him in the Same Breath": Relationships of adult survivors of sexual abuse with their perpetrating siblings. *Journal of Interpersonal Violence, 0*(0), 0886260518821462. https://doi.org/10.1177/0886260518821462

Tener, D., Katz, C., & Kaufmann, Y. (2020). "And I Let It All Out": Survivors' sibling sexual abuse disclosures. *Journal of Interpersonal Violence.* https://doi.org/10.1177/0886260519897326

Tener, D., Lusky, E., Tarshish, N., & Turjeman, S. (2018). Parental attitudes following disclosure of sibling sexual abuse: A child advocacy center intervention study. *American Journal of Orthopsychiatry, Advance online publication* https://doi.org/10.1037/ort0000311

Tener, D., Tarshish, N., & Turgeman, S. (2017). "Victim, Perpetrator, or Just My Brother?" Sibling sexual abuse in large families: A child advocacy center study. *Journal of Interpersonal Violence, Epub.* https://doi.org/doi: https://doi.org/10.1177/0886260517718831

Tidefors, I., Arvidsson, H., Ingevaldson, S., & Larsson, M. (2010). Sibling incest: A literature review and a clinical study. *Journal of Sexual Aggression, 16*(3), 347–360. https://doi.org/10.1080/13552600903511667

Weatherred, J. L. (2015). Child sexual abuse and the media: A literature review. *Journal of Child Sexual Abuse, 24*(1), 16–34. https://doi.org/10.1080/10538712.2015.976302

Worling, J. R. (1995). Adolescent sibling-incest offenders: Differences in family and individual functioning when compared to adolescent nonsibling sex offenders. *Child Abuse and Neglect, 19*(5), 633–643.

Yates, P. (2017). Sibling sexual abuse: Why don't we talk about it? *Journal of Clinical Nursing, 26*(15-16), 2482–2494.

Yates, P. (2018). 'Siblings as better together': Social worker decision-making in cases involving sibling sexual behaviour. *British Journal of Social Work, 48*(1), 176–194. https://doi.org/10.1093/bjsw/bcx018

Yates, P. (2020). "It's just the abuse that needs to stop": Professional framing of sibling relationships in a grounded theory study of social worker decision-making following sibling abuse. *Journal of Child Sexual Abuse, 29*(2), 222–245. https://doi.org/10.1080/10538712.2019.1692399

Yates, P., & Allardyce, S. (2021). *Sibling sexual abuse: Knowledge and Practice.* Centre of Expertise on Child Sexual Abuse.

Yates, P., Allardyce, S., & MacQueen, S. (2012). Children who display harmful sexual behaviour: Assessing the risks of boys abusing at home, in the community or across both settings. *Journal of Sexual Aggression, 18*(1), 23–35.

Part II

Assessment of People Who Have Committed a Sexual Offence

5

Using Indirect Measures of Sexual Interest in Forensic Contexts: Past, Present, and Future

Alexander F. Schmidt and Rainer Banse

Paraphilic interests in general and pedophilic interest in particular have been identified as among the most valid predictors of sexual reoffending in meta-analyses (Mann et al., 2010). Moreover, paraphilia has been cross-sectionally linked to self-reported sexual victimizations of children (Klein et al., 2015) or sexual coercion involving adults (Larue et al., 2014) in community males. The assessment of paraphilic

---

We have no known conflict of interest to disclose.

A. F. Schmidt (✉)
Department of Psychology, Social and Legal Psychology, Johannes Gutenberg University of Mainz, Mainz, Germany
e-mail: alexander.schmidt@uni-mainz.de

R. Banse
Department of Psychology, Social and Legal Psychology, University of Bonn, Bonn, Germany
e-mail: banse@uni-bonn.de

© The Author(s), under exclusive license to Springer Nature Switzerland AG 2022

K. Uzieblo et al. (eds.), *Challenges in the Management of People Convicted of a Sexual Offence*, Palgrave Studies in Risk, Crime and Society,
https://doi.org/10.1007/978-3-030-80212-7_5

inclinations, therefore, is a crucial diagnostic indicator in applied contexts involving individuals who have come into contact with the justice system.

Commonly, in applied forensic and clinical contexts sexual interests are inferred from known offending behaviour (for an overview of recent advances, see Lehmann et al., 2018) in combination with self- and other-reports (Kalmus & Beech, 2005). However, validity of self-reports is limited due to the associated legal and psychosocial repercussions for the respondent. Furthermore, the link between offending behaviour and paraphilic interest is equivocal. For example, not every individual with pedophilic sexual interest is sexually victimizing children (Dombert et al., 2016), and the majority of convicted individuals who have sexually abused children (CISAC) do not exhibit a pedophilic disorder (e.g., Schmidt et al., 2013). Finally, with at least roughly one out of three routine care diagnoses of pedophilic disorder being invalid due to lacking interrater reliability (Mokros et al., 2018), the diagnostic accuracy for this disorder falls short of the desirable validity for single case assessments informing sentencing, (mandatory) treatment, and risk management decisions.

Past Developments: Validation of Indirect Measures of Sexual Interest

One answer to the above-mentioned problems in assessing categorical paraphilic interest (Marshall & Kingston, 2018) was the development of easy-to-apply, continuous, indirect measures of sexual interest over the last two decades. In contrast to direct measures that rely on self-reported sexual interests, fantasies, or behaviours, indirect measures are based on behaviours that are believed to be causally driven by sexual interest but do not require a report of subjective sexual inclinations or physical arousal (De Houwer, 2006). To this end, response latencies or accuracy rates are most frequently used as dependent variables from which sexual interests are inferred. Thus, the term *indirect measure* denotes that the construct in question is not directly derived from self-report, but indirectly from another type of behaviour; hence, it is not the same as physiological or subjectively perceived sexual arousal.

Since the early 1990s, a number of latency-based paradigms, mostly developed in social cognition research, have been adapted and validated to assess constructs relevant for the forensic context. These developments were motivated by the hope that these approaches based on unobtrusively measured response latencies or accuracy rates may overcome the problem of strategic self-presentation in the forensic assessment of individuals who have committed sexual offences. Although preliminary attempts have been made in other construct domains (such as aggressiveness, psychopathy, criminal identity, and sexual self-regulation), the overwhelming majority of research hitherto has focused on indirect measures of paedohebephilic interest (see Table 5.1 for an overview).

Table 5.1 Overview of indirect measures of paedohebephilic interest comparing groups of convicted males who sexually victimized children against various control groups

Measure	First validation study
Task-relevant measures	
Viewing Time	Harris et al. (1996)
Implicit Association Test	Nunes et al. (2007)
Implicit Relational Assessment Procedure	Dawson et al. (2009)
Eye-Tracking (fixations)	Fromberger et al. (2012)
Task-irrelevant measures	
Emotional Stroop	Smith and Waterman (2004)
Rapid Serial Visual Presentation/Attentional Blink	Beech et al. (2008)
Choice Reaction Task	Mokros et al. (2010)
Picture Association Task (validated with self-identified men with pedophilic interests)	van Leeuwen et al. (2013)
Go/No-Go Association Task	Bartels et al. (2018)
Approach-Avoidance Task	Weidacker et al. (2018)

Criterion, Convergent, and Predictive Validity

Prototypical validation rationales compare samples of CISAC with other types of offending and non-offending control groups. However, most indirect measures have undergone only preliminary validation based on single or few empirical tests (for comprehensive overviews of effect sizes of indirect measures of paedohebephilic interest see Bartels et al., 2017; Schmidt et al., 2015). Notable exceptions are Implicit Association Tests (IATs) and Viewing Time (VT) measures of sexual interest in children and adults for which meta-analytic reviews exist (Babchishin et al., 2013; Nunes & Pedneault, 2020; Schmidt et al., 2017), although the underlying database with $k < 15$ studies for each measure is still small.

In terms of *criterion validity*, the average meta-analytic VT effect size for discriminating CISAC from controls is $d = 0.60$. This effect size increases to $d = 1.03$ when using sexual preference indices for children over adults (i.e., the difference between the maximum adult and child categories; Schmidt et al., 2017; see below for advantages of this scoring approach). The IATs yield discriminatory effects of $d = 0.63$ (Babchishin et al., 2013). Gauging the validity of VTs and IATs against penile plethysmographic measures ($d = 0.67$, increasing to $d = 1.01$ when using a z-standardized preference index; McPhail et al., 2019) reveals that all these measures show roughly similar criterion validity. Notably, as these validity estimations are based on convictions for child sexual abuse as a proxy of paedohebephilic[1] sexual interest, validity will most probably be underestimated because unselected CISAC groups also contain a considerable amount of individuals with teleiophilic sexual preferences (Schmidt et al., 2013, 2017). In line with this reasoning, studies involving *self-identified* paedohebephilic and teleiophilic men from the community showed substantially larger group differences (*ds* between 1.24 and 1.79; VT: Jahnke et al., 2020; IAT: van Leeuwen et al., 2013).[2]

[1] Pedophilic interests refer to sexual interest in prepubescent children and hebephilic interests to pubescent children. The term *pedohebephilia* is used to refer to sexual interests in both target maturity categories.

[2] Comparing CISACs with versus without clinical diagnoses of pedophilic disorder revealed *ds* of 0.61 and 0.69 for VT and IAT preference indices (recalculated from Schmidt et al., 2010), respec-

In terms of *convergent validity*, VT measures are meaningfully associated with offence-behavioural indicators (Screening Scale for Pedophilic Interests [SSPI]; Seto & Lalumiére, 2001), self-report, penile plethysmographic assessment, and IATs of paedohebephilic interest (Schmidt et al., 2017) as well as other indirect latency-based and oculomotoric measures of sexual interest in children and adults (Ó Ciardha et al., 2018). Concerning the *predictive validity* of indirect measures of pedophilic sexual interest, only for VT it has been demonstrated that the measure prospectively predicts sexual reoffending over a 15-year observation period (Harrel's $c = 0.68$; Gray et al., 2015).

Present Developments: Using Indirect Measures of Sexual Interest

Combining Indirect Measures into Test Batteries

To take the leap from measurement validation to using indirect measures in real-life forensic assessments, psychometric quality is paramount. It is a fact that any single measure is amenable to personal and situational moderators. Therefore, using single measures for diagnostic decisions should be avoided. According to the aggregation principle, diagnostic inferences can be drawn with greater confidence if they are based on conceptually different, reliable, valid, and convergent measures. To this end, the *Explicit and Implicit Sexual Interest Profile* (EISIP; Banse et al., 2010) combines the best-validated indirect measures (VT, IAT) as well as a self-report questionnaire into a computer-based test battery of sexual interests ranging from children to adults. To ease the EISIP's practical applicability, we have developed a software tool that graphically displays individual profile charts of sexual interests (for a detailed description of EISIP measures and their single-case application, see Schmidt & Perkins, 2020).

The validity of the EISIP as a measure of paedohebephilic interest has been demonstrated using a range of criteria such as distinguishing CISAC

tively. But note that this clinical criterion suffers from decreased validity as outlined above (Mokros et al., 2018).

from controls, (Banse et al., 2010) and between subgroups of CISAC varying in paedohebephilic interest (Schmidt et al., 2014). The EISIP correlates with clinicians' diagnoses of pedophilic disorder, the SSPI, and static actuarial risk assessment measures (Schmidt et al., 2010, 2014; Banse et al., 2010). Taxometric analyses of EISIP assessments among men with and without sexual interests in children revealed a taxonic structure of paedohebephilic interests (Schmidt et al., 2013). Importantly, EISIP indirect measures were incrementally valid beyond self-report measures in non-denying samples (Banse et al., 2010) and routine-care forensic settings (Schmidt et al., 2010).

Although the EISIP is not related to social desirability (Banse et al., 2010), it certainly can be willfully altered—much like any psychological measure—if the measurement rationales are known and the respondent has the cognitive abilities and the motivation to do so. Strikingly, in CISAC who denied or admitted sexual interest in children or sexual behaviour involving minors, EISIP VT and IAT paedohebephilic preference indexes as well as SSPI scores were decreased in deniers (Schmidt & Perkins, 2020). Hence, the objective measure based on offending behaviour dovetailed with indirect measures in revealing lower sexual preferences for children in the deniers. This underscores that CISAC's denial of paedohebephilic interest might be more valid than generally supposed—at least in forensic research contexts.

Scoring Approaches for Indirect Measures

Indirect measures tapping into sexual interests in children and adults can be scored absolutely or relatively. *Absolute measures* of sexual interest have the advantage to assess within-individual differences in the strength of sexual interest across classes of specific sexual targets (e.g., boys > men > girls = women). Their disadvantage is that between-individual differences are difficult to attribute solely to sexual interests, as absolute category latencies are confounded with factors that unspecifically affect response times in the assessment situation (individual differences in processing speed, accuracy/speed trade-offs, etc.).

Relative measures of sexual preferences compare target categories against each other (e.g., a girl-women IAT assesses the sexual preference of girls compared to women) either by subtraction or by division of both target categories. This indicates to what extent children are sexually preferred over adults. Additionally, relative measures statistically control for factors impacting general response speed. Hence, relative indices are particularly suited for between-individual comparisons as evidenced by the increased validity for sexual preference indices outlined above. Their disadvantage, however, is that they *must not* be interpreted in absolute terms: A preference score of zero may be caused by equally high or by equally low absolute sexual interest in both categories.

Absolute measures of sexual interest can always be transformed into relative measures but not necessarily vice versa in cases where absolute scores are not available—as is conceptually the case for IATs where it remains obscure which category drives a certain sexual preference, for example increased interest in girls or decreased interest in women. For example, for VT measures subtracting the maximum adult category score from the maximum child category score irrespective of target gender results in a relative sexual preference index that is independent of sexual orientation (i.e., sexual gender preferences). This implies that the relative term *sexual preference* and the absolute term *sexual interest* address different conceptualizations of sexual inclinations.

Reliability Matters

According to classical test theory, reliability limits the maximum validity of measures. Latency-based measures are notoriously fraught with low reliabilities (e.g., LeBel & Paunonen, 2011). At present, data on reliability—particularly test-retest reliability—is seldom reported in research on indirect measures of sexual interest in the forensic field (Schmidt et al., 2015). This practice hampers not only research as low reliability restricts evaluations of replicability or change but also the application of indirect measures in forensic assessments due to the fact that large confidence intervals due to high measurement error prevent precise (i.e., informative) diagnostic conclusions.

Among indirect sexual interest measures, VT measures and the IAT stand out as most reliable (i.e., internally consistent; Schmidt et al., 2015). However, for some of the other measures the data base is very limited. Utilizing EISIP sexual preference indices, Welsch, Schmidt, and colleagues (2020a) ran the first comprehensive study on the temporal stability of indirect measures of paedohebephilic interest in CISAC and community controls. Internal consistencies were satisfactory to good for all EISIP sexual preference measures (based on VT, IAT, and self-report). Relative test-retest reliabilities (i.e., rank orders) were surprisingly high over a 14-day interval: Intraclass correlation coefficients for sexual preference indices ranged from marginally satisfactory to good (IAT 0.66; VT 0.78; self-reports 0.87; full EISIP aggregate score 0.90). However, assessing absolute temporal agreement revealed that effects from roughly a third to three-quarters of a standardized mean difference unit will be needed to rule out artificial change induced by transient measurement error. This means that the EISIP is currently the only existing indirect measure for which the impact of measurement error on repeated assessments can be specified and taken into account—a necessary prerequisite for meaningful evaluations of (therapy-induced) change of sexual interests over time[3] (Welsch et al., 2020a).

Underlying Psychological Processes

Indirect measures of sexual interest can be distinguished into (1) task-relevant and (2) task-irrelevant measures (Schmidt et al., 2015; also Table 1). *Task-relevant* indirect measures involve the explicit categorization or evaluation of sexual target categories as the respondent's primary task—either in terms of sexual attractiveness (e.g., VT) or in combination with classification trials of sexual attributes (e.g., IAT). Due to the explicit task requirement to process sexual relevance, it is particularly transparent to the respondents that sexual interest is the diagnostic focus,

[3] Whether change of pedohebephilic preferences is possible at all is a debated, empirically open question. Although most clinicians doubt that psychologically significant change can be achieved, it might be possible for subtypes who develop paraphilic sexual preferences only later in life (Imhoff et al., 2017; Smid & Wever, 2019).

although they are not informed that response latencies are unobtrusively recorded.

Task-irrelevant measures (e.g., choice reaction time) are based on the detection of sexually irrelevant characteristics (e.g., location, colour, and semantic meaning) of target stimuli that are presented together with distracting sexually relevant versus irrelevant background stimuli (e.g., adults and children). The underlying rationale is that sexually attractive background stimuli cause larger interference with the non-sexual primary detection task resulting in increased response latencies. There is preliminary support for the idea that task-relevant indirect measures are psychometrically superior to task-irrelevant measures (Schmidt et al., 2015; Rönspies et al., 2015) due to their increased structural similarity between task and assessment aim.

Currently, particularly the underlying psychological processes of VT measures of sexual interest have been examined (for a primer on the large social psychological literature on general IAT processes, see Gawronski et al., in press). It is a robust finding that for more sexually attractive stimuli, raters will take longer to reach their decision about subjective sexual attractivity (Imhoff et al., 2010). Notably, these decision latencies are not caused by attentional engagement or holding effects (Imhoff et al., 2010) as often supposed in the literature, but are the result of a feature checking process that is induced by the structure of the VT-task (Imhoff et al., 2012). In order to decide about stimuli's sexual attractiveness, respondents need to check a set of idiosyncratic stimulus features such as, for example, age, gender, and sexual attractiveness. In case that one of these features does not fit the interest of the respondent, the rating process can be terminated faster. However, as long as these feature checks remain positive, the process continues and prolongs the rating process. Hence, the VT effect is not stimuli-driven but a cognitive byproduct of the structure of the rating task (Imhoff et al., 2012). Therefore, VT measures produce meaningful results only as long as participants comply with the instructions to rate targets' sexual attractiveness from their own personal perspective. If participants perform rating tasks not relevant to their own sexual perspective (e.g., rating stimuli from a vicarious perspective [Imhoff et al., 2012]) or determine only single stimulus properties such as age or hair colour [Pohl et al., 2016]), VT latency patterns become non-interpretable.

The Future of Indirect Measures

Summarizing past evidence corroborates that indirect measures of sexual interest have clearly passed the proof-of-concept phase. As opposed to indirect measures in other fields, over the last decade the EISIP has found its way into first practical applications in pioneering forensic institutions to inform their diagnostic and administrative decisions. Notwithstanding this, researchers emphasize the lack of standardized scoring for indirect measures, whereas practitioners miss yet lacking norms or cut-offs that aid their clinical single-case decisions of how to demarcate preferential from non-preferential paedohebephilia or data on critical differences between absolute sexual interest categories. There is headroom for research on how indirect measures of sexual interest relate to risk assessment where more prospective studies are needed. Particularly, due to the ease of measurement application not only associations with baseline risk will be of interest but also whether paedohebephilia is amenable to change and how such change is related to future reoffending (Welsch et al., 2020a; see Forscher et al., 2019 for a general discussion of how well indirect measures tap into individual [behaviour] change). Another question concerns whether pharmacological treatment impacts sexual interests as indirectly inferred from cognitive byproducts (i.e., latencies, accuracy rates) of the measurement. Finally, most stimulus sets for indirect measures consist of White individuals only. It hitherto remains an open empirical question whether matching respondents' and target stimuli's ethnic origins influences sexual interest assessments in ethnically diverse samples.

We firmly encourage researchers to focus more on issues of reliability and the underlying psychological processes of indirect measures (Meissner et al., 2019). On the one hand, low reliability is among the biggest concerns for a majority of these measures. On the other hand, once we will better understand how certain processes drive the outcomes of indirect measurements, this may open a venue to modify these measures in terms of increased faking-resistance.

Fakeability of indirect measures remains an under-researched topic specifically in applied forensic contexts where practitioners have to balance respondents' civil rights and society's interest to be protected. Against this background, in order to be an effective diagnostic tool it is paramount that the underlying measurement rationales (i.e., focus on response latencies) and actual names of indirect measures are protected from public awareness. It is unfortunate, for example, that the DSM-5 literally mentions VT as a valid diagnostic tool in the introductory section on pedophilic disorder, thus giving away the rationale of these tasks. Note, although this recommendation might sound as if we were actively deceiving respondents, clinicians never reveal scoring keys of any diagnostic interview or psychometric scale to respondents in order to protect their assessments' diagnostic potential. Importantly, most indirect measures, but certainly the EISIP, are rather transparent about their assessment purpose, namely sexual interest in children and adults. An ethically satisficing way of achieving informed consent for participating in an EISIP assessment might be to refer to individual differences in information processing that are revealed in classification and sorting tasks—without mentioning response latencies—in case the underlying measurement rationales become part of a debate (Schmidt & Perkins, 2020).

Last but not least, there are preliminary developments that might be promising for applied forensic contexts such as potentially highly faking-resistant oculomotoric measures based on pupil dilation (Attard-Johnson et al., 2016), saccadic eye movements (Oberlader et al., 2017), or virtual reality-based interpersonal distance and approach behaviour (Welsch et al., 2020c). Moreover, extending the available measures to tap into the sexual coercion–sexual sadism spectrum (Larue et al., 2014) or other forensically relevant constructs such as sexual excitability/sex drive (Imhoff et al., 2020), aggressiveness (Banse et al., 2017), and psychopathy (Krüppel et al., 2020; Welsch et al., 2020b) illustrates the potential that these fascinating measures may offer for the applied forensic field.

References

Attard-Johnson, J., Bindemann, M., & Ciardha, C. Ó. (2016). Pupillary response as an age-specific measure of sexual interest. *Archives of Sexual Behavior, 45*(4), 855–870. https://doi.org/10.1007/s10508-015-0681-3

Babchishin, K. M., Nunes, K. L., & Hermann, C. A. (2013). The validity of Implicit Association Test (IAT) measures of sexual attraction to children: A meta-analysis. *Archives of Sexual Behavior, 42*(3), 487–499. https://doi.org/10.1007/s10508-012-0022-8

Banse, R., Schmidt, A. F., & Clarbour, J. (2010). Indirect measures of sexual interest in child sex offenders: A multimethod approach. *Criminal Justice and Behavior, 37*(3), 319–335. https://doi.org/10.1177/0093854809357598

Banse, R., Schmidt, A. F., & Imhoff, R. (2017). Aggression in the perspective of the Reflective-Impulsive Model: Testing predictions using indirect measures. In R. Deutsch, B. Gawronski, & W. Hofmann (Eds.), *Reflective and impulsive determinants of human behaviour* (pp. 239–256). Routledge Psychology Press.

Bartels, R. M., Beech, A. R., Harkins, L., & Thornton, D. (2018). Assessing sexual interest in children using the go/no-go association test. *Sexual Abuse, 30*(5), 593–614. https://doi.org/10.1177/1079063216686119

Bartels, R. M., Gray, N. S., & Snowden, R. J. (2017). Indirect measures of deviant sexual interest. In L. A. Craig & M. Rettenberger (Eds.), *The Wiley handbook on the theories, assessment, and treatment of sexual offending—Volume II: Assessment* (pp. 965–993). Wiley-Blackwell.

Beech, A. R., Kalmus, E., Tipper, S. P., Baudouin, J. Y., Flak, V., & Humphreys, G. W. (2008). Children induce an enhanced attentional blink in child molesters. *Psychological Assessment, 20*(4), 397–402. https://doi.org/10.1037/a0013587

Dawson, D. L., Barnes-Holmes, D., Gresswell, D. M., Hart, A. J., & Gore, N. J. (2009). Assessing the implicit beliefs of sexual offenders using the Implicit Relational Assessment Procedure: A first study. *Sexual Abuse: A Journal of Research and Treatment, 21*(1), 57–75. https://doi.org/10.1177/1079063208326928

De Houwer, J. (2006). What are implicit measures and why are we using them. In R. W. Wiers & A. W. Stacy (Eds.), *The handbook of implicit cognition and addiction* (pp. 11–28). Sage Publishers.

Dombert, B., Schmidt, A. F., Banse, R., Briken, P., Hoyer, J., Neutze, J., & Osterheider, M. (2016). How common is men's self-reported sexual interest in prepubescent children? *The Journal of Sex Research, 53*(2), 214–223. https://doi.org/10.1080/00224499.2015.1020108

Forscher, P. S., Lai, C. K., Axt, J. R., Ebersole, C. R., Herman, M., Devine, P. G., & Nosek, B. A. (2019). A meta-analysis of procedures to change implicit measures. *Journal of Personality and Social Psychology, 117*(3), 522–559. https://doi.org/10.1037/pspa0000160

Fromberger, P., Jordan, K., Steinkrauss, H., von Herder, J., Witzel, J., Stolpmann, G., Kröner-Herwig, B., & Müller, J. L. (2012). Diagnostic accuracy of eye movements in assessing paedophilia. *The Journal of Sexual Medicine, 9*(7), 1868–1882. https://doi.org/10.1111/j.1743-6109.2012.02754.x

Gawronski, B., De Houwer, J., & Shermann, J. (2020). Twenty-five years of research using implicit measures. *Social Cognition, 38* (Supplement), s1–s25. https://doi.org/10.1521/soco.2020.38.supp.s1

Gray, S. R., Abel, G. G., Jordan, A., Garby, T., Wiegel, M., & Harlow, N. (2015). Visual reaction time™ as a predictor of sexual offense recidivism. *Sexual Abuse: A Journal of Research and Treatment, 27*(2), 173–188. https://doi.org/10.1177/1079063213502680

Harris, G. T., Rice, M. E., Quinsey, V. L., & Chaplin, T. C. (1996). Viewing time as a measure of sexual interest among child molesters and normal heterosexual men. *Behaviour Research and Therapy, 34*(4), 389–394. https://doi.org/10.1016/0005-7967(95)00070-4

Imhoff, R., Banse, R., & Schmidt, A. F. (2017). Toward a theoretical understanding of sexual orientation and sexual motivation. *Archives of Sexual Behavior, 46*, 29–33. https://doi.org/10.1007/s10508-016-0881-5

Imhoff, R., Barker, P., & Schmidt, A. F. (2020). To what extent do erotic images elicit visuospatial versus cognitive attentional processes? Consistent support for a (non-spatial) Sexual Content-Induced Delay. *Archives of Sexual Behavior, 49*(2), 531–550. https://doi.org/10.1007/BF02229209

Imhoff, R., Schmidt, A. F., Nordsiek, U., Luzar, C., Young, A. W., & Banse, R. (2010). Viewing time effects revisited: Prolonged response latencies for sexually attractive targets under restricted task conditions. *Archives of Sexual Behavior, 39*(6), 1275–1288. https://doi.org/10.1007/s10508-009-9595-2

Imhoff, R., Schmidt, A. F., Weiß, S., Young, A. W., & Banse, R. (2012). Vicarious viewing time: Prolonged response latencies for sexually attractive targets as a function of task- or stimulus-specific processing. *Archives of Sexual Behavior, 41*(6), 1389–1401. https://doi.org/10.1007/s10508-011-9879-1

Jahnke, S., Schmidt, A. F., Klöckner, A., & Hoyer, J. (2020). *Disentangling neurodevelopmental differences, sexual offending, and paedophilia: Findings from two online surveys*. Manuscript submitted for publication.

Kalmus, E., & Beech, A. R. (2005). Forensic assessment of sexual interest: A review. *Aggression and Violent Behavior, 10*(2), 193–217. https://doi.org/10.1016/j.avb.2003.12.002

Klein, V., Schmidt, A. F., Turner, D., & Briken, P. (2015). Are sex drive and hypersexuality associated with paedophilic interest and child sexual abuse in a male community sample? *PLoS One, 10*(7), e0129730. https://doi.org/10.1371/journal.pone.0139533

Krüppel, J., Yoon, D., Zerres, K., & Mokros, A. (2020). *Implicit and explicit assessment of psychopathy: Results from two community samples.* Manuscript submitted for publication.

Larue, D., Schmidt, A. F., Imhoff, R., Eggers, K., Schönbrodt, F. D., & Banse, R. (2014). Validation of direct and indirect measures of preference for sexualized violence. *Psychological Assessment, 26*(4), 1173–1183. https://doi.org/10.1037/pas0000016

LeBel, E. P., & Paunonen, S. V. (2011). Sexy but often unreliable: The impact of unreliability on the replicability of experimental findings with implicit measures. *Personality and Social Psychology Bulletin, 37*(4), 570–583. https://doi.org/10.1177/0146167211400619

Lehmann, R. J. B., Dahle, K.-P., & Schmidt, A. F. (2018). Primer on the contribution of crime scene behavior to the forensic assessment of sexual offenders. *European Psychologist, 23*(2), 154–166. https://doi.org/10.1027/1016-9040/a000324

Mann, R. E., Hanson, R. K., & Thornton, D. (2010). Assessing risk for sexual recidivism: Some proposals on the nature of psychologically meaningful risk factors. *Sexual Abuse, 22,* 191–217. https://doi.org/10.1177/1079063210366039

Marshall, W. L., & Kingston, D. A. (2018). Diagnostic issues in the paraphilias. *Current Psychiatry Reports, 20,* 54. https://doi.org/10.1007/s11920-018-0919-6

McPhail, I. V., Hermann, C. A., Fernane, S., Fernandez, Y. M., Nunes, K. L., & Cantor, J. M. (2019). Validity in phallometric testing for sexual interests in children: A meta-analytic review. *Assessment, 26*(3), 535–551. https://doi.org/10.1177/1073191117706139

Meissner, F., Grigutsch, L. A., Koranyi, N., Müller, F., & Rothermund, K. (2019). Predicting behaviour with implicit measures: Disillusioning findings, reasonable explanations, and sophisticated solutions. *Frontiers in Psychology, 10,* 2483. https://doi.org/10.3389/fpsyg.2019.02483

Mokros, A., Dombert, B., Osterheider, M., Zappala, A., & Santtila, P. (2010). Assessment of paedophilic sexual interest with an attentional choice reaction time task. *Archives of Sexual Behavior, 39*(5), 1081–1090. https://doi.org/10.1007/s10508-009-9530-6

Mokros, A., Habermeyer, E., & Küchenhoff, H. (2018). The uncertainty of psychological and psychiatric diagnoses. *Psychological Assessment, 30*(4), 556–560. https://doi.org/10.1037/pas0000524
Nunes, K. L., Firestone, P., & Baldwin, M. W. (2007). Indirect assessment of cognitions of child sexual abusers with the Implicit Association Test. *Criminal Justice and Behavior, 34*(4), 454–475. https://doi.org/10.1177/0093854806291703
Nunes, K. L., & Pedneault, C. I. (2020). Indirect and physiological approaches to assessing deviant sexual interests. In J. Proulx, F. Cortoni, L. A. Craig, & E. J. Letourneau (Eds.), *The Wiley handbook of what works with sexual offenders: Contemporary perspectives in theory, assessment, treatment, and prevention* (pp. 123–138). Wiley-Blackwell.
Ó Ciardha, C., Attard-Johnson, J., & Bindemann, M. (2018). Latency-based and psychophysiological measures of sexual interest show convergent and concurrent validity. *Archives of Sexual Behavior, 47*(3), 637–649. https://doi.org/10.1007/s10508-017-1133-z
Oberlader, V. A., Ettinger, U., Banse, R., & Schmidt, A. F. (2017). Development of a cued pro-and antisaccade paradigm: An indirect measure to explore automatic components of sexual interest. *Archives of Sexual Behavior, 46*(8), 2377–2388. https://doi.org/10.1007/s10508-016-0839-7
Pohl, A., Wolters, A., & Ponseti, J. (2016). Investigating the task dependency of viewing time effects. *The Journal of Sex Research, 53*(8), 1027–1035. https://doi.org/10.1080/00224499.2015.1089429
Rönspies, J., Schmidt, A. F., Melnikova, A., Krumova, R., Zolfagari, A., & Banse, R. (2015). Indirect measurement of sexual orientation: Comparison of the implicit relational assessment procedure, viewing time, and choice reaction time tasks. *Archives of Sexual Behavior, 44*(5), 1483–1492. https://doi.org/10.1007/s10508-014-0473-1
Schmidt, A. F., Babchishin, K. M., & Lehmann, R. J. (2017). A meta-analysis of viewing time measures of sexual interest in children. *Archives of Sexual Behavior, 46*(1), 287–300. https://doi.org/10.1007/s10508-016-0806-3
Schmidt, A. F., Banse, R., & Imhoff, R. (2015). Indirect measures in forensic contexts. In T. M. Ortner & F. J. R. van de Vijver (Eds.), *Behavior-based assessment in psychology* (pp. 173–194). Hogrefe.
Schmidt, A. F., Bonus, P., & Banse, R. (2010, July). *Indirect measures of sexual interest in child sex offenders: A multimethod approach and its clinical implications*. Paper presented at the International Summer Conference in Forensic Psychiatry, Regensburg, Germany.

Schmidt, A. F., Gykiere, K., Vanhoeck, K., Mann, R. E., & Banse, R. (2014). Direct and indirect measures of sexual maturity preferences differentiate subtypes of child sexual abusers. *Sexual Abuse, 26*(2), 107–128. https://doi.org/10.1177/1079063213480817

Schmidt, A. F., Mokros, A., & Banse, R. (2013). Is paedophilic sexual preference continuous? A taxometric analysis based on direct and indirect measures. *Psychological Assessment, 25*(4), 1146–1153. https://doi.org/10.1037/a0033326

Schmidt, A. F., & Perkins, D. (2020). Using the Explicit and Implicit Sexual Interest Profile in applied forensic or clinical contexts. In G. Ackerman, D. Perkins, & R. M. Bartels (Eds.), *Assessing and managing problematic sexual interests—A practitioner's guide* (pp. 57–81). Routledge.

Seto, M. C., & Lalumière, M. L. (2001). A brief screening scale to identify paedophilic interests among child molesters. *Sexual Abuse: A Journal of Research and Treatment, 13*(1), 15–25. https://doi.org/10.1023/A:1009510328588

Smid, W. J., & Wever, E. C. (2019). Mixed emotions: An incentive motivational model of sexual deviance. *Sexual Abuse, 31*(7), 731–764. https://doi.org/10.1177/1079063218775972

Smith, P., & Waterman, M. (2004). Processing bias for sexual material: The emotional Stroop and sexual offenders. *Sexual Abuse: A Journal of Research and Treatment, 16*(2), 163–171. https://doi.org/10.1023/B:SEBU.0000023064.54397.d6

van Leeuwen, M. L., van Baaren, R. B., Chakhssi, F., Loonen, M. G., Lippman, M., & Dijksterhuis, A. (2013). Assessment of implicit sexual associations in non-incarcerated pedophiles. *Archives of Sexual Behavior, 42*(8), 1501–1507. https://doi.org/10.1007/s10508-013-0094-0

Weidacker, K., Kärgel, C., Massau, C., Weiß, S., Kneer, J., Krueger, T. H. C., & Schiffer, B. (2018). Approach and avoidance tendencies toward picture stimuli of (pre-) pubescent children and adults: An investigation in paedophilic and nonpedophilic samples. *Sexual Abuse, 30*(7), 781–802. https://doi.org/10.1177/1079063217697134

Welsch, R., Schmidt, A. F., Turner, D., & Rettenberger, M. (2020a). Test–retest reliability and temporal agreement of direct and indirect sexual interest measures. *Sexual Abuse*. Advance online publication. https://doi.org/10.1177/1079063220904354

Welsch, R., von Castell, C., & Hecht, H. (2020b). Interpersonal distance regulation and approach-avoidance reactions are altered in psychopathy. *Clinical Psychological Science, 8*(2), 211–225. https://doi.org/10.1177/2167702619869336

Welsch, R., von Castell, C., Rettenberger, M., Turner, D., Hecht, H., & Fromberger, P. (2020c). Sexual attraction modulates interpersonal distance and approach-avoidance movements towards virtual agents in males. *PloS One, 15*(4), e0231539. https://doi.org/10.1371/journal.pone.0231539

6

Working with Individuals Who Have Accessed Child Sexual Exploitation Material: Assessment Strategies and Future Developments

Hannah L. Merdian and Derek E. Perkins

Sexual violence against children is a significant global threat to the health and protection of children, with online Child Sexual Exploitation Material (CSEM) representing a record of the sexual abuse. In their latest annual report, the Internet Watch Foundation (IWF, 2020) reported an increase of 26% for webpages confirmed to contain images and videos of child sexual abuse. This rate highlights the significant number of victims,

I have no known conflict of interest to disclose.

H. L. Merdian
University of Lincoln, Lincoln, UK
e-mail: hmerdian@lincoln.ac.uk

D. E. Perkins (✉)
Royal Holloway, University of London, Egham, UK
e-mail: derek.perkins@rhul.ac.uk

© The Author(s), under exclusive license to Springer Nature Switzerland AG 2022

K. Uzieblo et al. (eds.), *Challenges in the Management of People Convicted of a Sexual Offence*, Palgrave Studies in Risk, Crime and Society,
https://doi.org/10.1007/978-3-030-80212-7_6

and points to the large number of individuals who are accessing, distributing, and creating this material.

Over the last twenty years or so, the understanding of CSEM offending behaviour has grown substantially, including offence motivations (e.g., Seto et al., 2010), offending pathways (e.g., Winder et al., 2015), and offence-supportive cognitions (e.g., Paquette et al., 2020). Two meta-analyses (Babchishin et al., 2010, 2015) provided the empirical foundation on the differences between individuals who had accessed CSEM and those who had engaged in contact offending behaviour. There have been theoretical advances: Seto's (2019) expanded his Motivation-Facilitation Model of sexual offending (which outlines and exemplifies the distinction of motivational and facilitative contributors to sexual offending behavior) as an explanation for CSEM offending. Bartels and Merdian (2016) conceptualized the first set of implicit theories unique to CSEM offending behavior. Recent years saw the release of the first validated risk assessment tool for individuals who had CSEM offences (Child Pornography Offender Risk Tool, CPORT; Eke et al., 2019), and the development of the first validated tool for CSEM-related offence-supportive cognitions (Cognitions of Internet Sexual Offending, C-ISO; Paquette & Cortoni, 2019). This growing research body developed alongside a professional and public debate on appropriate terminology (e.g., Greijer et al., 2016), legal classification (e.g., International Centre for Missing and Exploited Children, 2018), treatment approaches (e.g., Beier et al., 2015), and preventative approaches (e.g., Quayle & Koukopoulos, 2019).

The research on CSEM offending behaviour is embedded in and informs the wider empirical context. There has been some discussion concerning the concept of internet addiction (e.g., Warden et al., 2004) or pornography addiction (e.g., Duffy et al., 2016). The significant numbers of individuals engaging in CSEM offending have raised questions concerning the community prevalence of sexual interest in children (e.g., Dombert et al., 2016), its manifestation and assessment (e.g., Rosburg et al., 2020), and theoretical conceptualisation (e.g., Seto, 2016). There is an emerging research body on the definition and role of sexual fantasy (see Bartels, 2021). There is a better differentiation and understanding of other technology-facilitated offending behaviours such as online solicitation (see, Winters et al., 2021) and transnational sexual abuse (Wefers et al., 2019), and an increased focus on how young people engage with the internet (e.g., Finkelhor et al., 2020). There is a strong debate on public health prevention approaches and help-seeking behaviour (e.g., Levenson et al., 2017). Despite the rapid increase in non-academic and academic outputs related to CSEM offending behaviour, knowledge generation in this area is ongoing and adaptive to technological advances. This provides a particular challenge for professionals working with individuals who have engaged in, or are at risk of engaging in, CSEM offending behaviour.

Exploring Pathways to CSEM Offending Behaviour

Our own research had a predominant focus on understanding individuals' pathways to CSEM offending behaviour as the basis for case formulation. We were presented with the challenge that people in a variety of professional roles (e.g., police, probation, treatment providers) were required to engage in informed risk and needs assessments and treatment planning—often on a daily basis—without a sound empirical basis for their decision-making. We were aware from the existing literature (e.g., Hanson, 2005) that the development and validation of actuarial risk assessment tools takes time, and needs to take its time, given the significant implications risk assessments have on an individual's trajectory in the criminal justice system. As we have outlined elsewhere (Merdian et al., 2020), we focused on developing a case formulation framework—using similar principles to Structured Professional Judgement Tools (Beech et al., 2003)—aimed to support professionals in their decision-making with regard to developing individualised case formulations and associated interventions. The resulting CSEM Pathways Tool (CPT; Merdian et al., 2018) can be used to complement assessments of an individual's risks, needs, and responsivity (see Andrews et al., 1990). In summary, it was designed as a case formulation (as opposed to risk assessment) tool that provides a general structure to the assessment process, highlights particular areas of concern, and provides a focus for future interventions. Most importantly, it allows the professional and client to make sense of each client's pathway to CSEM offending behaviour and gain insight into the steps necessary to support future desistance behaviour.

The CPT and its Assessment Domains

In our initial research on pathways to CSEM offending behaviour (Merdian et al., 2018), the analysis of the detailed case histories of 20 individuals who had committed CSEM offending behaviour highlighted seven themes as crucial to their offending pathways alongside the offending behaviour itself: Developmental Context, Psychological Vulnerabilities, Personal Circumstances, Permission-Giving Thoughts, Internet Environment/Behaviour, Evaluation of Consequences, and Desistance. Alongside the Offending Behaviour itself, these themes present the eight assessment sections of the CPT.

The primary aim of the CPT is to provide a framework of developmentally coherent sections that potentially interact with each other in ways that can vary between individuals who have committed CSEM offences. This can then be used as a collaborative exercise with each individual to help them identify connections between different parts of the framework. The CPT, in addition to assisting them move towards a comprehensive and personally coherent account of how they have come to commit offences, provides possible routes into a future, offence-free life. For example, individuals in our research stated they have been able to formulate how their use of CSEM fulfils a number of functions linked to their earlier development, such as avoiding interpersonal stressors, providing anticipatory excitement in otherwise unexciting lives, gaining sexual gratification free from the complexities (but also pleasures) of achieving interpersonal intimacy. Understanding these connections can in its own right be helpful to bring about change as well as signposting the specific mechanisms for behaviour change.

Offending Behaviour

This section refers to the offending behaviour(s) in which the person engaged in and an exploration of the function(s) this behaviour served for them. Glasgow (2010) pointed to the importance of evaluating the digital evidence in CSEM cases. Such an analysis may inform about victim preferences, engagement with the material (e.g., size and arrangement of material), the length and intensity of collecting behaviour, contact with other individuals accessing CSEM, the ratio of illegal to legal material, and so on. This information can help formulate possible future risk scenarios, on the basis that past behaviours typically predict future behaviours, but more importantly how these potential risks can be managed through the development of opportunities and strategies to support desistance—such as behaviours that are incompatible with offending or activities that meet the individual's needs that were previously met by the offending behaviour. Where appropriate, we also recommend the exploration of opportunities for further offending, either online or offline, including any activities indicating potential cross-over into contact sex offending, for example seeking out opportunities to have unsupervised contact with children that are not readily explained by the person's family and social network.

Developmental Context and Psychological Vulnerabilities

This section refers to the identification of key learning events that may have contributed to an individual's propensity for offending. In this context, psychological vulnerabilities refer to certain behaviours or thinking patterns resulting from a person's learning history that may increase their individual risk of offending in that they lead to, for example, anxieties about emotional intimacy or dysfunctional coping styles throughout a person's development. In line with Seto's (2019) theoretical concept, this should include the exploration of motivational (e.g., assessment of self-reported offence motivation, sexual interest, and sexual fantasy) and facilitative aspects, which are factors thought to increase the likelihood of offending behaviour (e.g., antisocial traits; Babchishin et al., 2015). However, besides these 'offending accelerators', a person's learning history also informs about 'offending preventers', including protective and resilience factors (e.g., pro-social friendships and capacity for empathy for others).

Permission-giving Thoughts

Permission-giving thoughts refer to thinking patterns that the individual uses to give themselves permission to offend, such as "I am not the one committing the abuse". The literature on sexual offending behaviour often refers to such cognitions has "offence-supportive cognitions" or "cognitive distortions" and has focused on such cognitions as pivotal in initialising and maintaining the abusive behaviour (Mann & Beech, 2003). As outlined, Bartels and Merdian (2016) identified a theoretical account of CSEM-specific implicit theories underpinning permission-giving thinking of individuals engaging in CSEM offending behaviour, including 'Unhappy World', 'Children as Sexual Objects', 'Nature of Harm (CSEM variant)', 'Self as Uncontrollable', and 'Self as Collector', each of which is contextualized by a general assumption about the 'Reinforcing Nature of the Internet'.

In establishing the nature of an individual's permission giving thoughts in the analysis of their CSEM offending, it is important to try and position these within the chain of events leading to the offending behaviour. For example, it may be that these thoughts precede or follow the individual finding opportunities to offend and related sexual arousal. Such differences in the offending pathway will have implications for assessing possible treatment interventions.

Sexual Arousal

This section refers to establishing the role of sexual arousal in the offending process. Whilst there is a need for more research on the role of sexual arousal in CSEM offending, it is believed to be an important facilitator, and to exacerbate the use of CSEM (Babchishin et al., 2018). There is a growing body of research on the impact of sexual arousal on decision-making (e.g., Imhoff & Schmidt, 2014). In contrast, some CSEM offenders may report not being sexually aroused by the content of CSEM, but instead, take enjoyment from the collecting, organising, and trading of CSEM (e.g., Seto et al., 2010). It is therefore pivotal to establish in the assessment what role sexual arousal played in the offending behaviour.

Offending Environment

This section refers to an exploration of the physical and technological context of the offending behaviour, in order to identify what situational factors acted as a physical enabler to offending. The first could refer to the types of devices used (e.g., a laptop or a smart phone) and location and access (e.g., a computer in a private office). The second part of this refers to the online environments the client used for their offending behaviour, for example type of search engines, use of 'the dark web'/'ToR', file sharing, and so on.

Personal Situation

This section refers to an exploration of the individual's personal context at the time of the offending behaviour. Alongside sexual arousal (see above), Pullman et al. (2016) identified negative affect and intoxication as state facilitators of offending behaviour. Our research also highlighted social-emotional dysfunction as a key consideration, including being unable to manage emotional difficulties within relationships, feeling unable to share emotional information and meet emotional needs in functional rather than dysfunctional ways.

Evaluation of Consequences

This section refers to the individual's personal evaluation of the consequences resulting from their offending behaviour, based on the principles of classical and operant conditioning. The CPT postulates that offending behaviour is reinforced by the individual's evaluation of the consequences of their behaviour, and we therefore recommend identifying the person's immediate and subsequent perceptions and experiences after offending (e.g., immediate sexual gratification, with only later feelings of guilt). This is particularly crucial when exploring obstacles to desistance from offending behaviour. Consider, for example, a man who loses out on time with his wife because of his obsessive use of CSEM online. In behavioural analysis terms, losing contact with his wife might at first be assumed to be a 'punishment' (an unpleasant consequence for him), but if he is having emotional problems with his wife, then less contact with her might actually represent 'negative reinforcement', that is, the CSEM use 'turns off' an unpleasant outcome, in this case the pain of ineffectively trying to communicate his emotions to his wife. Being distant from his wife, in this example, is therefore more likely to maintain the offending behaviour. In summary, the nature of consequences needs to be analysed in terms of their effects on behaviour, not on what they might initially appear to be, and clinicians and clients can sometimes find this information harder to determine than the precursors to the offending behaviour.

Protective Factors

Above, we introduced the concept of "offending preventers", factors that make a person less likely to offend. Key amongst these protective factors are the capacity to self-monitor, self-regulate, and generate personalised solutions to desistence and achieving a satisfying and offence-free life. Dervley et al. (2017), for example, in a psychoeducational group context, found that individuals working with others in a supportive and self-actualising environment were able to overcome emotional inhibitions, communicate more openly, and become committed to preventative solutions that were generated by themselves. It is important to note, as Yates and Ward (2008) have demonstrated, that building protective factors (as in Good Lives) and risk management approaches are not incompatible and are indeed essential components of a bigger picture that is necessary to accurately formulate risks, needs, and appropriate interventions. Similarly, Circles UK, which oversees Circles programmes running in the

UK, focuses on the need for social connectedness and reintegration back into the community of those who have sexually offended (known as the 'core member') through a combination of collaborative risk monitoring and self-management with the support of professionally supported community volunteer members of the Circle (McCartan, 2016).

CPT and Functional Analysis

The question as to "why" offending occurred aligns the CPT with the concept of Functional Analysis (FA; Sturmey, 1996). In its core profession, that is, clinical psychology, FA defines a framework which enables the therapist to develop a systematic and organised problem formulation of a client, by identifying the critical causal contributors to behaviour, and their interrelations, in order to deduce appropriate interventions and measures to assess the problem and to evaluate change (Hanley et al., 2003). By embedding this process into the existing theoretical and empirical context, resulting problem formulations are aimed to minimise personal and organisational biases in clinical judgement while enabling a flexible and individualised assessment focus (e.g., Godoy & Gabino, 2003); there are attempts to enhance this through increased formalisation of this process (e.g., computational modelling; Burger et al., 2020). FA is being used across the range of clinical presentations (e.g., anxiety, Friman & Dymond, 2020; alcoholism and paedophilia; Wulfert et al., 1996), and has further been applied beyond its individual focus, for example in the conceptualisation of broader societal topics (e.g., AIDS-related stigma; Herek & Capitanio, 1998).

FA therefore is also a key part of offence formulation, in which the antecedents to the offence behaviour and its consequences for the individual are assembled from all available data. Antecedents, in this context, mean all those things that proceed, and increase the probability of the initial offending. In the case of CSEM offending, it is important to understand its antecedents for each individual and to establish if there are common themes that are relevant to designing treatment and desistence approaches. It is generally possible to identify positive experiences deriving from the offending behaviour, such as sexual gratification, social connectedness, and an enjoyment of the risky nature of their behaviour. In behavioural analysis terms, these 'positive reinforcers' are defined as those precursors that make the behaviour in question more likely; offence-supportive consequences are similarly defined as things occurring after the offending that make the behaviour more likely to be repeated, and this is not always straightforward to determine. Helping offenders identify and understand these issues can be facilitated through individual or group therapies, and it is in that context that we developed the CPT, as an aid to this kind of case formulation and treatment planning.

Conducting FA posits several demands to the practitioner. It is a time-consuming process that requires a thorough understanding of the literature, in order to draw conclusions between observed behaviours and underlying factors and to generate hypotheses about implied behaviour change. Human behaviour is complex, and equally complex to describe and predict. The literature concerning FA is deeply embedded within behavioural science and its terminology, using terms such as "motivational conditions" and "concomitant behavioural repertoires" (see Wulfert et al., 1996), an engagement with which may require a familiarity with these concepts. Tools such as the CPT can therefore provide useful shortcuts in relating a functional analysis model to the specific area of CSEM research and assessment practice, in the hope to provide both (1) a focused, evidence-based tool aimed to optimise and standardise clinical decision-making and (2) the communication of a general research-informed approach to problem formulation that is based on exploring evidence, collecting relevant data, deriving and systematically testing hypotheses about the case, and reviewing one's formulation accordingly. We hope that, as the specific content of the former will change with new empirical knowledge, legal guidelines, technologies, and so on, professionals who engage with the CPT will adapt their approach through the latter. In line with the sentiment expressed above, by no means do we claim comprehensiveness of our approach; indeed, the presented information is likely updated in some way or other by the time the chapter is published, however, we hope the concept and method will continue to offer value.

Lessons Learnt and Future Directions

In summary, we developed the CPT and the related assessment guidance to support a systematic exploration of a person's CSEM offending behaviour within the context of their unique learning history. The aims were both to understand more about how and why individuals engage in this increasingly prevalent form of offending and to provide some practical support for those working with users of CSEM to achieve desistance. At its core is the "why" of the offending behaviour: What needs does the individual meet by their offending and how can they be assisted to generate a pathway to desistance and a satisfying pro-social life? Research with a community treatment centre has shown the feasibility of integrating the tool into standard treatment (Merdian et al., 2020).

Following publication and presentation of our pathways model, we were approached for training on CSEM offending and how our model might be helpful to different groups of practitioners from and services in the community and closed settings, with adults and some with young people who had engaged in sexually harmful behaviours. Through this engagement, we learnt that the benefits of this training were not confined to the specifics of the CPT but often included developing a sound knowledge base, higher-order concepts and critical thinking about CSEM, together with acquiring sufficient knowledge and confidence to pose relevant questions within and outside their organisations. Feedback indicated that introducing the CPT into practice settings needs to be integrated within the objectives and procedures of those organisations, and the nature of their client and staff groups.

So Where Do We See the Field Going?

Europol (2020) highlighted that child sexual exploitation is shaped by developments in technology, including mobile connectivity, increased internet coverage in developing countries, and pay-as-you-go streaming, which provide high-level anonymity and are exacerbating increases in the commercial live-streaming of child sexual abuse. Europol has identified key threat areas as the following: (a) peer-to-peer networks; (b) anonymized access through Darknet networks such as Tor, which are the main platforms for accessing CSEM and non-commercial distribution; (c) live-streaming of child sexual abuse, facilitated by new technology, with some evidence that commercial child sexual exploitation such as live-streaming is also contributing to the rise in CSEM online; (d) online solicitation and sexual extortion, linked to the growing number of children and young people who own smartphones and use them for self-generated indecent material, which can be hijacked by those who then exploit the victim, notably by means of extortion; and (e) networking and forensic awareness of offenders, in which offenders learn from the mistakes of those who have been apprehended. Data from the IWF (2020) also confirmed the increase in self-produced images and commercially produced CSEM. These are all factors, and often rapidly changing factors, that need to be kept in mind in working at an individual level or in policy development aimed at CSEM prevention or desistance (Brennan et al., 2019).

The Online Harms White Paper (Department of Digital Culture, Media, and Sport & Home Office, 2020) sets out the current challenges to managing online harm, including CSEM offending, and makes the suggestion that first-time CSEM offenders to be given the opportunity to attend therapy rather than being automatically processed through the criminal justice system. In a review of services for those engaging in online CSEM offending, Perkins et al. (2018) reported that interventions for perpetrators of online child sexual exploitation, including CSEM offending, remain limited, largely similar in their client focus, scope, and funding, but are very limited in published treatment evaluation research. Professionals reported feeling overwhelmed by the large numbers of perpetrators needing help, with insufficient staff and a lack of appropriate decision-making support tools. Interventions and services needed to be prepared and equipped to respond to rapidly changing technological developments which continue at pace.

For our work, we see the future as merging the detailed clinical research work in which we have been engaged, within this wider context of CSEM offending prevention and desistance. Part of this has been engagement with a range of statutory and charitable services on the utilization and development of the scientist-practitioner approach to develop evidence-based practice and policy. For now, we have completed the work on the CPT and look forward to seeing what it can contribute to the developments in professional practice.

References

Andrews, D. A., Bonta, J., & Hoge, R. D. (1990). Classification for effective rehabilitation: Rediscovering psychology. *Criminal Justice and Behavior, 17*, 19–52. https://doi.org/10.1177/0093854890017001004

Babchishin, K. M., Hanson, K. R., & VanZuylen, H. (2015). Online child pornography offenders are different: A meta-analysis of the characteristics of online and offline sex offenders against children. *Archives of Sexual Behavior, 4*, 45–66. https://doi.org/10.1007/s10508-014-0270-x

Babchishin, K. M., Hanson, R. K., & Herrmann, C. A. (2010). The characteristics of online sex offenders: A meta-analysis. *Sexual Abuse: A Journal of Research and Treatment, 23*(1), 92–123. https://doi.org/10.1177/1079063210370708

Babchishin, K. M., Merdian, H. L., Bartels, R. M., & Perkins, D. (2018). Child sexual exploitation offenders: A Review. *European Psychologist, 23*(2), 130–143. https://doi.org/10.1027/1016-9040-a000326

Bartels, R. M. (2021). Understanding sexual fantasising: Implications for forensic practice and research. In K. Uzieblo, W. Smid, & K. McCartan (Eds.), *Crossroads to the management of people convicted of a sexual offence* (pp. 19–33). Palgrave Macmillan.

Bartels, R. M., & Merdian, H. L. (2016). The implicit theories of child sexual exploitation material users: An initial conceptualization. *Aggression and Violent Behavior, 26*, 16–25. https://doi.org/10.1016/j.avb.2015.11.002

Beech, A. R., Fisher, D. D., & Thornton, D. (2003). Risk assessment of sex offenders. *Professional Psychology: Research and Practice, 34*(4), 339–352. https://doi.org/10.1037/0735-7028.34.4.339

Beier, K. M., Grundmann, D., Kuhle, L. F., Scherner, G., Konrad, A., & Amelung, T. (2015). The German Dunkelfeld Project: A pilot study to prevent child sexual abuse and the use of child abusive images. *The Journal of Sexual Medicine, 12*(2), 529–542. https://doi.org/10.1111/jsm.12785

Brennan, M., Merdian, H. L., Perkins, D., Babchishin, K., Brown, J., Hammond, S., Kelly, R., Ludvigsen, B. E., & McCartan, K. (2019). *The International Working Group for the Best Practice in the Management of Online*

Sex Offending. Project Report. https://pearl.plymouth.ac.uk/bitstream/handle/10026.1/14331/IWG_OSO_17.06.19%20%28V6%29.pdf?sequence=1&isAllowed=y

Burger, J., van der Veen, D. C., Robinaugh, D. J., Quax, R., Riese, H., Schoevers, R. A., & Epskamp, S. (2020). Bridging the gap between complexity science and clinical practice by formalizing idiographic theories: A computational model of functional analysis. *BMC Medicine, 18*(99). https://doi.org/10.1186/s12916-020-01558-1

Department of Digital Culture, Media, and Sport & Home Office. (2020). *Online harms white paper—initial consultation response*. https://www.gov.uk/government/consultations/online-harms-white-paper/public-feedback/online-harms-white-paper-initial-consultation-response

Dervley, R., Perkins, D., Whitehead, H., Bailey, A., Gillespie, S., & Squire, T. (2017). Themes in participant feedback on a risk reduction programme for child sexual exploitation material offenders. *Journal of Sexual Aggression, 23*(1), 46–61. https://doi.org/10.1080/13552600.2016.1269958

Dombert, B., Schmidt, A. F., Banse, R., Briken, P., Hoyer, J., Neutze, J., & Osterheider, M. (2016). How common is men's self-reported sexual interest in prepubescent children? *The Journal of Sex Research, 53*(2), 214–223.

Duffy, A., Dawson, D., & Das Nair, R. (2016). Pornography addiction in adults: A systematic review of definitions and reported impact. *Journal of Sexual Medicine, 13*(5), 760–777. https://doi.org/10.1016/j.jsxm.2016.03.002

Eke, A. W., Helmus, L. M., & Seto, M. C. (2019). A validation study of the child pornography offender risk tool (CPORT). *Sexual Abuse, 31*(4), 456–476. https://doi.org/10.1177/1079063218762434

Europol. (2020). https://www.europol.europa.eu/crime-areas-and-trends/crime-areas/child-sexual-exploitation

Finkelhor, D., Walsh, K., Jones, L., Mitchell, K., & Collier, A. (2020). Youth internet safety education: Aligning programs with the evidence base. *Trauma, Violence, & Abuse*, 1–15. https://doi.org/10.1177/1524838020916257

Friman, P. C., & Dymond, S. (2020). The fear factor: A functional perspective on anxiety. In P. Sturmey (Ed.), *Functional analysis in clinical treatment (2nd Ed.): Practical resources for the mental health professional* (pp. 375–397). Academic Press. https://doi.org/10.1016/B978-0-12-805469-7.00016-4

Greijer, S., Doek, J., & the Interagency Working Group. (2016). *Terminology guidelines for the protection of children from sexual exploitation and sexual abuse*. https://www.unicef.org/protection/files/Terminology_guidelines_396922-E.pdf

Glasgow, D. (2010). The potential of digital evidence to contribute to risk assessment of internet offenders. *Journal of Sexual Aggression, 16*(1), 87–106. https://doi.org/10.1080/13552600903428839

Godoy, A. & Gavino, A. (2003). Information-gathering strategies in behavioral assessment. *European Journal of Psychological Assessment, 19*(3), 204–209. https://doi.org/10.1027/1015-5759.19.3.204

Hanley, G. P., Iwata, B. A., & McCord, B. E. (2003). Functional analysis of problem behavior: A review. *Journal of Applied Behavioural Analysis, 36*(2), 147–185. https://doi.org/10.1901/jaba.2003.36-147

Hanson, R. K. (2005). Twenty years of progress in violence risk assessment. *Journal of Interpersonal Violence, 20*(2), 212–217. https://doi.org/10.1177/0886260504267740

Herek, G. M., & Capitanio, J. M. (1998). Symbolic prejudice or fear of infection? A functional analysis of AIDS-related stigma among heterosexual adults. *Basic and Applied Social Psychology, 20*(3), 230–241. https://doi.org/10.1207/s15324834basp2003_5

Imhoff, R., & Schmidt, A. F. (2014). Sexual disinhibition under sexual arousal: Evidence for domain-specificity in men and women. *Archives of Sexual Behavior, 43*(6), 1123–1136. https://doi.org/10.1007/s10508-014-0329-8

International Centre for Missing and Exploited Children. (2018). *Child sexual abuse material: Model legislation and global review*. https://www.icmec.org/wp-content/uploads/2018/12/CSAM-Model-Law-9th-Ed-FINAL-12-3-18.pdf

Internet Watch Foundation. (2020). *The Internet Watch Foundation Annual Report 2019*. https://www.iwf.org.uk/sites/default/files/reports/2020-04/IWF_Annual_Report_2020_Low-res-Digital_AW_6mb.pdf

Levenson, J. S., Willis, G. M., & Vicencio, C. P. (2017). Obstacles to help-seeking for Sexual offenders: Implications for prevention of sexual abuse. *Journal of Child Sexual Abuse, 26*(2), 99–120.

Mann, R., & Beech, A. (2003). Cognitive distortions, schemas, and implicit theories. In D. Ward, R. Laws, & S. M. Hudson (Eds.), *Sexual deviance: Issues and controversies* (pp. 135–153). Sage.

McCartan, K. (2016). *Circles of support and accountability social impact evaluation: Final report.* https://uwe-repository.worktribe.com/output/921364

Merdian, H. L., Perkins, D., Dustagheer, E., & Glorney, E. (2018). Development of a case formulation model for individuals who have viewed, distributed and/or shared child sexual exploitation material. *International Journal of Offender Therapy and Comparative Criminology, 64*(10–11), 1055–1073. https://doi.org/10.1177/0306624X17748067

Merdian, H. L., Perkins, D., McCashin, D., & Stevanovic, J. (2020). Integrating structured individual offending pathway analysis into group treatment for individuals who have accessed, shared, and/or distributed Child Sexual Exploitation Material: A feasibility study and preliminary outcome evaluation. *Psychology, Crime and Law, 27*, 579–605.
Paquette, S., & Cortoni, F. (2019). The development and validation of the cognitions of internet sexual offending (C-ISO) Scale. *Sexual Abuse.* https://doi.org/10.1177/1079063219862281
Paquette, S., Longpré, N., & Cortoni, F. (2020). A billion distorted thoughts: An exploratory study of criminogenic cognitions among men who sexually exploit children over the Internet. *International Journal of Offender Therapy and Comparative Criminology, 64*(10–11), 1114–1133. https://doi.org/10.1177/0306624X19873082
Perkins, D., Merdian, H. L., Schumacher, B., Bradshaw, H., & Stefanovic, J. (2018). *A scoping review and gap analysis of interventions for perpetrators of online child sexual exploitation*. Project Report. Centre for Expertise in Child Sexual Abuse.
Pullman, L., Stephens, S., & Seto, M. C. (2016). A motivation-facilitation model of adult male sexual offending. In C. A. Cuevas & C. M. Rennison (Eds.), *The Wiley handbook on the psychology of violence* (pp. 482–500). Wiley-Blackwell.
Quayle, E., & Koukopoulos, N. (2019). Deterrence of online child sexual abuse and exploitation. *Policing: A Journal of Policy and Practice, 13*(3), 345–362.
Rosburg, T., Pflueger, M. O., Mokros, A., Boillat, C., Deuring, G., Spielmann, T., & Graf, M. (2020). Indirect and neuropsychological indicators of pedophilia. *Sexual Abuse*. https://doi.org/10.1177/1079063220931822
Seto, M. (2016). The puzzle of male chronophilias. *Archives of Sexual Behavior, 46*(1). https://doi.org/10.1007/s10508-016-0799-y
Seto, M. C. (2019). The motivation-facilitation model of sexual offending. *Sexual Abuse, 31*(1), 3–24. https://doi.org/10.1177/1079063217720919
Seto, M. C., Reeves, L., & Jung, S. (2010). Explanations given by child pornography offenders for their crimes. *Journal of Sexual Aggression, 16*(2), 169–180. https://doi.org/10.1080/13552600903572396
Sturmey, P. (1996). *Wiley series in clinical psychology: Functional analysis in clinical psychology*. John Wiley & Sons.
Warden, N. L., Phillips, J. G., & Ogloff, J. R. P. (2004). Internet addiction. *Psychiatry, Psychology, and Law, 11*(2), 280–295. http://find.galegroup.com.ezproxy.waikato.ac.nz/itx/start.do?prodId=AONE

Wefers, S., Gerard, F. J., Whitfield, K., & Drabble, J. (September 2019). *Offender characteristics associated with transnational child sex offending: A systematic review* [paper presentation]. 29th Annual International Conference, National Organisation of Treatment of Abuse. Belfast, UK.

Winder, B., Gough, B., & Seymour-Smith, S. (2015). Stumbling into sexual crime: The passive perpetrator in accounts by male internet sex offenders. *Archives of Sexual Behavior, 44*(1), 167–180. https://doi.org/10.1007/s10508-014-0302-6

Winters, G. M., Spriggs, S., & Jeglic, E. L. (2021). The complexities of understanding sexual grooming behaviours. In K. Uzieblo, W. Smid, & K. McCartan (Eds.), *Crossroads to the management of people convicted of a sexual offence* (pp. 3–18). Palgrave Macmillan.

Wulfert, E., Greenway, D. E., & Dougher, M. J. (1996). A logical functional analysis of reinforcement-based disorders: Alcoholism and pedophilia. *Journal of Consulting and Clinical Psychology, 64*(6), 1140–1151. https://doi.org/10.1037/0022-006X.64.6.1140

Yates, P. M., & Ward, T. (2008). An integrated model of sexual offender assessment and treatment. *Sexual Abuse in Australia and New Zealand, 1*(1), 3–20. ISSN 0833-8488

7

We Are Not There Yet: Contemporary Challenges for Risk Assessment and Management

Kasia Uzieblo, Tamara de Beuf, Minne De Boeck, and Wineke J. Smid

No offending creates greater public concern than sexual offending (e.g., Pickett et al., 2013). People convicted of sexual offences (PCSO) are feared, and their release into the community has been met with public consternation and vigilante actions. The public dismay prompts legislators to quickly install legislations, often inspired and biased by atypical, high-profile cases of horrific nature. A common factor in these public outcries and legislations is the need to identify individuals who pose a significant threat to society. This requirement has pushed

We have no known conflict of interest to disclose.

K. Uzieblo (✉)
Van der Hoeven Kliniek, Utrecht, The Netherlands

Free University of Brussels, Brussels, Belgium
e-mail: kuzieblo@dfzs.nl

© The Author(s), under exclusive license to Springer Nature Switzerland AG 2022

K. Uzieblo et al. (eds.), *Challenges in the Management of People Convicted of a Sexual Offence*, Palgrave Studies in Risk, Crime and Society,
https://doi.org/10.1007/978-3-030-80212-7_7

considerable international research in the area of risk assessment in PCSO and has driven the development and optimization of numerous tools. This focus on predictive validity has resulted in a booming body of research, and although this is of tremendous value, it has diverted attention from the implementation and use of these tools in clinical and legal practice. In this chapter, we argue that some aspects of risk assessment deserve more attention: interrater reliability, adequate risk management strategies, and the implementation of risk assessment tools into practice.

Back to Basics

Given the prognostic nature of risk assessment tools, it is no surprise that research mainly focuses on the predictive accuracy of risk information. In practice, however, confusion and misunderstanding regarding the predictive value of these tools often lead to inappropriate applications and unfeasible expectations from the public, policymakers, and even professionals in the field. Hence, it is important to recapitulate what these tools can and cannot do.

T. de Beuf
Maastricht University, Maastricht, Netherlands
e-mail: t.debeuf@pactum.org

M. De Boeck
Stop it Now!, Flanders, Belgium

University Forensic Centre, University Hospital Antwerp, Edegem, Belgium

Collaborative Antwerp Psychiatric Research Institute (CAPRI), University of Antwerp, Antwerp, Belgium
e-mail: minne.deboeck@uza.be

W. J. Smid
The Forensic Care Specialists, Utrecht, Netherlands
e-mail: wsmid@dfzs.nl

Risk assessment tools are prognostic rather than diagnostic measures; they are built to forecast the probability that a future event will occur, instead of determining whether the condition of interest is present or absent. Uncertainty is inherent to prognostic tools. This implies that risk estimates cannot be expressed in dichotomous terms (will recidivate or not), but as probabilities. Risk is continuous, someone exhibits lower or higher risk, and this can change over time (Helmus, 2018). To the best of our knowledge, there is no psychiatric condition, no behaviour or personality feature nor crime characteristic that *guarantees* a person will reoffend. In practice, however, these basic principles are often forgotten or ignored with practitioners speaking in absolute terms when discussing an individual's risk of recidivism, often to meet the expectations and requests of decision-makers who are expected to make a dichotomous decision. Yet, it is up to the evaluator to correctly communicate about their risk evaluation and clarify what the estimates mean.

Risk assessment tools are typically divided into two categories: actuarial tools and structured clinical judgement (SPJ) tools. Actuarial instruments are developed based on risk factors that are empirically related to (sexual) violent recidivism. The items of these instruments are coded according to fixed rules and total scores are calculated with an algorithm. The evaluator reaches a conclusion on the risk of recidivism by comparing the sum score to a norm group, which provides a reference to interpret the results in a meaningful, evidence-based way. SPJ is described as an ideographic approach. Like actuarial tools, SPJ tools include risk factors that are empirically related to (sexual) violent behaviour, but, unlike the actuarial approach, the evaluator can consider extra, person-specific risk factors. In addition, the overall decision on the risk level is left at the discretion of the professional judgement of the assessor, guided by the identified risk factors. No normative group data are being used to interpret the risk for recidivism. Actuarial risk assessment has generally been found to predict recidivism in PCSO more accurately than SPJ (Hanson & Morton-Bourgon, 2009).

Interrater Reliability: The Elephant in the Room

The primary psychometric concerns in risk assessment scales are the interrater reliability (IRR) and the predictive accuracy. For understandable reasons, most research has been focusing on the predictive validity (i.e., the extent to which a tool predicts a certain outcome, here, sexual recidivism). An in-depth overview of the predictive validity of risk assessment tools for sexual recidivism is beyond the scope of this chapter and can be consulted elsewhere (Hanson & Morton-Bourgon, 2009; van den Berg et al., 2018). Instead, we will explore the topic of IRR, referring to the extent to which evaluators agree with each other when scoring a particular case.

Although IRR and validity are distinct properties, they are intertwined. The correlation of a risk score with recidivism cannot be higher than its IRR. Instruments that are found to be unreliable also exhibit lower validity. Hanson and Morton-Bourgon's (2009) meta-analysis, including 125 studies, found a significant positive correlation between reported inter-rater agreement and predictive accuracy. A similar pattern can also be found on item level: Smid et al. (2014) found a significant positive association between the predictive accuracy of the 64 items of nine tools and the inter-rater agreement of their scores.

Several, but not all, validity studies report on IRR. Hanson and Morton-Bourgon's (2009) meta-analysis reported a median intraclass correlation coefficient (ICC) over 125 studies of 0.90 (reflecting excellent IRR), ranging from 0.60 (moderate) to 1.00 (excellent). By contrast, the systematic review of Tully et al. (2013), including 43 studies, reported that less than half of their included empirical studies reported good or acceptable IRR. Although differences in methodologies may explain these divergent findings, they deserve attention. The good news is that studies specifically focusing on IRR also suggest moderate to strong agreement among evaluators (Boccaccini et al., 2012; Levenson, 2004). But it should be noted that field studies on this topic are mainly limited to the IRR of the STATIC-99(R), among Sexually Violent Predator (SVP) evaluators in the USA.

Even when studies report satisfactory levels of IRR, it is important to focus not only on how often scores are *similar* but also on how often scores are *identical*. Studies reporting high ICC values for the STATIC-99 total score still find that identical scores were assigned in 45 to 55% of the cases (Boccaccini et al., 2012). This is of interest, given that a 1-point difference may put the offender in a different risk category and may substantially affect decisions about their management. Indeed, Quesada et al. (2014) report that about half of the cases in which there was a discrepancy, this discrepancy resulted in scores falling into different risk categories. This urges us to reflect on the factors that may explain rater disagreement. Below, we will discuss five important factors.

Not Everyone Strictly Follows the Guidelines

We know that even with very strict coding guidelines, there is no guarantee that the presence of risk factors is unambiguously assessed. If we look at the STATIC-99(R), a risk assessment tool that is particularly known for its well-defined coding guidelines and its historical items that are relatively strictly defined, only two items consistently elicit excellent agreement across studies: Item 1 (age of the offender) and item 10 (any male victims) (Boccaccini et al., 2012; Fernandez & Helmus, 2017; Miller et al., 2012). Studies with other risk assessment tools also indicate that discrepancies on most items can be found (Fernandez & Helmus, 2017; Miller et al., 2012).

Quesada et al. (2014) explored the disagreement on STATIC-99 item scores between researchers and practitioners. Disagreements were mainly attributable to misapplication of the coding instructions in the manual. But other reasons were also found, including simple calculation errors and discrepancies between file data and the given score, indicating that some information was probably overlooked. No studies to date have focused on the effect on IRR of the translations of risk assessment instruments or the effect of differences in culture and language between various countries using risk assessment.

Similarity in Scoring is More Difficult to Obtain with Some Items and Tools

Although no item of any instrument is consistently scored without error, some items are considerably harder to score reliably than others. Items that require some subjective judgement, more in-depth file investigation, and calculations seem to evoke most disagreement among raters (Quesada et al., 2014).

Evaluators do Not Always Rely on the Same Information

Evaluators vary considerably in the information sources they use for their risk assessment (Neal & Grisso, 2014). Research studies often use convenient summaries of file information and provide the exact same information to all cooperating researchers, thus producing flatteringly high IRRs. But unruly clinical practice often encompasses more information than can be read within the given time or provides contradictory information. When interview information is used, discrepancies arise because the interviewee provides varying information across interviews (Fernandez & Helmus, 2017). Also, the available information varies across settings. For instance, evaluators conducting risk assessments for court generally have access to less information compared to clinicians working with forensic patients daily.

Evaluators differ in how they deal with insufficient information or with discrepancies found in files and/or through interviews. Evaluators should be aware of possible reliability issues that may arise from such instances; that said, awareness and introspection are not always sufficient (Neal & Brodsky, 2016).

Human Beings are Biased

Experts tend to view themselves as free from bias and able to compensate for any biases they may have (Commons et al., 2004). Nevertheless, empirical evidence finds that evaluators' personality traits, ideology, personal beliefs, and personal attitudes influence their judgements (Neal & Brodsky, 2016). Moreover, studies suggest that forensic evaluators in adversarial proceedings seem to reach—intentionally or unintentionally—opinions that support the party who retained them (i.e., adversarial allegiance), with higher levels of interrater disagreement as a result (Murrie & Boccaccini, 2015). This allegiance has primarily been studied in court cases, but there is no reason to believe that an allegiance effect cannot be found in treatment and management contexts as well.

Remedial Actions in Practice

Overall, validity studies do not question the IRR of risk assessment tools. However, in practice, rater disagreement occurs and can be worrisome, especially on a case level. So, what remedial actions can be taken in order to improve IRR in practice? First, evaluators need to use the instruments with the most reliable items and methods. This seems obvious, but it is not. Various institutions use tools that are developed specifically for their setting but often lack (good) validation. Second, evaluators need to apply the tools' guidelines rigorously. Third, clinical practice needs to accommodate evaluators with continued training, supervision, peer-to-peer coaching, and enough assessment time to ensure adherence to the coding rules and allow for retrieving all relevant information. Fourth, evaluators should specify the sources of information used for the assessment in their report and acknowledge the unreliability of the obtained information by not scoring items in case of too much uncertainty or inconsistency. Finally, evaluators can try to minimize the potential influence of biases by self-monitoring such as careful notetaking and considering alternative hypotheses (Neal & Brodsky, 2016).

To address most of these problems, organizations could facilitate a multidisciplinary consensus methodology, which entails that multiple evaluators independently conduct a risk assessment of the same individual, followed by a collective discussion of the item ratings and final consensus on the risk estimate. There are reasons to believe that consensus ratings provide the most accurate ratings in predicting violence (de Vogel & de Ruiter, 2006); however, it is laborious and expensive and may not be feasible in every setting.

From Risk Assessment to Risk Management: Lost in Translation

Over the years, the focus has moved from the assessment of risk to its reduction and management. Consequently, the question how risk assessment can be translated into effective risk management strategies has become increasingly important. Professionals, however, struggle to find proper ways to develop risk-assessment-informed management strategies. Viljoen et al. (2018) conducted a systematic review on 73 studies to evaluate whether risk assessment tools demonstrably direct management. The results were sobering. Many professionals do not seem to adhere to risk assessment tools to guide their risk management efforts. Consequently, many criminogenic needs, as identified by the risk assessment tools, remain unaddressed. According to the authors, this may be due to a lack of guidelines on how to translate risk information into management. This is problematic, given that merely identifying risk factors will not decrease recidivism. More recently, developers of SPJ risk assessment tools (e.g., HCR-20:V3) have provided clinical guidelines to formulate specific risk scenarios and risk management strategies. Formulating a risk management plan is a complex process that can be divided into four steps: (1) gathering information, (2) identifying the presence of risk and protective factors, (3) risk formulation (e.g., imminence, severity, and nature), and (4) risk management plan (e.g., treatment, monitoring, and supervision) (Doyle & Duffy, 2006). While the field of sexual offending has made clear progress on steps (1) and (2), steps (3) and (4) are still understudied.

To facilitate the transition from risk assessment to management, attention should be given to risk communication. If the outcome of a risk assessment is well understood, it is more likely that the management plan will sufficiently adhere to the risk assessment. Evidence-based and best practices for communicating the results of risk assessment tools have yet to be established. However, three general issues concerning risk communication have been identified.

First, the most common risk communication formats are categorical risk levels (e.g., low, moderate, and high) and numerical estimates (e.g., frequencies, likelihood ratios, and percentages). Other methods that have gained attention are the description of specific risk management strategies (instead or in addition to risk estimates) as well as visual representations of risk (e.g., graphs and figures). It is unclear which format is the most effective, yet each format has its own (dis)advantages. For instance, management and categorical formats tend to produce higher estimates of risks than numerical descriptions; numerical estimates are often interpreted incorrect; using visual aids to contextualize base rates is not necessarily helpful (Batastini et al., 2019; Hilton et al., 2017). Second, a wide range of other factors related to the crime (e.g., severity) and to the receiver of the message (e.g., beliefs and experience) are believed to influence people's understanding of risk (Douglas & Ogloff, 2003; Glik, 2007); however, it remains unclear to what extent. And third, the use of a wide variety of risk assessment instruments in practice hampers a univocal terminology to describe and define risk categories across instruments. For instance, some instruments use three nominal risk categories, whereas other use five. To address these inconsistencies, Hanson et al. (2017) developed a standardized five-level system for communicating about risk for sexual reoffending. They provide a common language that is applicable across instruments. The five levels range from Level I: very low risk, through Level III: average risk level, to Level IVb: well above average risk. Risk ratio's and recidivism rates approximately double with each increasing risk level. This system has so far been adapted for use with the STATIC-99R/STATIC-2002R, STABLE-2007, and VRS:SO. It certainly holds promise, and time will tell how this system will be adopted in practice and to what extent it will advance risk communication.

Viljoen et al. (2018) conclude that professionals should receive more guidance on how to adhere to management strategies that align with risk assessment outcomes. Hanson et al. (2017) acknowledge this and provide suggestions for adequate interventions and management strategies by risk level, in line with the RNR principles (see Chap. 10). These suggestions are described in broad terms and mainly focus on the intensity and duration of the risk management.

The possibilities to execute desired risk management strategies for PCSO are susceptible to international differences. A study in the Netherlands (Bouman et al., 2021), including 518 professionals from various settings, lists factors that help or hinder the formulation of adequate risk management plans. Professionals included lack of technical support, high employee turnover and absenteeism, and limited opportunities for further education and training in risk assessment and management due to a shortage in offered courses and high workload, as factors that prohibit the development of proper risk management strategies in their setting.

In sum, formulating an adequate risk management plan is anything but obvious, even with good risk assessment. More research into the factors facilitating and prohibiting this process is needed. However, in the meantime, best practices could be shared and promoted. Evaluating the presence of risk factors is of great importance, but identification is just one part of the risk management puzzle. Developers of risk assessment tools could offer more specific guidelines to formulate/communicate risks and develop risk management plans and include these in their training programs. Managers could stimulate and facilitate the development of a univocal method to communicate about risks within and preferably also across institutions. Settings could develop frameworks to enable the development of risk management strategies that align with risk identification and case conceptualization. And last but not least, a sound implementation process could ensure the actual use of these tools and best practices.

Implementing a Tool in Practice: More than Meets the Eye

The impact of implementation quality should not be underestimated. Good fidelity to a risk administration protocol has been found to impact the performance of the Static-99R, STABLE-2002 and STABLE-2007, with significantly better predictive accuracy for complete assessments than incomplete assessments (Hanson et al., 2015). Implementation quality may also set the tone for staff's commitment to risk assessment. In a context of good implementation, staff may be more compliant with the risk assessment practice and its application to intervention planning. Indeed, research has shown that when the instrument was better integrated into local procedures, it resulted in better risk management outcomes, such as fewer unnecessary restrictive placements and reduced supervision levels (Vincent et al., 2016). Altogether, good implementation may improve an instrument's performance as well as its utility for risk management. So how can implementation be facilitated?

To achieve successful implementation, an organization benefits from appointing a committee willing to take responsibility and granted with jurisdiction/authority—and time—to lead the project. The committee prepares an implementation plan and oversees the process. Implementation starts with creating stakeholder buy-in, selecting the most suitable risk assessment instrument, and integrating the new practice in local policy and standard procedures, followed by training staff, running a pilot implementation, and, finally, rolling out the risk assessment organization-wide (Vincent et al., 2012). The initial implementation is reinforced by continuing efforts to actively support the new practice, albeit with decreasing intensity. The implementation committee's responsibility does not end until there is sufficient integration and sustainability. Thus, an implementation process requires considerable investment of time and resources, and is estimated to take two to four years (Fixsen et al., 2007).

Before embarking on the implementation, success needs to be defined: When is the implementation considered successful and how can we measure that? The development of validated measures of implementation outcomes is marked as a key area for future research in risk assessment (Viljoen & Vincent, 2020). Drawing from the field of implementation science, eight implementation outcomes are suggested (Proctor et al., 2011). In short, implementing agencies can assess *user satisfaction* and *uptake* as well as the *relevance* and *practical utility* of the instrument to the service. Other indicators of success are the *quality of delivery*, *cost-effectiveness*, *integration*, and *maintenance* of the instrument in practice. To reach satisfactory results on these outcomes, barriers have to be overcome stemming from the risk assessment instrument itself (e.g., complexity and laboriousness), the users (e.g., resistance and attitudes towards risk assessment), the inner setting of the implementing service (e.g., learning climate and resources), the outer setting to which the service belongs (e.g., governmental guidelines and requirements), and the implementation process itself (e.g., planning and timing). Rather than elaborating on the barriers that have been identified in risk assessment implementation (De Beuf et al., 2020; Levin et al., 2016), we present the following recommendations addressing those barriers. For more implementation strategies, we refer to the "CFIR-ERIC implementation strategy matching tool", freely available on https://cfirguide.org.

Involvement

Identify stakeholders at all levels (e.g., staff, government, and court) and engage them early in the process. Be aware of their potential influence on the implementation, hear them, and make them responsible. Involve future users in the selection process of a suitable risk assessment instrument.

Leadership

Ensure both formal mandate and informal support from top management, and make sure they communicate their engagement openly to all stakeholders. Build on the central role of middle management to spread this supportive leadership further into the organization.

Communication

Communicate with stakeholders on all levels in a transparent and inclusive manner. Tailor the message to staff characteristics and needs. Reiterate the relevance and value of structured risk assessment whenever appropriate. Keep communicating throughout the implementation process and provide feedback about progress.

Resources

Allocate sufficient time, money, and human resources. Especially the initial stages will demand resources.

Training

Provide digestible information, education, and training tailored to the various stakeholders. Include general information on evidence-based risk assessment followed by instructions on how to complete the instrument as well as on how to translate the risk findings into risk management planning. Develop local expertise by fostering master trainers who are equipped to train staff within the organization.

Human Factor

Promote a positive attitude towards the innovation by focusing on its advantages and usefulness for the setting. Take into consideration that, when confronted with change, staff will go through phases that stir different emotions (e.g., denial and frustration; Belyh, 2020).

Integration

Incorporate the risk assessment practice in the workflow, and make it an essential part of the procedures in place. Invest in user-friendly technology to facilitate the integration and accommodate users.

Monitoring

Besides evaluating implementation effectiveness, monitoring of the quality of assessments is essential to ensure they are completed as prescribed, for instance, by conducting IRR checks. Motivation to deliver high-quality assessments can be increased by providing incentives.

Follow-up Training

Various forms of continued education can promote sound risk assessment, such as booster-sessions, workshops, conferences, mentorship by experienced colleagues, and peer reviews such as reliability checks.

Overall, the implementation of a risk assessment practice is a long-term and comprehensive process that requires considerable planning and collaboration.

To Conclude

The increased importance of risk assessment over the last decades has primarily encouraged rapid developments in research on predictive validity of risk assessment instruments. Now, the time has come to move beyond the predictive value of risk assessment tools, and to attend more thoroughly to the issues that increase their validity in practice, such as interrater reliability and implementation, and to issues that promote risk management strategies to adequately align with the risk assessment. With proper attention to these issues in practice and research, we will further increase the usefulness of our risk assessment tools.

References

Batastini, A. B., Vitacco, M. J., Coaker, L. C., & Lester, M. E. (2019). Communicating violence risk during testimony: Do different formats lead to different perceptions among jurors? *Psychology, Public Policy, and Law, 25*(2), 92–106. https://doi.org/10.1037/law0000196

Belyh, A. (2020, July 28). Understanding the Kubler-Ross Change Curve. *Cleverism.* https://www.cleverism.com/understanding-kubler-ross-change-curve/

Boccaccini, M. T., Murrie, D. C., Mercado, C., Quesada, S., Hawes, S., Rice, A. K., & Jeglic, E. L. (2012). Implications of STATIC-99 field reliability findings for score use and reporting. *Criminal Justice and Behavior, 39*(1), 42–58. https://doi.org/10.1177/0093854811427131

Bouman, Y. H. A., Hutten, J., Uzieblo, K., van der Veeken, F. C. A., Verschuur, J., te Mebel, L., & van Horn, J. E. (2021). *Risk assessment done: What's next? The translation from risk assessment to risk management.* Quality Forensic Care.

Commons, M. L., Miller, P. M., & Gutheil, T. G. (2004). Expert witness perceptions of bias in experts. *Journal of the American Academy of Psychiatry and the Law, 32*(1), 70–75.

De Beuf, T. L. F., de Ruiter, C., & de Vogel, V. (2020). Staff perceptions on the implementation of Structured Risk Assessment with the START: AV: Identifying barriers and facilitators in a residential youth care setting. *International Journal of Forensic Mental Health*, https://doi.org/10.1080/14999013.2020.1756994

de Vogel, V., & de Ruiter, C. (2006). Structured professional judgment of violence risk in forensic clinical practice: A prospective study into the predictive validity of the Dutch HCR-20. *Psychology, Crime & Law, 12*(3), 321–333. https://doi.org/10.1080/10683160600569029

Douglas, K. S., & Ogloff, J. R. P. (2003). Multiple facets of risk for violence: The impact of judgmental specificity on structured decisions about violence risk. *International Journal of Forensic Mental Health, 2*(1), 19–34. https://doi.org/10.1080/14999013.2003.10471176

Doyle, M., & Duffy, D. (2006). Assessing and managing risk to self and others. In National Forensic Nurses' Research and Development Group (Ed.), *Aspects of forensic mental health nursing: Interventions for people with personality disorder*. Quay Books.

Fernandez, Y. M., & Helmus, L. M. (2017). A field examination of the inter-rater reliability of the Static-99 and STABLE-2007 scored by Correctional Program Officers. *Sexual Offender Treatment, 12*(2). http://www.sexual-offender-treatment.org/181.html

Fixsen, D. L., Naoom, S. F., Blase, K. A., & Wallace, F. (2007). Implementation: The missing link between research and practice. *APSAC Advisor, 19*(1 & 2), 4–11.

Glik, D. C. (2007). Risk communication for public health emergencies. *Annual Review of Public Health, 28*, 33–54. https://doi.org/10.1146/annurev.publhealth.28.021406.144123

Hanson, R. K., Babchishin, K. M., Helmus, L. M., Thornton, D., & Phenix, A. (2017). Communicating the results of criterion referenced prediction measures: Risk categories for the Static-99R and Static-2002R sexual offender risk assessment tools. *Psychological Assessment, 29*(5), 582–597. https://doi.org/10.1037/pas0000371

Hanson, R. K., Helmus, L. M., & Harris, A. J. R. (2015). Assessing the risk and needs of supervised sexual offenders: A prospective study using STABLE-2007, Static-99R, and Static-2002R. *Criminal Justice and Behavior, 42*(12), 1205–1224. https://doi.org/10.1177/0093854815602094

Hanson, R. K., & Morton-Bourgon, K. E. (2009). The accuracy of recidivism risk assessments for sexual offenders: A meta-analysis of 118 prediction studies. *Psychological Assessment, 21*(1), 1–21. https://doi.org/10.1037/a0014421

Helmus, L. M. (2018). Sex offender risk assessment: Where are we and where are we going. *Current Psychiatry Reports, 20*(6), 46–55. https://doi.org/10.1007/s11920-018-0909-8

Hilton, N. Z., Ham, E., Nunes, K. L., Rodrigues, N. C., Frank, C., & Seto, M. C. (2017). Using graphs to improve violence risk communication. *Criminal Justice and Behavior, 44*(5), 678–694. https://doi.org/10.1177/0093854816668916

Levenson, J. S. (2004). Reliability of sexually violent predator civil commitment criteria in Florida. *Law and Human Behavior, 28*(4), 357–368. https://doi.org/10.1023/B:LAHU.0000039330.22347.ad

Levin, S. K., Nilsen, P., Bendtsen, P., & Bulow, P. (2016). Structured risk assessment instruments: A systematic review of implementation determinants. *Psychiatry, Psychology and Law, 23*(4), 602–628. https://doi.org/10.1080/13218719.2015.1084661

Miller, C. S., Kimonis, E. R., Otto, R. K., Kline, S. M., & Wasserman, A. L. (2012). Reliability of risk assessment measures used in sexually violent predator proceedings. *Psychological Assessment, 24*(4), 944–953. https://doi.org/10.1037/a0028411

Murrie, D. C., & Boccaccini, M. T. (2015). Adversarial allegiance among expert witnesses. *Annual Review of Law and Social Science, 11*(*November 2015*), 37–55. https://doi.org/10.1146/annurev-lawsocsci-120814-121714

Neal, T., & Grisso, T. (2014). Assessment practices and expert judgment methods in forensic psychology and psychiatry: An international snapshot. *Criminal Justice and Behavior, 41*(12), 1406–1421. https://doi.org/10.1177/0093854814548449

Neal, T. M. S., & Brodsky, S. L. (2016). Forensic psychologists' perceptions of bias and potential correction strategies in forensic mental health evaluations. *Psychology, Public Policy, and Law, 22*(1), 58–76. https://doi.org/10.1037/law0000077

Pickett, J. T., Mancini, C., & Mears, D. P. (2013). Vulnerable victims, monstrous offenders, and unmanageable risk: Explaining public opinion on the social control of sex crime. *Criminology, 51*(*3*), 729–759. https://doi.org/10.1111/1745-9125.12018

Proctor, E., Silmere, H., Raghavan, R., Hovmand, P., Aarons, G., Bunger, A., Griffey, R., & Hensley, M. (2011). Outcomes for implementation research: Conceptual distinctions, measurement challenges, and research agenda. *Administration and Policy in Mental Health and Mental Health Services Research, 38*, 65–76. https://doi.org/10.1007/s10488-010-0319-7

Quesada, S. P., Calkins, C., & Jeglic, E. L. (2014). An examination of the inter-rater reliability between practitioners and researchers on the static-99. *International Journal of Offender Therapy and Comparative Criminology, 58*(11), 1364–1375. https://doi.org/10.1177/0306624X13495504

Smid, W. J., Kamphuis, J. H., Wever, E. C., & Van Beek, D. J. (2014). A comparison of the predictive properties of nine sex offender risk assessment instruments. *Psychological Assessment, 26*(3), 691–703.

Tully, R. J., Chou, S., & Browne, K. D. (2013). A systematic review on the effectiveness of sex offender risk assessment tools in predicting sexual recidivism of adult male sex offenders. *Clinical Psychology Review, 33*(2), 287–316. https://doi.org/10.1016/j.cpr.2012.12.002

van den Berg, J. W., Smid, W., Schepers, K., Wever, E., van Beek, D., Janssen, E., & Gijs, L. (2018). The predictive properties of dynamic sex offender risk assessment instruments: A meta-analysis. *Psychological Assessment, 30*(2), 179–191. https://doi.org/10.1037/pas0000454

Viljoen, J. L., Cochrane, D. M., & Jonnson, M. R. (2018). Do risk assessment tools help manage and reduce risk of reoffending? A systematic review. *Law and Human Behavior, 42*(3), 181–214. https://doi.org/10.1037/lhb0000280

Viljoen, J. L., & Vincent, G. M. (2020). Risk assessment for violence and reoffending: Implementation and impact on risk management. *Clinical Psychology: Science and Practice*. https://doi.org/10.1111/cpsp.12378

Vincent, G. M., Guy, L. S., & Grisso, T. (2012). *Risk assessment in juvenile justice: A guidebook for implementation*. John D. & Catherine T. MacArthur Foundation. http://modelsforchange.net/publications/346

Vincent, G. M., Guy, L. S., Perrault, R. T., & Gershenson, B. (2016). Risk assessment matters, but only when implemented well: A multisite study in juvenile probation. *Law and Human Behavior, 40*(6), 683–696. https://doi.org/10.1037/lhb0000214

8

Towards an Integration of Risk Assessment, Case Formulation, and Forensic Neuroscience

Leam A. Craig and Martin Rettenberger

A case formulation (CF) communicates a 'story' of the individual's development leading up to the present time and considers the various developmental influences, which have impacted on the trajectory of the problem behaviour. A CF is essentially a working hypothesis about the aetiology of the problem behaviour which allows the clinician to understand and empathise with the individual and provides a rationale for treatment and risk management interventions by identifying trigger

We have no known conflict of interest to disclose.

L. A. Craig (✉)
Forensic Psychology Practice Ltd, The Willows Clinic, Sutton Coldfield, UK

Centre for Applied Psychology, University of Birmingham, Birmingham, UK

School of Social Sciences, Birmingham City University, Birmingham, UK

School of Psychology, University of Lincoln, Lincoln, UK
e-mail: LeamCraig@forensicpsychology.co.uk

© The Author(s), under exclusive license to Springer Nature Switzerland AG 2022

K. Uzieblo et al. (eds.), *Challenges in the Management of People Convicted of a Sexual Offence*, Palgrave Studies in Risk, Crime and Society,
https://doi.org/10.1007/978-3-030-80212-7_8

factors associated with the problem behaviour. Some essential features of CF include a summary of the individual's core problems, suggest how the individual's difficulties may relate to one another, aim to explain, on the basis of psychological theory, the development and maintenance of the individual's difficulties, and indicate a plan of intervention (Johnstone & Dallos, 2006).

Craig and Rettenberger (2018) proposed an aetiological approach in the assessment of people convicted of sexual offences (PCSO) incorporating developmental theory, offence behaviour, and risk assessment theory into one model, referred as the CAse Formulation Incorporating Risk Assessment (CAFIRA) model. The model was further refined with the inclusion of neurobiological considerations (Craig et al., 2020). In this chapter, we expand on the neurobiological influences when understanding the history of trauma in PCSO.

Case Formulation and Offending Behaviour

There are several methods of conducting a CF including cognitive, behavioural, behaviour analytic, cognitive analytic, psychodynamic, and cognitive-behavioural approaches (Sturmey, 2009). For the sake of brevity, this chapter will focus on cognitive-behavioural approaches, which are the most often used methodology. Common across all approaches is that the CF should clearly state and seek to explain the problem behaviour based on a range and quality of evidence and provide an account of developmental history, psychological explanations of problem behaviour, hypotheses to facilitate change, and be clearly understood. One CF approach commonly discussed in the literature is

---

M. Rettenberger
Centre for Criminology (Kriminologische Zentralstelle—KrimZ), Wiesbaden, Germany

Department of Psychology, Johannes Gutenberg University Mainz (JGU), Mainz, Germany
e-mail: m.rettenberger@krimz.de

the Five P's method (Macneil et al., 2012), which stands for presenting problem, predisposing factors, precipitating factors, perpetuating factors, and protective/positive factors. We will now describe each of the areas in more detail.

Presenting Problem

The Presenting Problem section simply identifies the current problem behaviour or the reason for the referral. For example, the current problematic behaviour may be self-injurious behaviour in a PCSO who has a history of trauma. In this case, the current problematic behaviour would be the self-injurious behaviour rather than the factors that contributed to the index offence. CFs are behaviour specific and more than one CF will need to be completed to explain idiosyncratic behaviours.

Predisposing Factors

Neurobiological Influences

Psychological inquiry usually begins with birth, however, there is established evidence to indicate that investigators should consider prenatal as well as post- and perinatal risk factors which are often caused by problematic development and can create disturbances in the neurobiological processes of the brain, sometimes in combination with genetic factors (for discussion, see Beech et al., 2018).

Children prenatally exposed to substances (e.g., teratogens) can suffer from serious cognitive deficits, including deficits in information processing and memory tasks, and behavioural problems verified by brain imaging studies which have identified structural changes in various brain regions of these children, including the basal ganglia, corpus callosum, cerebellum, and hippocampus (Mattson et al., 2001).

Developmental Influences

In addition to neurobiological considerations, psychological inquiry will also consider environmental and developmental influences on the origin of the problem behaviour. These will include historical events that might be linked to the problem: events and behaviours from childhood, experiences and relationships with parents or other caregivers, psychiatric issues, and living situations. Often practitioners working within a forensic context will need to draw upon theories of psychosocial development across the lifespan including attachment theory (Bowlby, 1969), social learning models (Bandura, 1977), cognitive and affective development theory (Piaget, 1990), as well as theories of personality development and socialisation (Hurrelmann, 1988), to name but a few.

The impact of adverse developmental influences on adulthood psychopathology is well recognised, and it is not uncommon for people who have committed serious sexual or violent offences to present with a history of trauma resulting in dysfunctional attachment styles. In samples of PCSO, preoccupied or fearful attachment style (Bartholomew, 1990) are commonly found in child molesters (Marshall & Marshall, 2010), whereas rapists were indiscriminable in some respects from violent nonsexual offenders (i.e., both tended to be dismissive in attachment style). The assessment of the impact of trauma (abuse, neglect, or deprivation) is also relevant to the understanding of the developmental trajectory of behaviour. There is a well-established body of literature which documents the relationship between childhood sexual abuse and perpetration of sexual abuse (Jespersen et al., 2009) and childhood trauma and later antisocial behaviour (Finkelhor, 2008). Multiple types of abuse also increase the odds of serious problems, suggesting a higher lifetime prevalence of psychopathology in PCSO (Kahn et al., 2020). Experiences of multiple trauma can have a cumulative effect on the developing brain resulting in impairments in multiple brain structures, which could lead to significantly more severe mental health difficulties (Negele et al., 2015).

Offence Behaviour-Related Theory

The information obtained from enquiries into the individuals' history would then be considered against one of the more specific offence-related theories in attempt to explain the origins and development of problem behaviour, for example the Integrated Theory of Sexual Offending (Ward & Beech, 2006). This is not an exhaustive list but given to illustrate there are numerous offence-related theories which could be used when completing CF in a forensic context.

Risk Assessment

Risk, we would argue, is a complex interaction between psychological problems (stable dynamic risk factors), an individual's history (static risk factors), and current life circumstances (acute or contextual risk factors). In developing a theory of (sexual) offender risk assessment, Beech and Ward (2004) proposed an aetiological model of risk informed by theories of sexual offending. The model emphasises a chain of events from a distal developmental factors section, through a vulnerability factors section, a triggering factors section, and finally an acute risk factors section. The concept of long-term vulnerabilities which may activate in response to environmental triggers (Thornton & Knight, 2015) as well as its recent development in terms of a theoretically more elaborated propensities model (Thornton, 2016) provide further support of this idea. These aetiological considerations, represented by different theoretical and conceptual approaches, can be incorporated into a mixed risk assessment and CF model which we introduce in Fig. 8.1, the CAse Formulation Incorporating Risk Assessment-Sexual (CAFIRA–S) model.

CAFIRA-S considers static risk factors, or predisposing factors of the Five P's model, where previous convictions act as historical markers for stable dynamic risk factors (Mrazek & Haggerty, 1994). Here, static risk factors are representations of psychological vulnerabilities in the here and now from the individual's past. The model posits that static risk factors, when measured using actuarial risk assessment instruments, act as proxies

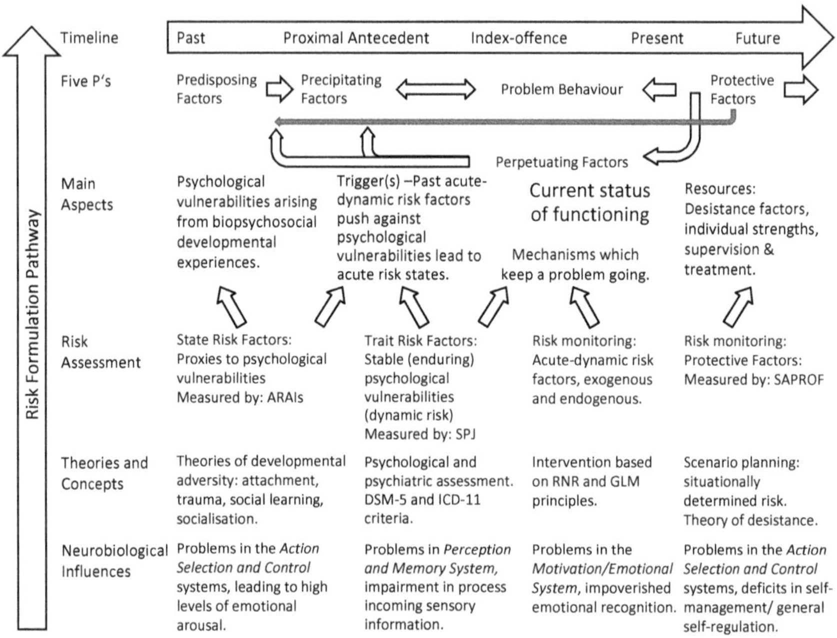

Fig. 8.1 CAse Formulation Incorporating Risk Assessment-Sexual (CAFIRA–S) model (Adapted from Craig et al., 2020, with permission from Wiley-Blackwell)

or historical markers of risk. Several of these instruments are now available when assessing risk of recidivism for PCSO, such as the STATIC family of measures (Hanson & Thornton, 2003).

Perpetuating Factors

These factors are the mechanisms that keep a problem going or unintended consequences of an attempt to cope with the problem. The concept of implicit theories of PCSO is useful here and posits that sexual offenders' cognitive distortions emerge at the interface between implicit motivation and cognition (Ward & Keenan, 1999). These implicit theories are used to explain people's actions and how they interpret the world around them, drawing on the idea of schema development. Negative cognitive beliefs are maintained by negative bias cognitive distortions, selective abstraction, arbitrary inferences, overgeneralisations, magnification of the negative, minimisation of the positive, and personalisation of negative outcomes. Factors such as intimacy (dysfunctional attachments) and socio-affective deficits (e.g., low self-esteem), poor self-management (e.g., poor impulse control), offence-supportive attitudes (e.g., sexual entitlement attitudes), and deviant sexual arousal are considered stable dynamic factors which denote psychologically meaningful risk factors (Mann et al., 2010) and have been identified as predictors of sexual recidivism (Craig et al., 2007), and therefore can be seen as perpetuating factors. The concept of dynamic factors operationalised as psychologically meaningful risk factors is today the psychometrically best way to capture perpetuating factors for offender risk assessment (Craig et al., 2007). These dynamic factors are often measured using Structured Professional Judgement (SPJ) frameworks which consist of empirically derived risk factors, underpinned by theoretical and empirical knowledge about (re) offending behaviour. Frameworks often used with PCSO include the Risk of Sexual Violence Protocol (RSVP: Hart et al., 2003) or the STABLE-2007 (Hanson et al., 2007).

Neurobiological Considerations

There is considerable evidence that childhood trauma (abuse, neglect or deprivation), often referred to as adverse childhood experiences (ACEs), causes enduring brain dysfunction that affects health and quality of life through the lifespan (Fox et al., 2015). Individuals with high ACE scores are more likely to be violent, and have more drug prescriptions, more depression, and more autoimmune diseases (Beech et al., 2018), and PCSO were three times more likely to have suffered from sexual abuse compared to the general population and have twice the odds of having suffered physical abuse (Levenson et al., 2016). Such early trauma produces neuronal and functional changes in the developing brain (Solomon & Heide, 2005). Because information processing in the brain is associated with protein synthesis, structural change at the molecular level is of particular relevance and can have lifelong implications when explaining aggressive behaviour (Nussbaum, 2020). Structural changes can include reduced size of the mid-portions of the corpus callosum, while functional consequences include increased 'electrical irritability' in the limbic structures of the brain (Teicher et al., 2003).

For a subset of PCSO against children, research has shown that there are considerable neuropsychological deficits, which seem to correlate with a particularly strong sexual interest in children (Turner et al., 2020). Similar neuropsychological anomalies were found in non-offending paedophiles compared against matched non-clinical controls (Abé et al., 2020). We will now examine the problems in terms of neuropsychological (dys)functions.

The Perception and Memory System

The perception and memory system is associated primarily with the hippocampal formation and the posterior neocortex, the major function of which is to process incoming sensory information and to construct representations of objects and events and make them available to the other two systems. Problems in this system can lead to maladaptive beliefs, attitudes, and problematic interpretations of social encounters and can distort a persons' experience of the world, the evaluation of reasons for action, and subsequent action plans. The presence of maladaptive beliefs that are chronically activated (i.e., frequently available to guide information processing) is likely to cause the subsequent activation of problematic goals and emotions, which in turn make it difficult for a person to effectively control their behaviour. We hypothesise that these cognitive structures can function as pre-attentive filters biasing the processing of social information and resulting in a variety of personal and social difficulties.

These problems may underlie the kinds of offence-supportive cognitions that Mann et al. (2010) regard as a particular type of stable dynamic risk factor for sexual offending. What have been termed "cognitive distortions" is arguably caused by entrenched beliefs and subsequent biased information-processing originating in the perception and memory system. An intriguing aspect of Ward and Beech's (2006) Integrated Theory of Sexual Offending is that different types of cognitive distortions are predicted to have their origins in different neuropsychological systems. However, strictly speaking it is only at the level of personal experience and agency that it is meaningful to speak of distorted beliefs or attitudes.

The Motivation/Emotional System

The Motivation/Emotional System is associated with cortical (motor, sensory, and visual functions), limbic (control of emotion, memories, and arousal), and brainstem (regulate body functions) structures. A major function of this system is to allow goals and values to influence both perception and action selection rapidly and to adjust motivational state to fit changing environmental circumstances (Pennington, 2002). Problems in an individual's genetic inheritance, cultural upbringing, or negative individual experiences may lead to defects in the motivational/emotional system. For example, someone from an emotionally impoverished environment might find it difficult to identify their emotions in an accurate manner and become confused when confronted with emotionally charged interpersonal situations. Another type of problem could be related to the range of needs or goals sought by a person. Impoverished early learning experiences could lead to an individual lacking the skills necessary (internal conditions) to establish strong interpersonal relationships and result in social isolation and further psychological and social deficits, such as intimacy or attachment problems (Marshall & Marshall, 2010). These deficits in interpersonal functioning are regarded as a type of stable dynamic risk factor or causal psychological risk factor (Beech & Ward, 2004).

The Action Selection and Control System

The action selection and control system is associated with the frontal cortex (implicated in planning complex cognitive behaviour, personality expression, decision-making, and impulse control), the basal ganglia (control of voluntary motor movements, habit learning, eye movements, cognition, and emotion), and parts of the thalamus (transmission of sensory nerves signals from the spinal cord and brainstem to the cerebral cortex). A major function of this system is to underpin individuals' capacity to plan, implement, and evaluate action plans, and to control behaviour, thoughts, and emotions in service of higher-level goals. This system is concerned with the formation and implementation of action plans designed to achieve individuals' goals. It draws heavily upon the motivation/emotional system for the goals that effectively energise behaviour and the perception and memory system for procedural and declarative knowledge (i.e., knowledge about how to do certain things). Problems that might arise from malfunctions in this system essentially span self-regulation problems such as impulsivity. These deficits in self-management/general self-regulation have been described as stable dynamic risk factors (Mann et al., 2010).

Precipitating Factors

This section focuses on the triggers of the problem behaviour which may be external (time or place) or internal (thoughts and feelings). Beech and Ward (2004) suggested that the distinction between stable (psychological vulnerabilities) dynamic and acute (trigger) risk factors might be better reframed in terms of the more psychologically rigorous definitions of trait risk factors (i.e., enduring personality problems) and transient state risk factors (i.e., the temporary, usually extreme expression of the more enduring stable dynamic risk factors). Beech and Ward (2004) posited that states of high risk are due to psychological traits operationalised as stable dynamic risk factors being pushed into states of high risk by an interaction with these acute triggering risk factors. A useful framework to structure acute risk factors is that of the ACUTE-2007 (Hanson et al., 2007). Of seven acute factors analysed, victim access, sexual preoccupation, rejection of supervision, and hostility were significantly related to sexual (and violent) recidivism.

Protective/Strength-Based Factors

In the last ten years there has been a groundswell of interest shown in strengths-based approaches in the caring professions with a particular interest in looking at 'resilience', that is, how people overcome adversity to lead healthy and successful lives (Masten & Reed, 2002).

Measuring Protective Factors

The range and prominence of protective factors can be more formally assessed using the Structured Assessment of PROtective Factors for violence risk (SAPROF: de Vogel et al., 2012), an assessment tool designed specifically for the assessment of protective factors. Although not designed as a risk assessment instrument, the SAPROF was developed primarily to assess future violence in adult forensic patients to be used alongside an existing SPJ risk assessment framework. While some studies have found positive support for the SAPROF in predicting a decrease in community recidivism (Coupland & Olver, 2020; de Vries Robbé et al., 2015), it should be emphasised that the strength of the scale is in organising protective risk factors information in a structured way rather than using it as a risk assessment measure.

Intervention

Protective/strength-based factors incorporate both future aspirations and the effects of intervention. The 'What Works' approach to offender rehabilitation for PCSO (Proulx et al., 2020) emphasises the Risk, Need, and Responsivity principles (RNR: Bonta & Andrews, 2017), where treatment intensity and approaches are adapted to match the assessed level risk of the individual. Neurobiological influences, again, become important when developing treatment approaches. When recalling or re-experiencing trauma, the left frontal cortex shuts down (especially Broca's area; Shin et al., 1997), while the parts of the brain associated with emotional states and autonomic arousal and the amygdala (centre for detecting threat) increases activity. Interventions where the offender is required to recount aspects of their trauma or provide offence accounts may be counterproductive where high emotional states are associated with increased neural activation and hyperarousal (right posterior insula, dorsal anterior cingulate cortex), regions involved in defensive responding (left postcentral gyrus) and areas responsible for cognitive control of emotions inducing feelings of shame (Lloyd et al., 2020). This may, in part, explain why offence disclosures have been phased out (Mann et al., 2010).

Williams and Carter (2018) described how correctional programmes are now being designed to take into account a biologically informed approach to offender intervention. A newly developed healthy sexual functioning programme takes into account the neurodevelopmental effects of ACE and adopts a multimodal, brain-friendly approach which is sensitive to shame and trauma. In brief, methods for sensory learning such as visual, auditory, and kinaesthetic are used as much as possible besides reading. This includes in-action 'body-movement' techniques, symbolising and signing, drawing, gesturing, and brain-breaks when challenging and redirecting deviant sexual fantasies (Walton, 2021).

Good Lives Model

The final step of CF is to consider personal strengths as part of a Good Lives Model (GLM) of offender rehabilitation (Ward & Gannon, 2006). The GLM was designed to augment the RNR principles of effective correctional interventions and has two primary aims: to reduce and/or manage criminogenic needs and to assist individuals in skill development, knowledge, and resources to achieve personally meaningful life goals in a prosocial manner. It is argued that human beings are naturally inclined to seek certain types of experiences or 'human/primary goods' and experience high levels of well-being if these goods are obtained. Although empirical research is limited, the success of the GLM appears to lie in how it is operationalised in treatment programmes as part of an integrated model having practice implications from beginning to end of a treatment programme through to follow-up and supervision (Willis et al., 2016).

Conclusions

The CAFIRA-S model considers theories of developmental adversity, biopsychosocial and neurobiological influences, offending behaviour, and risk assessment, and represents a coherent approach to the assessment of PCSO.

While most clinicians may not have ready access to neurological measuring equipment, an understanding of how ACE impact on neurological development and the developmental trajectory of problematic offending behaviour into adulthood will aid the clinician in constructing an accurate CF. Aspects of this model will have relevance to clinicians at different stages of the criminal justice process. Clinicians assessing PCSO at the pre-sentence stage will likely provide a clinical baseline considering recidivism of risk as well as highlighting any ACEs in the person's history from which a working hypothesis can be proffered. Clinicians working within correctional settings, such as prison or forensic psychiatric hospitals, will have more time to analyse and update the working hypothesis by focusing on the trajectory of the problematic behaviour and adapt their therapeutic style while taking into account the neurobiological influences when designing intervention approaches. For clinicians assessing individuals prior to release or as part of community management, the emphasis will be on the individual's ability to demonstrate insight into criminogenic factors, as well as identify and manage precipitating risk factors balanced against the development of protective/strength-based risk factors. At each stage, the working hypothesis is open to change based on the information available at that time.

We emphasise that the model is applicable to other groups of offenders with reference to offence specific theories of offending behaviour and offence specific risk assessments measures and frameworks.

References

Abé, C., Adebahr, R., Liberg, B., Mannfolk, C., Lebedev, A., Eriksson, J., Långström, N., & Rahm, C. (2020). Brain structure and clinical profile point to neurodevelopmental factors involved in pedophilic disorder. *Acta Psychiatrica Scandinavica*. https://doi.org/10.1111/acps.13273

Bandura, A. (1977). *Social learning theory*. Prentice Hall.

Bartholomew, K. (1990). Avoidance of intimacy: An attachment perspective. *Journal of Social and Personal Relationships, 7*, 147–178. https://doi.org/10.1177/0265407590072001

Beech, A. R., Nordstrom, N., & Raine, A. (2018). Developmental risk factors. In A. R. Beech, A. J. Carter, R. E. Mann, & P. Rotshtein (Eds.), *The Wiley Blackwell handbook of forensic neuroscience* (pp. 505–529). John Wiley & Sons Ltd..

Beech, A. R., & Ward, T. (2004). The integration of etiology and risk in sexual offenders: A theoretical framework. *Aggression and Violent Behavior, 10*, 31–63. https://doi.org/10.1016/j.avb.2003.08.002

Bonta, J., & Andrews, D. A. (2017). *The psychology of criminal conduct* (6th ed.). Routledge.

Bowlby, J. (1969). *Attachment and loss: Vol. 1. Loss*. Basic Books.

Coupland, R. B. A., & Olver, M. E. (2020). Assessing protective factors in treated violent offenders: Associations with recidivism reduction and positive community outcomes. *Psychological Assessment, 32*(5), 493–508. https://doi.org/10.1037/pas0000807

Craig, L. A., & Rettenberger, M. (2018). An etiological approach to sexual offender assessment: CAse Formulation Incorporating Risk Assessment (CAFIRA). *Current Psychiatry Reports, 20*(6), 20–43. https://doi.org/10.1007/s11920-018-0904-0

Craig, L. A., Rettenberger, M., & Beech, A. R. (2020). Neurobiological considerations on the etiological approach to sexual offender assessment: CAse Formulation Incorporating Risk Assessment–Version 2 (CAFIRA–v2). In J. Proulx, F. Cortoni, L. A. Craig, & E. Letourneau (Eds.), *The Wiley Handbook on what works with sexual offender: Contemporary perspectives in theory, assessment, treatment and prevention* (pp. 153–173). Chichester Wiley-Blackwell.

Craig, L. A., Thornton, D., Beech, A., & Browne, K. D. (2007). The relationship of statistical and psychological risk markers to sexual reconviction in child molesters. *Criminal Justice & Behavior., 34*(3), 314–329. https://doi.org/10.1177/0093854806291416

de Vogel, V., de Ruiter, C., Bouman, Y., & de Vries Robbé, M. (2012). *SAPROF. Guidelines for the assessment of protective factors for violence risk* (English version, 2nd Edn). Forum Educatief.

de Vries Robbé, M., de Vogel, V., Koster, K., & Bogaerts, S. (2015). Assessing protective factors for sexually violent offending with the SAPROF. *Sexual Abuse: A Journal of Research and Treatment, 27*, 51–70. https://doi.org/10.1177/1079063214550168

Finkelhor, D. (2008). *Childhood victimisation. Violence, crime and abuse in the lives of young people*. Oxford University Press.
Fox, B. H., Perez, N., Cass, E., Baglivio, M. T., & Epps, N. (2015). Trauma changes everything: Examining the relationship between adverse childhood experiences and serious, violent and chronic juvenile offenders. *Child Abuse & Neglect, 46*, 163–173. https://doi.org/10.1016/j.chiabu.2015.01.011
Hanson, R. K., Harris, A. J. R, Scott, T. L., & Helmus, L. (2007). *Assessing the risk of sexual offenders on community supervision: The Dynamic Supervision Project (Corrections research user report 2007-05)*. Public Safety Canada, Ottawa, Ontario. http://www.publicsafety.gc.ca/res/cor/rep/_fl/crp2007-05-en.pdf
Hanson, R. K., & Thornton, D. (2003). *Notes on the development of static-2002*. Department of the Solicitor General of Canada. https://www.publicsafety.gc.ca/cnt/rsrcs/pblctns/nts-dvlpmnt-sttc/index-en.aspx
Hart, S. D., Kropp, P. R., Laws, D. R., Klaver, J., & Logan, C. (2003). *The risk for sexual violence protocol (RSVP): Structured professional guidelines for assessing risk of sexual violence*. Mental Health, Law, and Policy Institute, Simon Fraser University.
Hurrelmann, K. (1988). *Social structure and personality development*. Cambridge University Press.
Jespersen, A. F., Lalumière, M. L., & Seto, M. C. (2009). Sexual abuse history among adult sex offenders and non-sex offenders: A meta-analysis. *Child Abuse and Neglect, 33*(3), 179–192. https://doi.org/10.1016/j.chiabu.2008.07.004
Johnstone, L., & Dallos, R. (2006). *Formulation in psychology and psychotherapy: Making sense of people's problems*. Routledge.
Kahn, R. E., Jackson, K., Keiser, K., Ambroziak, G., & Levenson, J. S. (2020). Adverse childhood experiences among sexual offenders: Associations with sexual recidivism risk and psychopathology. *Sexual Abuse*, first published online. https://doi.org/10.1177/1079063220970031
Levenson, J. S., Willis, G. M., & Prescott, D. S. (2016). Adverse childhood experiences in the lives of male sex offenders: Implications for trauma-informed care. *Sexual Abuse, 28*(4), 340–359. https://doi.org/10.1177/1079063214535819
Lloyd, C. S., Nicholson, A. A., Densmore, M., Théberge, J., Neufeld, R. W. J., Jetly, R., McKinnon, M. C., & Lanius, R. A. (2020). Shame on the brain: Neural correlates of moral injury event recall in posttraumatic stress disorder. *Depression and Anxiety*. Advanced Online Publication: https://doi.org/10.1002/da.23128
Macneil, C. A., Hasty, M. K., Conus, P., & Berk, M. (2012). Is diagnosis enough to guide interventions in mental health? Using case formulation in clinical practice. *BMC Medicine, 10*, 1–3. https://doi.org/10.1186/1741-7015-10-111

Mann, R. E., Hanson, R. K., & Thornton, D. (2010). Assessing risk for sexual recidivism: Some proposals on the nature of psychologically meaningful risk factors. *Sexual Abuse, 22*(2), 191–217. https://doi.org/10.1177/1079063210366039

Marshall, W. L., & Marshall, L. E. (2010). Attachment and intimacy in sexual offenders: An update. *Sexual and Relationship Therapy, 25*(1), 86–90. https://doi.org/10.1080/14681991003589568

Masten, A. S., & Reed, M.-G. J. (2002). Resilience in development. In C. R. Snyder & A. J. Lopez (Eds.), *The handbook of positive psychology* (pp. 74–88). Oxford University Press.

Mattson, S. N., Schoenfeld, A. M., & Riley, E. P. (2001). Teratogenic effects of alcohol on brain and behavior. *Alcohol Res Health, 25*(3), 185–191.

Mrazek, P. J., & Haggerty, R. J. (1994). *Reducing risks for mental disorders: Frontiers for preventive intervention*. National Academy Press.

Negele, A., Kaufhold, J., Kallenbach, L., & Leuzinger-Bohleber, M. (2015). Childhood trauma and its relation to chronic depression in adulthood. *Depression Research and Treatment*. 650804. https://doi.org/10.1155/2015/650804

Nussbaum, D. (2020). Aggression from a psychobiologicval perspective: Implications for enhanced violent risk assessment and intervention. In J. S. Wormith, L. A. Craig, & T. E. Hogue (Eds.), *The Wiley handbook of what works in violence risk management: Theory, research and practice* (pp. 315–348). Wiley-Blackwell.

Pennington, B. F. (2002). *The development of psychopathology: Nature and nurture*. Guilford Press.

Piaget, J. (1990). *The child's conception of the world*. Littlefield Adams.

Proulx, J., Cortoni, F., Craig, L. A., & Letourneau, E. (2020). *The Wiley handbook on what works with sexual offender: Contemporary perspectives in theory, assessment, treatment and prevention*. Wiley-Blackwell.

Shin, L. M., Kosslyn, S. M., McNally, R. J., Alpert, N. M., Thompson, W. L., Rauch, S. L., Macklin, M. L., & Pitman, R. K. (1997). Visual imagery and perception in posttraumatic stress disorder: A positron emission tomographic investigation. *Archives of General Psychiatry, 54*(3), 233–241. https://doi.org/10.1001/archpsyc.1997.01830150057010

Solomon, E. P., & Heide, K. M. (2005). The biology of trauma: Implications for treatment. *Journal of Interpersonal Violence, 20*(1), 51–60. https://doi.org/10.1177/0886260504268119

Sturmey, P. (2009). *Clinical case formulation: Varity of approaches*. Wiley.

Teicher, M. H., Andersen, S. L., Polcari, A., Anderson, C. M., Navalta, C. P., & Kim, D. M. (2003). The neurobiological consequences of early stress and childhood maltreatment. *Neuroscience & Biobehavioral Reviews, 27*(1–2), 33–44. https://doi.org/10.1016/S0149-7634(03)00007-1

Thornton, D. (2016). Developing a theory of dynamic risk. *Psychology, Crime and Law, 22*, 138–150.

Thornton, D., & Knight, R. A. (2015). Construction and validation of SRA-FV need assessment. *Sexual Abuse, 27*, 360–375. https://doi.org/10.1177/1079063213511120

Turner, D., Roszyk, A., Szumski, F., & Rettenberger, M. (2020). Deviant sexual interests but not antisocial behaviors are associated with neuropsychological deficits in individuals convicted of sexual offenses against children. *Neuropsychology, 34*(8), 906–916. https://doi.org/10.1037/neu0000703

Walton, J. S. (2021). Rehabilitating paraphilic disorder in prisons: Interventions sensitive to shame and trauma and the importance of safe prisons. In L. A. Craig & R. M. Bartels (Eds.), *Sexual deviance: Understanding and managing deviant sexual interests and paraphilic disorders*. Wiley-Blackwell.

Ward, T., & Beech, A. R. (2006). An integrated theory of sex offending. *Aggression and Violent Behavior, 11*, 44–63. https://doi.org/10.1016/j.avb.2005.05.002

Ward, T., & Gannon, T. A. (2006). Rehabilitation, etiology, and self-regulation: The comprehensive Good Lives Model of treatment for sexual offenders. *Aggression and Violent Behavior, 11*, 77–94. https://doi.org/10.1016/j.avb.2005.06.001

Ward, T., & Keenan, T. R. (1999). Child molesters' implicit theories. *Journal of Interpersonal Violence, 14*(8), 821–883. https://doi.org/10.1177/088626099014008003

Williams, F., & Carter, A. J. (2018). Engaging with forensic populations: A biologically informed approach. In A. R. Beech, A. J. Carter, R. E. Mann, & P. Rotshtein (Eds.), *The Wiley Blackwell handbook of forensic neuroscience* (pp. 577–600). Wiley-Blackwell.

Willis, G. M., Prescott, D. S., & Yates, P. M. (2016). Application of an integrated Good Lives Model to sexual offending treatment. In D. P. Boer, L. E. Marshall, & W. L. Marshall (Eds.), *Theories, assessment and treatment of sexual offending, Volume 3* (pp. 1355–1386). Wiley-Blackwell.

Part III

Treatment of People Exhibiting Deviant Sexual Interests and/or Behaviours

9

Future Directions in the Treatment of Sexual Self-Regulation Problems in People Who Have Sexually Offended

Wineke J. Smid

People convicted for sexual offenses (PCSO) are in many ways comparable to people who committed other types of offenses, and risk assessment instruments show ample overlap in relevant risk factors for both groups. However, it is the sexual aspect of the offenses that distinguishes these groups, and sexual self-regulation problems (SSRP) form the extra part of the risk assessment instruments specifically developed for PCSO. Following one of the internationally most widely used risk assessment instruments, the Stable-2007 (Fernandez et al., 2014), relevant SSRP consist of sexual preoccupation, sexualized coping, and sexual deviance (i.e., unusual and/or illegal[1] sexual interests). Over the past years, a lot of time and effort has

[1] The term 'illegal sexual interests' refers to sexual interests that are illegal if acted upon, such as pedophilia or coercion; interests are not illegal in and of themselves.

I have no known conflict of interest to disclose.

W. J. Smid (✉)
The Forensic Care Specialists, Utrecht, Netherlands
e-mail: wsmid@dfzs.nl

© The Author(s), under exclusive license to Springer Nature Switzerland AG 2022

K. Uzieblo et al. (eds.), *Challenges in the Management of People Convicted of a Sexual Offence*, Palgrave Studies in Risk, Crime and Society,
https://doi.org/10.1007/978-3-030-80212-7_9

been invested to increase our ability to assess SSRP (e.g., Chap. 5 on the assessment of deviance with indirect measures), theorize about their nature and aetiology (e.g., Smid & Wever, 2019), and improve their treatment (e.g., Levenson et al., 2018). Nevertheless, there is still room for improvement. This chapter proposes a way forward to develop our understanding and treatment of these risk factors.

Definitions

There is wide consensus on the importance of SSRP in PCSO; however, there is no consensus yet on the exact definitions of sexual deviance, sexual preoccupation, and sexual coping. For instance, in the literature, many concepts are gathered under the umbrella of 'sexual deviance', such as unusual but legal interests (e.g., diaper fetish) as well illegal but common interests (e.g., 14-year-old girls), and passing mild interests as well as lifelong exclusive preferences for deviant stimuli; these concepts are often used interchangeably. Drawing up definitions may seem a theoretical and abstract activity, but (the lack of) a clear and consistent definition can have real repercussions on clinical and scientific practice. Inadequate definitions automatically translate into problems regarding research and treatment: if we are not sure what it is we are aiming for, how can we measure it accurately, let alone try to change it?

Specific definitional discrepancies regarding paedophilia provide a good example. There is little doubt regarding the importance of sexual interest in children as a risk factor; however, it remains unclear whether we should focus on 'mere' interest in children or on the *preference* for children. There is also substantial variety in victim-age categories used in research, with ages deemed reflective of paedophilic interest sometimes set at under 13 (following the DSM 5), sometimes under 16 or under 18 (following the age of consent according to the law of the country/state), sometimes under 10, or sometimes described in terms as 'prepubescent', which in turn refers to an unclear age limit somewhere between 9 and 14. With regard to offending, in some studies subjects without criminal records who admitted to having accessed child sexual exploitation material (CSEM) are included in the offender group (Cantor et al., 2008), while in other studies they are included in the non-offender control group (Lett et al., 2018). The characteristics of subjects in various studies vary so widely that it may impede overarching conclusions. Sorting out these and other definitions is without doubt a difficult task, but it would be very beneficial to research, the development of theory and (the evaluation of) clinical practice regarding SSRP.

Non-Forensic Sexology

Difficulties regarding clear and consistent definitions for SSRP are not unique to the forensic field. Within non-forensic sexology, there are also numerous views on the exact nature of SSRP and definitions vary widely, for instance resulting in numerous terms for sexual preoccupation, including hypersexuality, sexual addiction, and sexual compulsivity. Furthermore, there is ample discussion whether or not 'sex addiction' or sexual deviance really exist or if the whole discussion is foremost normative/moral in nature and people are simply very diverse (Reay et al., 2013). Following the DSM 5 criteria (American Psychiatric Association, 2013), people who have *not* committed any sexual offenses (i.e., not made anyone else suffer) will only qualify for a paraphilic *disorder* if they suffer from their paraphilic interests themselves. The suggested criteria for a diagnosis of "hypersexual disorder" are also largely characterized by the subject's suffering (Kafka, 2013) and do not refer to an actual level of sexual activity that is deemed problematic in and of itself. Simply put, in non-forensic sexology there is only such a thing as 'deviant sex' or 'too much sex' if the subject feels it is. Following from this, non-forensic treatment of SSRP includes two approaches: (a) the reduction of the undesired sexual interest or behaviour and (b) the reduction of the subject's suffering. For example, subjective feelings of suffering are officially the primary treatment target in the Dutch "standard of care" regarding paraphilic and hypersexual disorders (Akwa, 2020).

This is profoundly different in forensic treatment. Although PCSO may suffer from their preferences and/or preoccupations, the actual sexual preference and the frequency of the sexual behaviours are of the essence here, because these have been found to be related to risk.

Consequently, non-offender research is not automatically informative for forensic purposes. If non-offender treatment was successful only in reducing the suffering and not the behaviour, it is clear that this would not help forensic treatment. Hence, our definitions of the problems and treatment goals need to be specifically tailored to the forensic field.

Treatment Effectiveness

Studies on the effectiveness of treatment of PCSO are mostly based on comprehensive treatment programs and far less on individual treatment of specific risk factors. These general findings indicate that treatment overall is (reasonably) effective, reducing recidivism rates by approximately one-third (Gannon et al., 2019). Treatment evaluations indicate cognitive behavioural therapy (CBT) as the most effective approach, and treatment effects increase if CBT is delivered following the risk-need-responsivity principles (RNR; Andrews & Bonta, 2017; see also Chap. 10). The core principles of the model entail that offenders with higher *risk* levels need more treatment, which needs to be tailored to the *responsivity* style of the individual offender and focused on their criminogenic *needs*, also described as the dynamic risk factors (Hanson et al., 2009). Building on this, a meta-analysis on dynamic risk factors (Van den Berg et al., 2018) found that reduction of offenders' total scores on dynamic risk assessment instruments, is indeed associated with lower recidivism rates.

Less studies are available about the effect of comprehensive CBT programs specifically on SSRP in PCSO. The available studies show that comprehensive CBT programs lower SSRP, and some studies find that these changes in SSRP from pre- to post-treatment are significantly associated with decreased recidivism (Olver & Stockdale, 2020). The remaining question is which specific treatment interventions best reduce SSRP.

In general sexology, many therapy approaches have been described and/or suggested for the specific treatment of SSRP/sexual preoccupation/sexual coping/sex addiction, including CBT, Relapse prevention, Supportive group therapy, Acceptance and Commitment therapy, Experiential psychotherapy, Psychoeducation, Surveillance Networks,

12-step programs, Mindfulness training, and Psychodynamic therapy. Of those treatments, CBT, Acceptance and Commitment therapy (ACT), experiential therapy, motivational interviewing, art therapy, and online psychoeducation have acquired some support. However, there is still a lack of rigorous research; there are hardly any sizable RCTs, and many studies have no control group. Most notably, there is evidence for the effectiveness of CBT in the treatment of (behavioural) addictions in general; however, there are limited data on treatment of sexual addiction specifically (e.g., Hook et al., 2014; Kaplan & Krueger, 2010; Rosenberg et al., 2014). Available evidence does indicate that CBT treatment for SSRP likely benefits from a strong behavioural component.

Behavioural Approaches

The importance of a strong behavioural component in CBT targeting SSRP also seems to translate to forensic treatment. A number of behavioural techniques have been developed that aim to directly reduce deviant arousal and/or promote normative/normophilic arousal (APA, 2013), such as covert sensitization, imaginal desensitization, aversive stimulation, aversive behavioural rehearsal, electrical aversion, satiation, fading, behavioural reconditioning, and guided masturbationS (Rosen & Hall, 1992).

McPhail and Olver (2020) meta-analysed interventions specifically aimed at 'paedohebephilic' arousal in men convicted for sexual offenses against children. They conclude that the largest reductions in pre-post deviant arousal (assessed by penile plethysmography) is found for behavioural interventions, followed by pharmacological interventions. The most recent meta-analysis on the effectiveness of comprehensive sex offender treatment (Gannon et al., 2019) underlines these results with the finding that treatment that includes "some form of arousal conditioning" appears to be more successful in reducing sexual recidivism than treatment that does not. Although this does not add up to irrefutable proof for the efficacy of these behavioural approaches, it certainly invites us to not disregard this option.

Behavioural arousal conditioning techniques are widely used in North America (McGrath et al., 2009), but (to my knowledge) far less in Europe, if at all. However, recently in Europe and Australia a different technique to directly influence deviant arousal has been used experimentally: eye movement desensitization and reprocessing (EMDR). EMDR is widely known as a validated method of treatment for trauma (Bisson et al., 2007), but can also be adapted to target deviant arousal. The patient recalls an arousing deviant memory while he is instructed to perform eye movements (usually by following horizontal hand movements with their eyes). The aim of the technique is to reduce the vividness and emotional charge of the memories and thus disconnect the deviant stimulus from its positive emotional load/sexual arousal (Smid et al., 2019). McPhail and Olver's meta-analysis of interventions aimed at "paedohebephilic" arousal (2020) included two small studies involving EMDR treatment ($N = 13$) with medium to large effect sizes, although not (yet) reaching statistical significance. This intervention seems worthy of further development and evaluation.

Medication

Currently, the more common way to tackle SSRP in PCSO is the administration of testosterone-lowering medication. Studies suggest the effectiveness of this treatment with respect to recidivism (e.g., Gallo et al., 2019), although more and more rigorous evaluation is needed. But there is certainly evidence to suggest that this medication reduces SSRP in PCSO (Landgren et al., 2020; McPhail & Olver, 2020), at least during the time the medication is used. However, there are serious negative effects to these medications as well; not limited to their medical/physical side effects, such as osteoporosis and gynecomastia (breast growth) (Turner & Briken, 2018). Foremost, testosterone-lowering medication suppresses sexual arousal continuously and for all stimuli. Therefore, it is difficult, for instance, to significantly reduce sexual preoccupation with this medication and yet allow the patient to have good-quality sexual arousal occasionally. Likewise, it is difficult to reduce sexual deviance with this medication and yet allow the patient to have good-quality normative sexual arousal. We could of course succumb to the notion that PCSO, as a result of their crimes, have forfeited their rights to all sexuality forever. But this seems rather rigorous, certainly if (a) it is far from certain whether they would recidivate without medication, (b) it is far from certain that the medication will stop them from doing so, besides the fact that livelong supervision may be necessary to ensure continued use, and (c) there may be other, possibly better (McPhail & Olver, 2020) and less damaging, ways to achieve the same goal.

A Legitimate Treatment Target

Besides clear and consistent definitions, specific (behavioural) treatment interventions and focused research, treatment could benefit from a more nuanced and differentiated view on SSRP and sexuality. For instance, sexual traits, especially deviant interests are often seen as absolutely unchangeable (Seto, 2012). In a way, it is mystifying we are convinced that we can have a substantial influence on a person's violent and impulsive proclivities but seem to render ourselves almost chanceless with regard to someone's sexual proclivities. Furthermore, given the existing evidence for the role of learning and conditioning in the development of sexual interests (Brom et al., 2014), and the possible effects of psychotherapeutic treatment (Gannon et al., 2019; McPhail & Olver, 2020), it is not unreasonable to assume that sexual interests may be amenable to at least some change through therapeutic treatment, and in some cases "some change" may just be enough. For instance, it is possible that a small decrease in deviant interest and a small increase in normative interest could 'flip' an illegal preference to a legal one and this, in turn, might help reduce risk.

Sexual Health

The World Health Organization (WHO, 2021) describes *sexual health* as "the possibility of having pleasurable and safe sexual experiences", and states that all people have "the right to the highest attainable standard of sexual health". This implies that anything that is satisfying for the individual and not harmful for them or for others is worthy of consideration. In my experience, most forensic patients do really want to control their illegal behaviour, even if only to stay out of trouble with the law. However, they also want to retain their sexuality and the possibility for satisfying sexual arousal. For some of them (only) deviant/illegal stimuli provide that particular satisfying arousal. The focus of treatment is to stop offending behaviour, and with regard to SSRP, there are a number of alternative ways to achieve this goal besides suppressing sexual arousal altogether.

Recent research suggests that (exclusive) deviant *preference* specifically seems to be the key risk factor for recidivism, while a mere coexisting deviant interest is not (McPhail et al., 2018). In other words: coexisting normative interests may provide an opportunity for protective influence. Therefore, treatment should also stimulate the enhancement of normative sexual interests and experiences. For instance, if a patient is engaged in seeking normative sexual contact, the occasional use of sildenafil (Viagra) is sometimes considered, to temporarily counter the effect of testosterone-lowering medication and enable the patient to gain positive experiences with normative sex (J. Troelstra (psychiatrist), personal communication, January 28, 2021).

In other cases, it may not be possible to enhance interest in normative sexual behaviour because there is no starting point. For some patients, the focus on sexual interests in illegal sexual stimuli can be deferred to coexisting unusual-but-legal interests, such as wearing women's lingerie or using sex toys (S. Noom (treatment supervisor), personal communication, January 19, 2021). The patient refrains from illegal sexual activity but retains the possibility for satisfying sexual arousal in a legal, albeit unusual, manner.

Even if it is impossible to move away from the desired illegal stimulus (e.g., children), it may still be possible to find ways to stop offending behaviour, while holding on to the possibility of occasional sexual arousal to the desired stimulus in a legal manner. For instance, masturbating to a sexual fantasy (in private) is never illegal. Most of the pornographic stories that float around the internet in every variation are also legal in most countries and so is owning a (child) sex doll in many countries (some countries prohibit the import of these dolls, but almost none prohibit the possession). Of course, these approaches involve complex moral issues that need to be considered and some may even consider this a 'cure worse than the disease'. On an equally important note, these efforts need to be carefully monitored and evaluated to make sure they do not cause opposite effects, for instance, by increasing the focus on offending behaviour and thus increasing risk. But despite these complications, it is still worth trying because life with alternative sexual expressions may be considerably easier to sustain than life with no sexuality at all, especially for younger patients. Moreover, in general sexology the finding is that patients' acceptance of their paraphilic interests and finding satisfying and not-harmful ways to express these interests will often *lower* the focus on these paraphilic interests (e.g., Coleman, 2012) and may sometimes even open the patient up to latent alternative interests (Van Lunsen & Laan, 2017). Given the limited evidence for all types of interventions directed at SSRP, there is no reason not to include these less rigorous approaches. We should aim to do well by society by increasing our knowledge and reduce sexual offending to the best of our abilities. At the same time, we should aim to do well by our patients by treating what is necessary to the best of our abilities, while leaving them intact as much as possible, including sexually.

Harm Reduction

As discussed earlier, non-forensic research and treatment is not automatically applicable to forensic samples; however, some aspects of non-forensic treatment could be helpful. For instance, non-forensic treatment of sexual preoccupation, or 'sex addiction', is firmly related to addiction therapy, and modern-day addiction therapy explicitly leaves room for the normalization of relapse. Relapse does not mean treatment has failed; on the contrary, adequately dealing with relapse is an essential part of treatment. Avoiding relapse is deemed important but finding one's way back to the right track as swiftly as possible following relapse is deemed even more important. In PCSO treatment, there is little to no room at all for any form of relapse, and of course, relapse in the form of new offending behaviour is unacceptable. However, there are also more benign forms of 'relapse' or 'breach' such as searching the internet for pornography or visiting a prostitute. In practice, these breaches are often regarded as treatment failure, a sign that nothing has really changed. However, this may not always be the case; change is a gradual process. Forensic treatment could benefit from normalizing the possibility of (some forms of) relapse and put more focus on dealing with these issues rather than exclusively focusing on avoiding them. Following the sexual health perspective, these 'relapses' can be helpful in the patient's active search for acceptable and sustainable expressions of sexuality.

On a related note, the outcome of non-forensic treatment, both regarding addiction and SSRP, is often assessed in terms of 'harm reduction', acknowledging the fact that less drinking, less drug use, or less sexualized coping also means progress. It is logical that forensic treatment focuses on harm elimination instead of harm reduction, because the harm is generally done to others. However, although harm reduction is not a valid treatment target for forensic treatment, it is a valid outcome measure for research, in addition to the mere presence or absence of recidivism. Because this dichotomous outcome may obscure potential positive effects of treatment on which we could build to improve. Future research could include more differentiated variables such as 'time to new offense', 'number of new offenses', and 'seriousness of new offenses'. Not to condone 'lighter' offenses, but to enable us to use the knowledge on how we managed, for instance, to extend the 'time to new offenses', to be able to extend that time further and further.

Moral Issues

One of the issues complicating a sexual health approach in the treatment of PCSO lies in the moral dilemmas surrounding sexual offending. This is a delicate topic that inspires the need to precede its discussion with the statement that I, as the author of this chapter, do not condone sexual offending behaviour in any way shape or form, and at the same time sincerely believe that it is everybody's right to engage in any legal sexual activity that does not hurt anybody. But isn't it strange that I, like so many others often do, feel the need to explain myself, and explain why I do what I do?

It often seems that we, following popular believe, feel the need to adhere to straight lines between good and bad, and want to place ourselves firmly on the good side. We want to strictly separate what is immoral/illegal and therefore must be 'deviant' and keep it on one side of the line, while keeping what is morally acceptable/legal and therefore must be labelled 'normal' on the other side of the line. There seems to be little room for doubt, nuances, or grey areas. In reality, there are, of course, many grey areas. For instance, relatively common sexual interests, such as interest in 13-year-old children or interest in coercion (Lalumière et al., 2005), do result in illegal behaviour if acted upon. There is nothing inherently wrong or special about having such a sexual interest, but everything is wrong with acting on it. On the other hand, there are many sexual interests that are completely legal to practice, that do not have to stand in the way of a healthy and productive life (although they certainly can), but are none the less very unusual, such as a diaper fetish or 'poop-play'.

We also tend to keep perpetrators and victims strictly separated; a person is either one or the other. It is implicitly assumed that it is always clear as day that perpetrators are wrong and they always know exactly what they are doing; again, there seems to be little room for doubt, nuances, or grey areas. If a perpetrator has himself also been a victim of abuse, this introduces a complicating discrepancy that is often disregarded for we don't want the trauma to be used as an excuse for their behaviour. Sometimes patients who have sexually offended are told to see a separate therapist for the treatment of their own trauma. In recent years, there has been a counter-reaction with increased calls for 'trauma informed care' for PCSO (Levenson et al., 2018). And this makes sense because the relationship between victimization and perpetration has been firmly established (e.g., Jespersen et al., 2009). Insufficient attention for offenders' own childhood traumas could impede our view on the possible risk-reducing effects of such treatment. There are certainly clinical examples of deviant interests that seem to 'fade' after properly addressing their related childhood traumas in treatment (N. ten Hoor (psychotherapist), personal communication, January 22, 2021; R. M. (former forensic patient), personal communication, February 2,

2021). Of course, this does not amount to hard evidence, but it seems worthy of further investigation.

Summarizing, it is important that we are aware of the moral issues surrounding our work and not let these get in the way of consistent definitions, good research, and effective treatment. Our job is not to decide between guilt and innocence or even between 'good' and 'bad' in general. Our job is to understand sexual offending behaviours as good as we can and help prevent them from happening (again). For that purpose, a pragmatic approach seems preferable that emphasizes clarity and accuracy, without moral judgement or at least clearly separated from moral judgement.

Conclusions

SSRP are considered essential factors in the treatment of PCSO. Despite the need for more and stronger research, there is no reason for definitive pessimism in the treatment of SSRP, including deviant sexual interests, as they seem amenable to (at least some) change. Behavioural interventions and testosterone-lowering medication currently have the most, albeit still limited, empirical support. However, medication has serious downsides and other possibly effective interventions, such as EMDR, deserve further evaluation. The field could also benefit from establishing clear and consistent definitions that facilitate research and communication and allow us to gather knowledge in a more consistent way. Clinical practice could benefit from more differentiation in treatment goals regarding SSRP that better match patients' sexual health and provide more sustainable lifestyles. Consequently, research will need to use more differentiated outcome measures to evaluate these treatments in better detail. At all times, it remains a challenge to avoid moral pitfalls, to pass judgement as little as possible, and to leave room for grey areas and nuances.

References

Akwa, G. G. Z. (2020, August 5). *Parafiele en hyperseksuele stoornissen*. GGZ Standaarden. [*Paraphilic and hypersexual disorders*. Mental Health Care Standards] https://www.ggzstandaarden.nl/zorgstandaarden/parafiele-en-hyperseksuele-stoornissen/introductie

American Psychiatric Association. (2013). *Diagnostic and statistical manual of mental dis- orders* (5th ed.). Author.

Andrews, D. A., & Bonta, J. (2017). *The psychology of criminal conduct* (6th ed.). Routledge.

Bisson, J. I., Ehlers, A., Matthews, R., Pilling, S., Richards, D., & Turner, S. (2007). Psychological treatments for chronic post-traumatic stress disorder: Systematic review and meta-analysis. *British Journal of Psychiatry, 190*, 97–104. https://doi.org/10.1192/bjp.bp.106.021402

Brom, M., Both, S., Laan, E., Everaerd, W., & Spinhoven, P. (2014). The role of conditioning, learning and dopamine in sexual behavior: A narrative review of animal and human studies. *Neuroscience & Biobehavioral Reviews, 38*, 38–59. https://doi.org/10.1016/j.neubiorev.2013.10.014

Cantor, J. M., Kabani, N., Christensen, B. K., Zipursky, R. B., Barbaree, H. E., Dickey, R., Klassen, P. E., Mikulis, D. J., Kuban, M. E., Blak, T., Richards, B. A., Hanratty, M. K., & Blanchard, R. (2008). Cerebral white matter deficiencies in pedophilic men. *Journal of Psychiatric Research, 42*(3), 167–183. https://doi.org/10.1016/j.jpsychires.2007.10.013

Coleman, E. (2012). Impulsive/compulsive sexual behavior: Assessment and treatment. In J. E. Grant & M. N. Potenza (Eds.), *The Oxford handbook of impulse control disorders* (pp. 375–388). Oxford University.

Fernandez, Y., Harris, A. J. R., Hanson, R. K., & Sparks, J. (2014). *STABLE-2007 coding manual: Revised 2014*. Unpublished manual, Public Safety Canada, Ottawa, Ontario.

Gallo, A., Abracen, J., Looman, J., Jeglic, E., & Dickey, R. (2019). The use of leuprolide acetate in the management of high-risk sex offenders. *Sexual Abuse, 31*(8), 930–951. https://doi.org/10.1177/1079063218791176

Gannon, T. A., Olver, M. E., Mallion, J. S., & James, M. (2019). Does specialized psychological treatment for offending reduce recidivism? A meta-analysis examining staff and program variables as predictors of treatment effectiveness. *Clinical Psychology Review, 73*, 101752. https://doi.org/10.1016/j.cpr.2019.101752

Hanson, R. K., Bourgon, G., Helmus, L., & Hodgson, S. (2009). The principles of effective correctional treatment also apply to sexual offenders: A meta-analysis. *Criminal Justice and Behavior, 9*, 865–891. https://doi.org/10.1177/0093854809338545

Hook, J. N., Reid, R. C., Penberthy, J. K., Davis, D. E., & Jennings, D. J. (2014). Methodological review of treatments for nonparaphilic hypersexual behavior. *Journal of Sex & Marital Therapy, 40*(4), 294–308. https://doi.org/10.1080/0092623X.2012.751075

Jespersen, A. F., Lalumière, M. L., & Seto, M. C. (2009). Sexual abuse history among adult sex offenders and non-sex offenders: A meta-analysis. *Child Abuse & Neglect, 33*, 179–192. https://doi.org/10.1016/j.chiabu.2008.07.004

Kafka, M. P. (2013). The development and evolution of the criteria for a newly proposed diagnosis for DSM-5: Hypersexual disorder. *Sexual Addiction & Compulsivity, 20*(1–2), 19–26. https://doi.org/10.1080/10720162.2013.768127

Kaplan, M. S., & Krueger, R. B. (2010). Diagnosis, assessment, and treatment of hypersexuality. *Journal of Sex Research, 47*(2–3), 181–198. https://doi.org/10.1080/00224491003592863

Lalumière, M. L., Harris, G., Quinsey, V., & Rice, M. E. (2005). *The causes of rape: Understanding individual differences in male propensity for sexual aggression*. American Psychological Association.

Landgren, V., Malki, K., Bottai, M., Arver, S., & Rahm, C. (2020). Effect of gonadotropin-releasing hormone antagonist on risk of committing child sexual abuse in men with pedophilic disorder: A randomized clinical trial. *JAMA Psychiatry, 77*(9), 897–905. https://doi.org/10.1001/jamapsychiatry.2020.0440

Lett, T. A., Mohnke, S., Amelung, T., Brandl, E. J., Schiltz, K., Pohl, A., Gerwinn, H., Kärgel, C., Massau, C., Tenbergen, G., Wittfoth, M., Kneer, J., Beier, K. M., Walter, M., Ponseti, J., Krüger, T. H. C., Schiffer, B., & Walter, H. (2018). Multimodal neuroimaging measures and intelligence influence pedophile child sexual offense behavior. *European Neuropsychopharmacology, 28*(7), 818–827. https://doi.org/10.1016/j.euroneuro.2018.05.002

Levenson, J. S., Willis, G. M., & Prescott, D. (2018). Incorporating principles of trauma- informed care into evidence-based sex offending treatment. In E. L. Jeglic & C. Calkins (Eds.) *New frontiers in offender treatment* (pp. 171–188). Springer. https://doi.org/10.1007/978-3-030-01030-0_9.

McGrath, R. J., Cumming, G. F., Burchard, B. L., Zeoli, S., & Ellerby, L. (2009). Current practices and emerging trends in sexual abuser management. *The Safer Society, 24*. https://robertmcgrath.us/files/6414/3204/5288/2009_Safer_Society_North_American_Survey.pdf

McPhail, I. V., & Olver, M. E. (2020). Interventions for pedohebephilic arousal in men convicted for sexual offenses against children: A meta-analytic review. *Criminal Justice and Behavior, 47*(10), 1319–1339. https://doi.org/10.1177/0093854820916774

McPhail, I. V., Olver, M. E., Brouillette-Alarie, S., & Looman, J. (2018). Taxometric analysis of the latent structure of Pedophilic interest. *Archives of Sexual Behavior, 47*(8), 2223–2240. https://doi.org/10.1007/s10508-018-1225-4

Olver, M. E., & Stockdale, K. C. (2020). Evaluating change in men who have sexually offended: Linkages to risk assessment and management. *Current Psychiatry Reports, 22*(5), 1–10. https://doi.org/10.1007/s11920-020-01146-3

Reay, B., Attwood, N., & Gooder, C. (2013). Inventing sex: The short history of sex addiction. *Sexuality & Culture, 17*(1), 1–19. https://doi.org/10.1007/s12119-012-9136-3

Rosen, R. C., & Hall, K. S. (1992). Behavioural treatment approaches for offenders and victims. In W. O'Donohue & J. H. Geer (Eds.), *The sexual abuse of children: Volume II: Clinical issues*. Routledge.

Rosenberg, K. P., Carnes, P., & O'Connor, S. (2014). Evaluation and treatment of sex addiction. *Journal of Sex & Marital Therapy, 40*(2), 77–91. https://doi.org/10.1080/0092623X.2012.701268

Seto, M. C. (2012). Is pedophilia a sexual orientation? *Archives of Sexual Behavior, 41*(1), 231–236. https://doi.org/10.1007/s10508-011-9882-6

Smid, W. J., ten Hoor, N., & Uzieblo, K. (2019). Eye Movement Desensitization and Reprocessing (EMDR): Exploring a new avenue for sex offender treatment. *Association for The Treatment of Sexual Abusers. The Forum Newsletter, 19*(4). http://newsmanager.commpartners.com/atsa/issues/2019-09-20/7.html

Smid, W. J., & Wever, E. C. (2019). Mixed emotions: An incentive motivational model of sexual deviance. *Sexual Abuse, 31*(7), 731–764. https://doi.org/10.1177/1079063218775972

Turner, D., & Briken, P. (2018). Treatment of paraphilic disorders in sexual offenders or men with a risk of sexual offending with luteinizing hormone-releasing hormone agonists: An updated systematic review. *The Journal of Sexual Medicine, 15*(1), 77–93. https://doi.org/10.1016/j.jsxm.2017.11.013

Van den Berg, J. W., Smid, W., Schepers, K., Wever, E., van Beek, D., Janssen, E., & Gijs, L. (2018). The predictive properties of dynamic sex offender risk assessment instruments: A meta-analysis. *Psychological Assessment, 30*(2), 179–191. https://doi.org/10.1037/pas0000454

Van Lunsen, R. H. W., & Laan, E. (2017). *Seks! Een leven lang leren [Seks! Life-long learning]*. Prometheus.

World Health Organization. (2021). *Sexual health.* https://www.who.int/teams/sexual-and-reproductive-health-and-research/key-areas-of-work/sexual-health/defining-sexual-health

10

Applying RNR Principles to Effectively Treat People Who Have Committed a Sexual Offence

Sandy Jung

Eradicating sexual abuse is a goal many of us aim to achieve in both our personal and professional lives. The most seasoned therapists often take time to figure out that quick fixes will not resolve larger societal problems, such as the prevention of sexual abuse. Therefore, it is critical that we use what is considered sound advice, and this advice must be evidence-based. One of the most widely regarded approaches in the effective rehabilitation of people who have committed a sexual offence (PCSO) involves a series of 18 principles that should guide our practice. These principles of effective rehabilitation comprise the following components: the overarching principles of effective rehabilitation, three core principles colloquially called the risk, need, and responsivity (RNR) principles, structured assessment, programme delivery, staff practices, and organization that houses

I have no known conflict of interest to disclose.

S. Jung (✉)
Department of Psychology, MacEwan University, Edmonton, AB, Canada
e-mail: jungs0@macewan.ca

© The Author(s), under exclusive license to Springer Nature Switzerland AG 2022

K. Uzieblo et al. (eds.), *Challenges in the Management of People Convicted of a Sexual Offence*, Palgrave Studies in Risk, Crime and Society,
https://doi.org/10.1007/978-3-030-80212-7_10

the service (see Andrews et al., 2011, for an overview of all 18 principles). This chapter provides a brief background and will focus on the core principles of RNR and why programmes should adhere to RNR to effectively reduce sexual reoffending. An exploration of the challenges faced in implementing this evidence-based model is explored, followed by a discussion as to how our field can move forward.

A Brief History and an Overview

In order to understand and appreciate the value of the RNR principles, a brief background on its origin may help demonstrate how they emerged out of need and necessity. In North America, the political perspectives in the early 1970s moved away from valuing rehabilitative efforts in correctional settings to an attitude of retribution and punishment. Like a perfect storm, sociologist Robert Martinson (1974) published his comprehensive literature review of 231 studies and concluded that we could only expect minimal, if any, changes brought about by offender rehabilitation as reviewed in his paper. Although not his intention, others interpreted his thesis as an endorsement to reduce spending on rehabilitative efforts in prisons and in the communities, and some even reframed his words into the idea that "nothing works" in the rehabilitation of offenders (Sarre, 2001). This reinterpretation led to an escalation of researchers and clinicians responding, which included a growth in published empirical studies evaluating correctional programmes and improved study of the complexity of factors that contribute to rehabilitative effectiveness. Despite efforts to address this criticism (Lipton et al., 1975) and to retract Martinson's earlier conclusions in subsequent publications (Martinson, 1979), Martinson continues to be misquoted from his 1974 publication.

Two Canadian researchers, Don Andrews and James Bonta, re-examined the body of treatment effectiveness research. Their efforts moved beyond a subjective account of the existing research, and instead they employed a meta-analytic approach to examine the data objectively. What they found led to establishing a framework for effective correctional interventions, which was eventually published in their seminal book on the subject, *The Psychology of Criminal Conduct* (Andrews & Bonta, 1994). The original framework and expanded model outlined in their text has been since condensed to three core RNR principles.

To gain an appreciation for the RNR principles, let's begin with a description of each principle. The first principle, the Risk Principle, argues that interventions are most effective in reducing reoffending when they target individuals who are at a higher risk to offend (Andrews & Bonta, 2010). In other words, the Risk Principle tells us who should receive the most treatment and supervision. Therefore, the intensity of service must match an individual's risk to reoffend. In order to adhere to this principle when working with PCSO, we must (1) properly assess sexual violence risk using validated risk tools and (2) apply an appropriate amount of service to that individual. For example, a probation officer would provide more frequent supervision of a client who scores high on a validated risk tool. In contrast, if an individual was scored at a low risk, it would not be beneficial to provide intense and frequent supervision, given that risk would not be further decreased in any meaningful way and intensive services may even be detrimental (e.g., Lovins et al., 2009).

The second principle, the Need Principle, emphasizes that treatment and supervision should address risk factors directly linked to offending behaviours, called criminogenic needs, and therefore tells us what we should target in the intervention (Andrews & Bonta, 2010). For example, criminogenic needs that are relevant to sexual reoffending include sexual preoccupation, deviant sexual interests, and sexualized coping (see Mann et al., 2010). In addition, there are a number of criminogenic needs associated with general or violent offending, and these are also valuable to monitor and to address in treatment (i.e., Central '8' from Bonta & Andrews, 2017; e.g., poor family relationships, poor use of leisure time, procriminal attitudes, and antisocial associates). It is important that criminogenic needs are not confused with responsivity issues that limit engagement in treatment or supervision but do not contribute directly to criminal behaviour. For example, clinical needs (e.g., depression, low self-esteem, poor social skills, and experienced childhood abuse) may be areas to address in treatment, although they are not linked with criminal behaviours, and they may limit one from engaging with treatment.

The third principle is the Responsivity Principle, and asserts that interventions are most effective when the intervention follows a social learning approach and the mode of the intervention matches the individual's characteristics (e.g., degree of motivation, learning capabilities, and personality features; Andrews & Bonta, 2010). Consequently, the Responsivity Principle informs us on how we should treat and supervise the individual. This principle has two components: *general responsivity* refers to the strategy used to influence behaviours and emphasizes that social learning approaches should be used (e.g., cognitive behavioural interventions, and rapport-infused working alliance) and *specific responsivity* refers to specific characteristics of the individual that pose a threat to treatment engagement and include poor treatment motivation, denial or minimization, developmental delays, learning disabilities, personality disorders (e.g., psychopathy and borderline personality disorder), culture-specific concerns, mental health instability, and adverse childhood experiences (including trauma) (Jung, 2017). Hence, treatment and supervision should be structured to address and monitor criminogenic needs but should also be individualized to ensure there are no responsivity issues that serve as obstacles, which may limit engagement.

Adopting RNR: Survey and Rationale

Although the RNR principles are nearly three decades old, implementation of RNR has not consistently been adopted by all institutions and community agencies that offer treatment. For example, despite the fact that researchers had developed the RNR principles in Canada, not all provinces have adopted supervision and treatment practices that align with RNR principles for people who have engaged in any form of offending behaviours (Rugge et al., 2019). With regards to programmes that are employed to specifically treat PCSO, a survey of community and residential treatment programmes in North America was conducted in 2009 by Safer Society Press (McGrath et al., 2010). In the US, the survey revealed that only a third or fewer programmes identified that RNR principles were one of the top three approaches used in their practice (18.5% of community, 31.6% of residential) while only 10% or fewer programmes indicated that RNR was their primary approach (3.1% of community, 10.1% of residential). Surprisingly, in Canada, the proportion of programmes that listed RNR as one of their top approaches was also quite small (26.3% of community; 37.5% of residential) with only 5.3% of community and none of the residential programmes noting that RNR was their primary approach.

Despite these data showing limited adoption in the US and Canada, RNR principles are widely accepted as part of effective practices to guide intervention practices with PCSO (see Association for the Treatment of Sexual Abusers [ATSA] Practice Guidelines, 2014). In some U.S. states, RNR principles are weaved into policies, such as those outlined by the Colorado Sex Offender Management Board (2020); however, many other large U.S. states with similar boards do not highlight these principles (e.g., California, New York, and Illinois). Moreover, there is little evidence that RNR is being widely translated into practice in European countries or other parts of the world (e.g., see Rettenberger, 2018, for Germany; Smid, 2018, for Netherlands; Uzieblo et al., 2018, for Belgium; Zara et al., 2020, for Italy).

So why is it important to use evidence-based practices and specifically RNR principles to guide practice? The RNR principles is not a magical formula to eradicate sexual abuse. The principles provide us with an evidence-based guide on what we must follow to ensure we are effectively reducing sexually violent behaviours, as it is human nature to resort to intuition or other pseudoscientific, feel-good approaches. These three principles inform us on who should receive services, what factors should be targeted to reduce reoffending, and how services should be delivered to PCSO. Early meta-analytic studies have shown that adherence to two or three of the principles can lead to small to moderate effects in reducing recidivism among inmates with heterogeneous offending histories (Dowden et al., 1990). Further, adherence to the principles has been empirically examined for PCSO, and research has shown that interventions adhering to all three principles have an appreciable effect reducing risk for sexual offending (Hanson et al., 2009). Given the strong support for interventions that adhere to the RNR principles, two parsimonious reasons for adopting RNR follow, namely efficiency and accountability.

In light of the empirical evidence supporting the effectiveness of interventions that adhere to RNR principles, we should consequently follow these principles for two parsimonious reasons: efficiency and accountability. Efficiency refers to the idea that we must allocate our limited resources to those who require more service. It is rare to hear that any organization or institution has a plethora of unlimited funds to support the rehabilitation and management of PCSO. There are practical reasons for why programmes should adhere to the RNR principles. Efficiently using resources and applying them to the individuals who need it the most because they are at a higher level of risk to victimize another human being is a strong reason to apply these principles. We would get more "bang for our buck" if we thoughtfully utilized such limited criminal justice resources. Romani et al. (2012) examined the cost-effectiveness of employing services that commensurate with the RNR principles, and they found that appropriate correctional services significantly reduced recidivism without a cost increase. Their results highlight the importance of adherence to RNR and the advantages associated with doing so and conclude that "the bang of RNR services is definitely worth the buck" (p. 162). A second reason why we should adhere to RNR principles is the sheer need for accountability. We have strong evidence to know that adherence to RNR is supported by the research, so it is our ethical responsibility to use methods that are evidence-based. Further, we must accept that there would be consequences if we decided to abort sound decisions and practices in favour of pseudoscientific approaches. Poor decisions would not be defensible and any consequences that are injurious to public safety would be scrutinized and irreversible.

Challenges in Implementation

There are many challenges in the implementation and adherence of RNR principles in practice. Some of these difficulties have to do with political and government pressures and policies (countries where basic evidence-based practices have yet to be implemented, let alone maintained). Others have to do with the challenge of translating these principles into settings where practitioners are not well versed in interpreting research and require concrete solutions and procedures. There are also settings where practitioners are scientifically minded but a paradigm shift must take place in order for progress to take place.

General Concerns Adopting Evidence-Based Practices

At a basic level, many clinicians and researchers alike would concur that evidence-based practices (EBP) should be used to assess and treat individuals who are incarcerated or supervised in the community (e.g., using validated risk tools and applying treatment approaches supported by treatment effectiveness studies). Yet, Viglione's (2017) study highlights that both organizational and individual factors play a role in limiting the use of EBP, along with the fact that many do not really understand what "evidence-based practices" really mean and how it should translate into practice, often using discretion to determine when such practices should be utilized. Lilienfeld et al. (2013) highlighted several potential reasons for why clinicians do not adopt EBP, and they include, but are not limited to, naïve realism (i.e., deeply embedded in our intuitions is the belief that the world is exactly how we see it, so unguided clinical intuition supersedes systematic research in one's decision-making), difficulty applying group probabilities to individuals (i.e., underlying EBP is the application of group-based findings to the individual yet a difficulty is presuming, erroneously, that group probabilities cannot apply to the individual case), and misunderstandings of what EBP entails (e.g., construing EBP as "one size fits all" approach, EBP stifles innovations, and findings cannot be generalized beyond individuals in the studies).

Translating RNR into Practical Decisions

For countries that have adopted some level of adherence to RNR principles, there remains the caveat of translating the principles into direct practice. In fact, clarity on how much treatment (e.g., hours, number of sessions, and intensity of sessions) should be administered is not always explicitly outlined. Only recently has translation of the principles into practice become more readily available. For example, there is some guidance on what RNR principles may look like in practice (Jung, 2017) and even session-by-session prepackaged programmes with resources for both the clinician and the client (e.g., Ward & Groener, 2018). However, specificity of threshold to identify who receives intensive services or how much treatment would be considered intensive have yet to be established by leading organizations or governments. Without defined guidelines, variance can be found in practice. For example, Maltais and Jung (2019) found that treatment intensity, in terms of the number of hours and sessions, assigned to individuals with low, moderate, and high risk for sexual violence varied greatly among practitioners in this field. There is some guidance provided by the proposed five-level standardized risk categories outlined by Hanson and Bourgon (2016), which provides the number of hours of treatment that should be administered to offenders of varying risk levels with the goals of allocating resources to higher risk individuals and promoting public protection. However, this has yet to be reliably established for PCSO. Another issue is a lack of consensus on what are meaningful criminogenic needs for an individual. For example, some studies have shown that practitioners, who work with PCSO, have difficulty identifying risk factors that are criminogenic versus non-criminogenic (Dyck et al., 2018; Maltais & Jung, 2019).

Obstacles to Implementation

For any implementation of something new, there will always be the potential for pushback. Andrews and Bonta (2010) foretold this issue, noting that major policy and organizational changes, along with buy-in from key players in the organization (often at the front line of implementation), are not only beneficial but necessary. The available evidence regarding RNR implementation demonstrates that this is a significant issue, especially with paraprofessionals who are expected to adopt the RNR principles in their supervision and management of PCSO. Despite strong empirical support for RNR principles and the endorsement of several organizations, implementation and adherence is a common challenge (Dyck et al., 2018). One caveat that is common among most practitioners is the tendency to continue with old practices despite new training. Familiarity with old methods and lack of time to translate these principles into contemporary practice are often contributing factors. Sometimes lack of time is all it takes for people to resort to old and unfounded practices. The workload concerns that accompany new skills, policies, and procedural changes on top of caseloads, which are already high, are rarely addressed.

Others have observed that there are significant gaps between risk assessment and risk management efforts, suggesting that beyond a proper assessment of an individual's risk factors and needs, there should also be a service delivery plan in place that identifies and prioritizes treatment and supervision targets (Bonta et al., 2008). Viljoen et al. (2018) sought to examine underlying reasons for this gap and conducted a systematic review of the literature. Specifically, they asked whether the use of risk tools would increase professionals' level of adherence to the RNR principles and whether this adherence would, in turn, decrease offending. First, they found that professionals had mixed views about whether risk tools were useful, and that "slippage" seems to occur between assessment and the management of risk. They further found that when risk assessment tools were used, practitioners showed a greater adherence to the risk principle in their practice. However, the same could not be said about following the need principle (addressing criminogenic needs) or improving risk management practices, following the use of a tool, as many needs remained unaddressed in programming. Their findings point to the importance of training, establishment of in-house guidelines, and the need for an implementation process to improve adherence to all three of the RNR principles. Bosker and Witteman (2016) further found that the mere inclusion of a risk tool did not always translate to case management practices. However, when the tool contained a section for case management that facilitated an explicit outline of goals and how to achieve them, the match between risk of recidivism and the intensity of the plan greatly improved.

Sustainable RNR

In addition to the caveats of implementing evidence-based practices, translating principles and practice, and addressing possible pushback, it is also necessary to safeguard this work. To ensure implementation is sustainable, the larger criminal justice community of stakeholders should be involved in training and practice. This network of stakeholders may be from diverse backgrounds, which include, but are not limited to, professionals in correctional treatment facilities and programmes, law enforcement, victim services, judiciary, prosecutors and defence attorneys, and probation and parole—all of who make critical decisions. When stakeholders make decisions that work against each principle, then what happens next may counter the work establishing RNR adherence, such as assigning greater treatment intensity to higher-risk individuals, providing interventions that target criminogenic areas most relevant to that person, and using methods that promote the most change. Therefore, in order for there to be reductions in overall risk, the collective knowledge of RNR principles and adherence to them is needed.

Moving Forward

Recognizing that there will be implementation challenges, readers are reminded that the overarching goal of reducing crime and victimization is why it is essential that programmes adhere to RNR principles, which we know to be the best empirically supported paradigm for the treatment and management of individuals who have committed sexually abusive acts and which provides the 'best bang for our buck' in the efficient use of our limited resources. How the field should move forward, despite these challenges, requires several key recommendations.

Start Adopting One Practice

One should practice RNR principles at every stage of contact with their clients. So, starting at a basic level, examining what would be the most feasible ways to adopt what we know, such as obtaining training on a validated risk tool and begin assessing your current clients, would be a good start. However, it is also important to avoid stopping short of just implementing a risk tool, which can often be seen as a bureaucratic exercise. There must be a pathway built between risk assessment and risk management (Viljoen et al., 2018), and therefore decisions about what you should be prioritizing as treatment targets is a reasonable next step.

Facilitate Buy-In

A larger proactive step involves the implementation of procedural and policy changes, but this requires buy-in by both practitioners and administrators. Buy-in is necessary to ensure professionals perceive the use of risk tools, and adherence to RNR is useful in order for them to adopt these changes (Jung, 2017). A key argument that can be given is that there is a culpability of practitioners if evidence-based approaches are not employed. Non-adherence to RNR could potentially lead to increased rates of reoffending and possibly harm to the same victims or different victims that would be in essence, preventable if supportive practices were in place. The research suggests that when stronger adherence to the RNR model is achieved, the rate of general recidivism is lower (e.g., Luong & Wormith, 2011).

Increase Training Accessibility

Tied into the need for bringing in the key players who carry out the work in the decision-making process, it is critical to improve the access to quality field training in the application of RNR principles. Essentially, training should not only cover what RNR is but also emphasize (a) why adherence matters for risk reduction, (b) how non-adherence increases liability and terrible consequences, and (c) skills-based learning that goes beyond merely covering concepts and involves role-playing and practice to address responsivity needs (e.g., motivational interviewing and addressing denial and minimization). There should be an advanced skills level offered after the practitioner has a period of implementing these principles in practice where upgrading of skills and advanced booster sessions are involved. This type of training should be made accessible to mental health professionals and correctional staff, but also adapted to include judiciary, police, lawyers, probation, and parole in the form of workshops or webinars.

Use Tools that Commensurate with Practice

Several studies have shown that when the tool used to assess individuals did not match the risk management process, adherence to the risk and need principles was disrupted and led to needs being unaddressed and case plans that were poor in quality (see Viljoen et al., 2018). Therefore, using tools that fit with both the jurisdiction and case planning for community supervision led to clearer identification of both the dosage of treatment and supervision and what are relevant criminogenic needs that should be targeted. Unfortunately, risk assessment practices often vary, as seen in a Canadian study that showed provinces used different measures to assess risk of general offending, sexual offending, and domestic violence risk (Bourgon et al., 2018). An issue arises with using different tools as communication is weakened and sound decision-making can be challenged because different tools seldom lead to the same conclusions (e.g., Barbaree et al., 2006; Jung et al., 2013). Using assessments to drive treatments is needed. Beyond just merely using a risk assessment tool to establish treatment intensity, it is necessary to capture criminogenic needs and separate out responsivity issues that are clinically relevant but not necessarily relevant to reducing overall violence risk.

Widen Your Network

Lastly, moving in a direction that promotes the use of RNR principles in our practice should include widening one's network, in terms of other criminal justice branches and also organizations outside one's region. It is important to enhance the use of RNR in other criminal justice settings to ensure there is a common communication about managing an individual's case. Having the judge become aware of why you recommend a particular treatment programme because it would best address the individual's criminogenic needs would ensure they know your recommendations are based on cogent evidence-based decisions. Outlining to the parole board members why the interventions that an inmate completed did not address his criminogenic needs, and, therefore, does not lower his risk, makes it clear that the need principle was not addressed.

Furthermore, it is equally critical to increase collaborations with other organizations in other countries. This is particularly useful when working in relatively smaller countries with fewer resources and banding with other regions would increase the viability of training and overall resources.

Conclusion

The RNR principles comprise the best evidence-supported guidelines for the treatment and supervision of individuals who have sexually offended. We hope that with copious amounts of research, practices, and treatments evolve. Until then, it is essential that we continue to find ways to integrate these principles and to ensure that we maintain fidelity to them in our practices.

References

Andrews, D. A., & Bonta, J. (1994). *The psychology of criminal conduct*. Anderson.

Andrews, D. A., & Bonta, J. (2010). Rehabilitating criminal justice policy and practice. *Psychology, Public Policy, and Law, 16*, 39–55. https://doi.org/10.1037/a0018362

Andrews, D. A., Bonta, J., & Wormith, J. S. (2011). The risk-need-responsivity (RNR) model: Does adding the good lives model contribute to effective crime prevention? *Criminal Justice and Behaviour, 38*, 735–755. https://doi.org/10.1177/0093854811406356

Association for the Treatment of Sexual Abusers. (2014). *Practice guidelines for the assessment, treatment, and management of male adult sexual abusers*. Author.

Barbaree, H. E., Langton, C. M., & Peacock, E. J. (2006). Different actuarial risk measures produce different risk rankings for sexual offenders. *Sexual Abuse, 18*(4), 423–440. https://doi.org/10.1177/107906320601800408

Bonta, J., & Andrews, D. A. (2017). *The psychology of criminal conduct* (6th ed.). Routledge.

Bonta, J., Rugge, T., Scott, T.-L., Bourgon, G., & Yessine, A. K. (2008). Exporing the black box of community supervision. *Journal of Offender Rehabilitation, 47*(3), 248–270. https://doi.org/10.1080/10509670802134085

Bosker, J., & Witteman, C. (2016). Finding the right focus: Improving the link between risk/needs assessment and case management in probation. *Psychology, Public Policy, and Law, 22*(2), 221–233. https://doi.org/10.1037/law0000075

Bourgon, G., Mugford, R., Hanson, R. K., & Coligado, M. (2018). Offender risk assessment practices vary across Canada. *Canadian Journal of Criminology and Criminal Justice, 60*(2), 167–205. https://doi.org/10.3138/cjccj.2016-0024

Colorado Department of Public Safety. (2020). *Standards and guidelines for the assessment, evaluation, treatment and behavioral monitoring of adult sex offenders*. https://cdpsdocs.state.co.us/dvomb/SOMB/Standards/SAdult.pdf

Dowden, C., Zinger, I., Hoge, R. D., Bonta, J., Gendreau, P., & Cullen, F. T. (1990). Does correctional treatment work? A clinically relevant and psychologically informed meta-analysis. *Criminology, 28*(3), 369–404. https://doi.org/10.1111/j.1745-9125.1990.tb01330.x

Dyck, H. L., Campbell, M. A., & Wershler, J. L. (2018). Real-world use of the risk–need–responsivity model and the level of service/case management inventory with community-supervised offenders. *Law and Human Behavior, 42*(3), 258–268. https://doi.org/10.1037/lhb0000279

Hanson, R. K., & Bourgon, G. (2016). Advancing sexual offender risk assessment: Standardized risk levels based on psychologically meaningful offender characteristics. In F. S. Taxman (Ed.), *Handbook on risk and need assessment: Theory and practice* (pp. 244–268). Routledge.

Hanson, R. K., Bourgon, G., Helmus, L., & Hodgson, S. (2009). The principles of effective correctional treatment also apply to sexual offenders: A meta-analysis. *Criminal Justice and Behavior, 36*, 865–891. https://doi.org/10.1177/0093854809338545

Jung, S. (2017). *RNR principles in practice in the management and treatment of sexual abusers*. Safer Society Press.

Jung, S., Pham, A., & Ennis, L. (2013). Measuring the disparity of categorical risk among various sex offender risk assessment instruments. *Journal of*

Forensic Psychiatry and Psychology, 24, 353–370. https://doi.org/10.1080/14789949.2013.806567
Lilienfeld, S. O., Ritschel, L. A., Lynn, S. J., Cautin, R. L., & Latzman, R. D. (2013). Why many clinical psychologists are resistant to evidence-based practice: Root causes and constructive remedies. *Clinical Psychology Review, 33*, 883–900. https://doi.org/10.1016/j.cpr.2012.09.008
Lipton, D. S., Martinson, R., & Wilks, J. (1975). *The effectiveness of correctional treatment: A survey of treatment valuation studies*. Praeger Press.
Lovins, B., Lowenkamp, C. T., & Latessa, E. J. (2009). Applying the risk principle to sex offenders: Can treatment make some sex offenders worse. *The Prison Journal, 89*(3), 344–357. https://doi.org/10.1177/0032885509339509
Luong, D., & Wormith, J. S. (2011). Applying risk/need assessment to probation practice and its impact on the recidivism of young offenders. *Criminal Justice and Behavior, 38*, 1177–1199. https://doi.org/10.1177/0093854811421596
Maltais, N., & Jung, S. (2019, Summer). Perceptions on RNR. *The ATSA Forum, 31*(3).
Mann, R. E., Hanson, R. K., & Thornton, D. (2010). Assessing risk for sexual recidivism: Some proposals on the nature of psychologically meaningful risk factors. *Sexual Abuse, 22*(2), 191–217. https://doi.org/10.1177/1079063210366039
Martinson, R. (1974). What works? Questions and answers about prison reform. *The Public Interest, 35*, 22–54.
Martinson, R. (1979). New findings, new views: A note of caution regarding sentencing reform. *Hofstra Law Review, 7*, 243–258.
McGrath, R., Cumming, G., Burchard, B., Zeoli, S., & Ellerby, L. (2010). *Current practices and emerging trends in sexual abuser management: The safer society 2009 north American survey*. Safer Society Press.
Rettenberger, M. (2018). Understanding and managing risk of sexual offenders in Germany—A criminological success story or punitive hysteria? *Sexual Offender Treatment, 13*(1/2).
Romani, C. J., Morgan, R. D., Gross, N. R., & McDonald, B. R. (2012). Treating criminal behavior: Is the bang worth the buck? *Psychology, Public Policy, and Law, 18*(1), 144–165. https://doi.org/10.1037/a0024714
Rugge, T., Bourgon, G., & Bonta, J. (2019). Strategic Training Initiative in Community Supervision (STICS). In R. D. Morgan (Ed.), *The SAGE Encyclopedia of Criminal Psychology* (pp. 1466–1468). Sage. https://doi.org/10.4135/9781483392240.n476.

Sarre, R. (2001). Beyond 'what works?' A 25-year jubilee retrospective of Robert Martinson's famous article. *Australian and New Zealand Journal of Criminology, 34*(1), 38–46. https://doi.org/10.1177/000486580103400103

Smid, W. (2018). Attitudes towards sex offenders and their risk in the Netherlands. *Sexual Offender Treatment, 13*(1/2).

Uzieblo, K., Merckx, L., Vertommen, T., De Boeck, M., & Huys, W. (2018). A matter of shared responsibility: How practitioners, policy makers, and media shape sex offender risk assessment in Belgium. *Sexual Offender Treatment, 13*(1/2).

Viglione, J. (2017). Street-level decision making: Acceptability, feasibility, and use of evidence-based practices in adult probation. *Criminal Justice and Behavior, 44*(10), 1356–1381. https://doi.org/10.1177/0093854817718583

Viljoen, J. L., Cochrane, D. M., & Jonnson, M. R. (2018). Do risk assessment tools help manage and reduce risk of violence and reoffending? A systematic review. *Law and Human Behavior, 42*(3), 181–214. https://doi.org/10.1037/lhb0000280

Ward, J., & Groener, D. (2018). *Lattices: Clinicians' guide, an integrated treatment approach for high-risk forensic clients*. Safer Society Press.

Zara, G., Farrington, D., & Jung, S. (2020). Denial in sex offending treatment: Examining criminal career diversity. *Journal of Forensic Psychology: Research and Practice, 20*(5), 451–473. https://doi.org/10.1080/24732850.2020.1776050

11

Prison Climate and Rehabilitating Men with Sexual Convictions

Nicholas Blagden

For men convicted of a sexual offence, life in prison is not easy and can often be a brutal experience. They are despised by all for what they have done. They may have lost, or fear losing, the support of those who care for them. They will be at the bottom of the prison hierarchy, living in constant fear of being identified as a 'sex offender' and will often be the victim of physical and verbal assaults (Schwaebe, 2005). The difficulties facing these men are innumerable. Yet, despite all these issues, we still expect these men to be rehabilitated, to volunteer willingly for, and commit to, treatment where the most intimate details of their lives are laid bare (Ware & Blagden, 2016). The experience of prison and participating in treatment must seem like frightening prospects on many levels.

I have no known conflict of interest to disclose.

N. Blagden (✉)
Nottingham Trent University, Nottingham, UK
e-mail: Nicholas.blagden@ntu.ac.uk

© The Author(s), under exclusive license to Springer Nature Switzerland AG 2022
K. Uzieblo et al. (eds.), *Challenges in the Management of People Convicted of a Sexual Offence*, Palgrave Studies in Risk, Crime and Society,
https://doi.org/10.1007/978-3-030-80212-7_11

Some countries, for example North America, Canada, Australia, and United Kingdom, offer therapeutic interventions within prison. Rehabilitation in prison, however, is inherently complicated. Therapists have a dual role of protecting the public, but also looking after the prisoner's psychological needs. Prisons are also not ideal environments for therapy. Feeling threatened, anxious, and living in fear do not help to rehabilitate people and are unlikely to lead to personal change in individuals (Blagden et al., 2016). It is well known that harsh prison environments make people worse and not better and negatively impact both staff and prisoners (see e.g., Briere, 2012). Indeed, the environment where prison therapy takes place has often been underestimated and not sufficiently researched in terms of impact on rehabilitative outcomes.

Prison and Intervention

The evidence base for rehabilitative interventions for offenders has expanded over the decades, giving us clearer understanding of the treatment targets to address if intervention is to be effective (Mann et al., 2010). For example, there is now a much greater understanding of the treatment targets and dynamic risk factors for interventions with those with sexual convictions (Hanson et al., 2009; Mann et al., 2010). However, prison-based treatment for men with sexual convictions is contested. The study by Mews et al. (2017) found that the rate of overall sexual reoffending was larger in treated men with sexual convictions (10.0%) than for the control group (8.0%). High-quality studies have now consistently found that there are no significant effects of treatment in prison on the rate of sexual reoffending (Lösel et al., 2020; Schmucker & Lösel, 2015).

However, some of these findings are perhaps not unsurprising. Prison for most offenders does not work, it is one of the few truisms within criminological psychology. Most academics agree that imprisonment has, at best, no effect on reoffending and several studies have shown that imprisonment can increase reoffending (Cullen et al., 2011). While there has been much research into the risk factors of offenders and the individual changes offenders make during their treatment, there is much less examining the context or situation of that treatment. As Ware, Frost & Hoy (2010) argued a decade ago, the "context in which treatment is provided may actually prove to be quite important to the overall effectiveness of treatment" (p. 30). The prison climate, whether therapeutic (or not), and the attitudes of staff within the prison play a pivotal role in successful treatment and rehabilitation of offenders. Birgden (2004) has argued that such issues constitute an aspect of responsivity, which is underdeveloped and researched. Indeed, there are growing concerns that rehabilitative programmes and practice are being compromised by ineffective correctional environments, staff drift, organisational resistance, degree to which therapeutic integrity is maintained and the quality of programme implementation (Day et al., 2012; Smith et al., 2009). Thus, the rehabilitative climate of a prison could have serious implications for offender reform and treatment. This chapter will explore these issues in more detail. It will first consider the definitional issues when considering a rehabilitative climate, then move to consider the importance of accounting for prison climate in programme design, through to examining why considering wider environment is important for practice and future directions.

Defining Climate

There have been various definitions of institutional climates which have been put forward including social, therapeutic, and rehabilitative. As Day et al. (2012) point out, the definition of climate is difficult to "pin-down", define and operationalise with some using terms like "culture" and "climate" interchangeably. Furthermore, different authors have provided various types of climate including moral, social, and rehabilitative. A moral climate is about staff and prisoner experiences of fairness, decency, and respect in prison (Liebling & Arnold, 2004). A good social climate can be characterised as being supportive, offering a safe environment and opportunities for personal growth and development (van der Helm et al., 2011). Day et al. (2012) and Schalast et al. (2008) propose that a social and therapeutic climate has been taken to mean the extent to which the climate is perceived as supportive of therapy and therapeutic change, whether mutual support is typically seen as characteristic of the prison environment and the level of tension and perceived threat of fear, aggression, and violence within the prison.

However, much less frequently discussed in the literature is a rehabilitative climate. This has been defined as being conducive to human development or well-being in prison including access to rehabilitative/therapeutic programmes, education, provision of work activities, opportunities for personal development, and recreational activities (Pierce, 1974). Such a definition mirrors closely both social and moral climates, and this chapter contends that a rehabilitative climate be construed as the ways in which the correctional climate fosters and promotes positive personal change and ultimately how conducive it is to reducing reoffending (Blagden et al., 2016). The rehabilitative climate of a prison can be understood as the prison's social and therapeutic climate coupled with the prison's culture, philosophy, and fitness for purpose in relation to reducing reoffending and the role it plays in individual change.

Empirical Evidence for Accounting for Prison Climate in Programme Design

Despite empirical evidence to the contrary, prisons are expected to reduce reoffending—by the public, by politicians, by the media and by their own staff; and are repeatedly criticised when they fail to do so (Mann et al., 2019). There is a lack of research on the experience of imprisonment for men with sexual convictions, which has important ramifications for practice with this group (Blagden et al., 2019). As noted previously, individuals convicted of sexual offences reside at the bottom of the prison hierarchy (McNaughton Nicholls & Webster, 2018) and often report feeling victimised and marginalised by other prisoners (Schwaebe, 2005), as well as staff (Higgins & Ireland, 2009). The environment thus has ramifications for practice. Ware and Blagden (2016) argue that if we consider what is actually asked of an individual with sexual convictions within treatment, coupled with responsivity factors such as prison environment, then perhaps it is not surprising that the reported sex offender treatment non-completion rates range from 18.9% to 80% (Proulx et al., 2004). The threat of violence towards people with sexual convictions in prisons has resulted in them mainly residing on vulnerable prisoner units, where they are separated from other prisoners (Jewkes et al., 2016). Such prison environments are experienced as anxiety-provoking and hostile, and this makes therapy challenging (Duncan et al., 2020; Ware & Blagden, 2016).

If prisons and the rehabilitative programmes which run in them are to be successful, more work needs to be done in considering the wider environment. This is important as Blagden et al. (2016) found that prison climate predicted readiness for treatment and was correlated with beliefs that offenders can change. Williams et al. (2019) found that higher scores in prison climate were related to readiness to treatment and change. These results are particularly pertinent for prisons that have a focus on treatment interventions. Similarly, Stasch et al.'s (2018) study found that perception of prison climate significantly correlated with their attitudes towards treatment. More positive prison climate in terms of therapeutic hold (prisoner–staff relationships) and more positive treatment attitude in terms of trust in therapy were also the best predictors of stronger decreases in dynamic risk factors. Blagden et al. (2016, 2017) found that more positive views of "sex offenders" by both prisoners and staff correlated with beliefs that offenders can change, readiness for treatment and experiencing the prison as safe. Importantly, attitudes towards people with sexual convictions have been linked to therapeutic effectiveness and therapeutic alliance (Hogue, 2009; Kjelsberg & Loos, 2008), which is linked to positive treatment outcome (Serran et al., 2003).

Treatment motivation and readiness for treatment are important responsivity components of rehabilitative interventions and can be greatly impacted by wider prison environment. Prisoner and staff relationships, a crucial aspect of prison climate, have been found to have important effects on readiness. Gaab et al. (2020) found that the only strong predictor of internal readiness was relationships between prisoners and staff. Blagden et al. (2016) found that prisoner and staff relationships are important for helping to maintain treatment goals/gains. Previous research has found that the attitudes held by professionals towards prisoners can have a profound effect on their practice (Dirkzwager & Kruttschnitt, 2012). Outside of therapy, prisoner and staff relationships are important for maintaining treatment goals and can help with enacting important skills learned within programmes (see e.g., Tate et al.,

2017; Weaver & McNeill, 2015). These interactions outside of programmes could be considered testing grounds for future interaction with others (Blagden et al., 2016). Indeed, the general psychotherapeutic literature stresses the importance of meaningful relationships between therapist and patient, and, in offender behaviour programmes, emphasis is placed on the responsivity issue of the therapeutic alliance. The therapeutic alliance is pivotal for effective treatment with a constructive relationship characterised by warmth, empathy, respect, rewarding behaviour, and genuineness. Prisoner and staff relationships are thus pivotally important in prisons that have men with sexual convictions, as such a client group is widely stigmatised (Tewksbury, 2012). The expectations and beliefs of prison staff about prisoners are important. There is research on the Pygmalion effects (i.e., high expectation produces higher outcome) and interpersonal expectancy effects on prisoner outcome (LeBel et al., 2008).

The pains of imprisonment are well documented in the literature. Sykes (1958) stressed that the "destruction of the psyche" or the psychological pains of imprisonment (loss of liberty and autonomy) were as damaging as physical assaults. Various factors can contribute to well-being of incarcerated individuals, with prison environment and prison climate being particularly important. Van Ginneken et al. (2018) investigated the relationship between prison climate and well-being among a large sample of adults (male and female) incarcerated in the Netherlands. They found positive individual experiences of prison climate were related to higher well-being. Individual experiences of prison climate also had positive effects for perceptions of safety, autonomy (including the ability to self-cater), and good peer relationships.

What's Important for Rehabilitative Climate

While it is difficult for prisons to reduce reoffending (see e.g., Cullen et al., 2011), the last section highlights key aspects of the prison climate that impact on programme integrity. Important components in prison climate are, at least in part, relational. Relationships between prisoner–staff and prisoner–prisoner are two vital components in establishing a good prison climate. A third important component is how safe the environment is perceived (these comprise the dimensions on the EssenCES measure; Schalast et al., 2008). These dimensions also appear particularly relevant to men with sexual convictions experiences of imprisonment (Blagden et al., 2019). Furthermore, these relationships seem important for helping men who participate in treatment programmes in enacting more desirable identities, which assists with the "living" of those identities (McAdams, 1985).

Two things which have been important for creating reciprocity within prison are *peer support* and *active citizenship*. Indeed, the reciprocal aspects of these have been found to galvanise staff–prisoner and prisoner–prisoner relationships, which is important as the relational properties of both are linked to the "self-change" process (Mead et al., 2001).

Prisoner–Staff Relationships

The chapter has highlighted that prisoner–staff relationships are important for climate, but it is important to consider what 'good' prisoner–staff relationships look like. The staff–prisoner relationship has been described as integral to the prison system, with the interactions between prison officers and prisoners considered fundamental to effective prison management (Trotter, 1993). Gredecki and Ireland (2012) observed that the term "relationship" marked a difficult construct within prison research as the relationships observed in prisons are unavoidable and frequently occur between individuals who would not normally choose to interact. Being thrust into an unavoidable relationship, the staff–prisoner interaction could be viewed as artificial and developed mainly for instrumental purposes. This raises the question of whether relationships on prison wings can ever be pure and authentic (Crewe, 2011). For instance, the notion of "good" prisoner–prison officer relationships is a difficult one to define and perhaps even harder to operationalise, as context will often mediate what is perceived as "good" within a prison (Crewe et al., 2011). Indeed, just because a prisoner–prison officer relationship is "good", it doesn't necessarily mean it is "right", for example relationships can be too close or too informal, lacking boundaries and professional distance

(Liebling, 2011). However, "good" or perhaps rather "meaningful" relationships have been found within prisons (Blagden et al., 2016; Liebling, 2011). There is research which suggests that prisoners desire constructive and positive relationships with prison staff based on supportive, affirming, fair, and respectful relationships (Bennett & Shuker, 2010). In Blagden et al. (2016) and Blagden and Wilson (2020), meaningful and perceived genuine relationships were important features of "good" prisoner-staff relationships. Fostering relationships like this appears to be based on reciprocity, respect, genuineness, and congruence in the relationships (Blagden & Wilson, 2020).

Active Citizenship and Promoting Peer Support

While prison staff–prisoner relationships are crucial in a rehabilitative climate, prisoner–prisoner relationships are also an important dimension (Schalast et al., 2008). One important way that prisons can help foster such relationships is through active citizenship and peer support. The most effective prisoner–prisoner relationships are characterised by shared problem-solving and reciprocity (Mead et al., 2001). Active citizenship in prison can take the form of recognising, reinforcing, and recording acts seen to be doing good for the community, environment, and others.

One way of achieving active citizenship in prisons is through peer support. Peer support has existed in prisons both in the UK and abroad for decades, primarily in the form of discernible yet informal 'programmes' or 'schemes'. Through these programmes, prisoners can access support from fellow prisoners for issues ranging from emotional distress and addiction problems to practical and educational needs. The aim of peer mentoring is not only for mentees to receive support to develop skills but also to enhance the self-esteem of both the mentee and mentor. The reciprocal nature of the roles and the shared and collaborative working also help to enact more desirable possible selves, and such roles assist with fostering constructive relationships with others (Perrin & Blagden, 2014). In a study on peer support roles and individuals with sexual convictions, Perrin and colleagues (2018) found that having such a role helped cultivate constructive relationships with prison staff and other prisoners, allowed personal growth from "doing good" experiences, hone positive skills, and make meaning in prison settings. As LeBel et al. (2015) conclude, helping others appears to have adaptive consequences for prisoners and ex-prisoners, and. on these grounds, an argument can be made for increasing opportunities for reintegrating ex-offenders to engage in roles characterised by reciprocal helping. Thus, the prison environment and the relationships which constitute it have an important impact on how men participant in correctional programmes, with a safe and decent culture freeing up "headspace" for men to focus on the future (Blagden et al., 2016, 2017; Mann et al., 2019).

Active citizenship is also about recognising and promoting the 'voice' of the individuals within the prison and helping them take a sense of ownership of the well-being of others and their environment. Historically, criminal justice has paid little attention to the voice of service users, which often leads to the experience of things being done to individuals rather than with them, which can lead to resignation and disengagement (McCartan et al., 2020; S, 2019). This notion is important as feeling alienated and disconnected is unlikely to motivate change. However, including service user perspectives builds trust, leads to better perceptions of the institutional climate and there's growing evidence of the restorative properties of understanding the service user (McCartan et al., 2020). There is growing evidence that when people in prisons feel heard, when they see rules applied consistently, and when they experience respectful and authentic staff behaviour, they are more likely to cooperate and abide by rules (Walton, 2019; Mann et al., 2019).

Implementing Rehabilitative Environments

Smith and Schweitzer (2012) introduced the notion of "the therapeutic prison" where evidence-based interventions were supported by clearly articulated goals and a range of rehabilitative staff behaviours such as pro-social modelling, reinforcement of new behaviours, skills-building interactions, and open and respectful communication between staff and prisoners. On a practical level, Ware and Galouzis (2019) argue that prison climate can support and bolster intervention *before*, *during*, and *after* intervention. Before treatment, prison environments can assist with recruiting volunteers for treatment and fostering a climate supportive of therapy. They advocate the use of prison staff to help recruit into programmes, as well as increased training for non-programme staff. To ensure a positive prison climate supportive of rehabilitation *before* treatment, it is important to focus on the engagement and education of non-treatment staff (also attitudes) (Ware & Galouzis, 2019). Wider prison staff attitudes matter. Ware and Galouzis (2019) also contend wider input from psychological staff within senior prison management can also be important for distilling messages important for programme effectiveness. The last point is supported by Blagden et al. (2016) and Blagden and Wilson (2020), who found that greater cohesive working between prison senior management, wider input form psychologists, and greater joined up working with other prison departments can help with a more positive prison climate.

Frost et al. (2016) have suggested that there are two necessary conditions in providing a positive prison climate during treatment to allow for content rehearsal and practice. The first condition is that there must be a "safe" and containing environment that is conducive to openness, directness, and honesty. A prison climate where prisoners feel safe and the environment is not threatening and where offenders can have positive and validating contacts with others encourages offender agency and concentration on their own personal development (Needs & Adair-Stantiall, 2018; Blagden et al., 2016). The second condition is that prisons must create structured opportunities to develop attitudes and learn skills as an expedient forum for addressing interpersonal relationships. As programmes have been criticised for being too 'cognitive', prison needs to allow opportunities to support the development of positive practical identities and help enact them.

Future Directions: Recognising Trauma

Men with sexual convictions have high rates of Adverse Childhood Experiences (ACE) including traumas (Hamilton, 2020). Compared to the general population, men with sexual convictions are more likely to experience higher rates of ACE (Jespersen et al., 2009; Levenson et al., 2016). They are *2 times* as likely to have experienced physical abuse, *3 times* more likely to have experienced childhood sexual abuse, *4 times* more likely to have experienced emotional neglect, and *13 times* more likely to have experienced verbal abuse. Less than 16% endorsed zero ACE (Levenson et al., 2016).

Previously in criminal justice practice, prisoners' disclosures of their own abusive histories in treatment were seen as excuses, justifications, or cognitive distortions. There is now recognition of the real traumas experienced by men with sexual convictions, and a growing understanding of how rehabilitative environments including prisons can account for and work with those experiences (Levenson et al., 2016; Walton, 2019). Trauma-informed practice means recognising the impact that trauma, including but not limited to ACE, has on an individual and, in acknowledging this, providing appropriate support to that person. At the heart of this practice is a recognition that criminal justice practice can be re-traumatising, and so it is important to recognise strengths and skills, build confidence, and re-educate individuals—embedding new coping skills (McCartan et al., 2020). The punitive role and impact of the prison environment can pose a key challenge to the cornerstone of trauma-informed practice which is to actively avoid re-traumatisation (Vaswani & Paul, 2019).

Concluding Thoughts

Prison impacts on individuals in a myriad of ways. These impacts can have deleterious ramifications for *doing* therapy within prison. Mann et al. (2019) argue that a positive rehabilitative culture is one that supports involvement in formal programmes, but also provides a culture (through positive staff and prisoner interactions) that enables identity change in its own right. As Ward and Brown (2004) have argued, the prison environment is crucial for sustaining treatment gains. In particular, prisoner–staff relationships and prisoner–prisoner relationships appear vital in sustaining therapeutic gains (Blagden et al., 2017). Constructive relationships within prison are important in the desistance process where establishing social relationships is seen as vital to the triggering, enabling, and sustaining of change (Weaver & McNeill, 2015). In order for prison-based programmes to have the maximum impact on individuals, much more attention and focus is required on prison climate.

References

Bennett, P., & Shuker, R. (2010). Improving prisoner-staff relationships: Exporting Grendon's good practice. *The Howard Journal of Criminal Justice, 49*(5), 491–502. https://doi.org/10.1111/j.1468-2311.2010.00639.x

Birgden, A. (2004). Therapeutic jurisprudence and responsivity: Finding the will and the way in offender rehabilitation. *Psychology, Crime & Law, 10*(3), 283–295. https://doi.org/10.1080/10683160410001662771

Blagden, N., Perrin, C., Smith, S., Gleeson, F., & Gillies, L. (2017). "A different world" exploring and understanding the climate of a recently re-rolled sexual offender prison. *Journal of Sexual Aggression, 23*(2), 151–166. https://doi.org/10.1080/13552600.2016.1264633

Blagden, N., & Wilson, K. (2020). "We're all the same Here"—Investigating the rehabilitative climate of a re-rolled sexual offender prison: A qualitative longitudinal study. *Sexual Abuse, 32*(6), 727–750. https://doi.org/10.1177/1079063219839496

Blagden, N., Winder, B., & Hames, C. (2016). "They treat us like human beings"—Experiencing a therapeutic sex offenders prison: Impact on prisoners and staff and implications for treatment. *International Journal of Offender Therapy and Comparative Criminology, 60*(4), 371–396. https://doi.org/10.1177/0306624X14553227

Blagden, N., Winder, B., Hocken, K., Lievesley, R., Banyard, P., & Elliott, H. (Eds.). (2019). *Sexual crime and the experience of imprisonment*. Springer.

Briere, J., Agee, E., & Dietrich, A. (2012). Cumulative trauma and current post-traumatic stress disorder status in general population and inmate samples. *Psychological Trauma Theory Research Practice and Policy, 8*, 439–446. https://doi.org/10.1037/tra0000107

Crewe, B. (2011). Soft power in prison: Implications for staff–prisoner relationships, liberty and legitimacy. *European Journal of Criminology, 8*(6), 455–468. https://doi.org/10.1177/1477370811413805

Cullen, F. T., Jonson, C. L., & Nagin, D. S. (2011). Prisons do not reduce recidivism: The high cost of ignoring science. *The Prison Journal, 91*(3_suppl), 48S-65S.

Day, A., Casey, S., Vess, J., & Huisy, G. (2012). Assessing the therapeutic climate of prisons. *Criminal Justice and Behavior, 39*(2), 156–168. https://doi.org/10.1177/0093854811430476

Dirkzwager, A. J., & Kruttschnitt, C. (2012). Prisoners' perceptions of correctional officers' behavior in English and Dutch prisons. *Journal of Criminal Justice, 40*(5), 404–412. https://doi.org/10.1016/j.jcrimjus.2012.06.004

Duncan, K., Winder, B., Blagden, N., & Norman, C. (2020). "I've got the energy to change, but I Haven't got the energy for this Kinda therapy": A qualitative analysis of the motivations behind democratic therapeutic community drop-out for men with sexual convictions. *International Journal of Offender Therapy and Comparative Criminology*. https://doi.org/10.1177/0306624X20956957

Frost, A., Ware, J., & Boer, D. P. (2016). Sex offender treatment skills and approaches: Group therapy. In *The Wiley handbook on the theories, assessment and treatment of sexual offending* (pp. 1469–1487).

Gaab, S., Brazil, I. A., de Vries, M. G., & Bulten, B. H. (2020). The relationship between treatment alliance, social climate, and treatment readiness in long-term forensic psychiatric care: An explorative study. *International Journal of Offender Therapy and Comparative Criminology, 64*(9), 1013–1026. https://doi.org/10.1177/0093854811430476

Gredecki, N., & Ireland, J. L. (2012). Applications of interpersonal circumplex and complementarity theory to staff-prisoner relationships. *The British Journal of Forensic Practice, 14*(3), 180–191. https://doi.org/10.1108/14636641211254905

Hamilton, J. A. (2020). *Exploring the relationships between personality disorder, sexual preoccupation, and adverse childhood experiences among individuals who have previously sexually offended.* Doctoral dissertation, Nottingham Trent University.

Hanson, R. K., Bourgon, G., Helmus, L., & Hodgson, S. (2009). The principles of effective correctional treatment also apply to sexual offenders: A meta-analysis. *Criminal Justice and Behavior, 36*(9), 865–891.

Higgins, C., & Ireland, C. (2009). Attitudes towards male and female sex offenders: A comparison of forensic staff, prison officers and the general public in Northern Ireland. *The British Journal of Forensic Practice, 11*(1), 14–19. https://doi.org/10.1108/14636646200900004

Jespersen, A., Lalumiere, M., & Seto, M. (2009). Sexual abuse history among adult sex offenders and non-sex offenders: A meta-analysis. *Child Abuse & Neglect, 33*, 179–192. https://doi.org/10.1016/j.chiabu.2008.07.004

Jewkes, Y., Crewe, B., & Bennett, J. (Eds.). (2016). *Handbook on prisons*. Routledge.

Kjelsberg, E., & Loos, L. H. (2008). Conciliation or condemnation? Prison employees' and young peoples' attitudes towards sexual offenders. *International Journal of Forensic Mental Health, 7*(1), 95–103.

LeBel, T. P., Burnett, R., Maruna, S., & Bushway, S. (2008). The "chicken and egg" of subjective and social factors in desistance from crime. *European Journal of Criminology, 5*(2), 131–159. https://doi.org/10.1177/1477370807087640

LeBel, T. P., Richie, M., & Maruna, S. (2015). Helping others as a response to reconcile a criminal past the role of the wounded healer in prisoner re-entry programs. *Criminal Justice and Behavior, 42*, 108–120. https://doi.org/10.1177/0093854814550029

Levenson, J. S., Willis, G. M., & Prescott, D. S. (2016). Adverse childhood experiences in the lives of male sex offenders: Implications for trauma-informed care. *Sexual Abuse, 28*(4), 340–359. https://doi.org/10.1177/1079063214535819

Liebling, A. (2011). Moral performance, inhuman and degrading treatment and prison pain. *Punishment & Society, 13*(5), 530–550.

Liebling, A., & Arnold, H. (2004). *Prisons and their moral performance*. Oxford University Press.

Lösel, F., Link, E., Schmucker, M., Bender, D., Breuer, M., Carl, L., Endres, J., & Lauchs, L. (2020). On the effectiveness of sexual offender treatment in prisons: A comparison of two different evaluation designs in routine practice. *Sexual Abuse, 32*(4), 452–475. https://doi.org/10.1177/1079063219871576

Mann, R., Barnett, G., Box, G., Howard, F. F., O'Mara, O., Travers, R., & Wakeling, H. (2019). Rehabilitative culture in prisons for people convicted of sexual offending. In *Sexual crime and the experience of imprisonment* (pp. 1–33). Palgrave Macmillan.

Mann, R. E., Hanson, R. K., & Thornton, D. (2010). Assessing risk for sexual recidivism: Some proposals on the nature of psychologically meaningful risk factors. *Sexual Abuse, 22*(2), 191–217. https://doi.org/10.1177/1079063210366039

McAdams, D. P. (1985). *Power, intimacy, and the life story: Personological inquiries into identity*. Guilford Press.

McCartan, K., Harris, D. A., & Prescott, D. S. (2020). Seen and not heard: The service user's experience through the justice system of individuals convicted of sexual offenses. *International Journal of Offender Therapy and Comparative Criminology*. https://doi.org/10.1177/0306624X19851671

McNaughton Nicholls, C., & Webster, S. (2018). The separated location of prisoners with sexual convictions: Research on the benefits and risks. *HM Prison & Probation Service*.

Mead, S., Hilton, D., & Curtis, L. (2001). *Peer support: A theoretical perspective*. Mead Consulting. http://www.mentalhealthpeers.com/booksarticles.html

Mews, A., Di Bella, L., & Purver, M. (2017). *Impact evaluation of the prison-based core sex offender treatment programme*. Ministry of Justice.

Needs, A., & Adair-Stantiall, A. (2018). The social context of transition and rehabilitation. In *Transforming environments and offender rehabilitation: A guide for practitioners in forensic settings and criminal justice*. Routledge.

Perrin, C., & Blagden, N. (2014). Accumulating meaning, purpose and opportunities to change 'drip by drip': The impact of being a listener in prison. *Psychology, Crime & Law, 20*(9), 902–920.

Perrin, C., Blagden, N., Winder, B., & Dillon, G. (2018). "It's sort of reaffirmed to me that I'm not a monster, I'm not a terrible person": Sex offenders' movements toward desistance via peer-support roles in prison. *Sexual Abuse, 30*(7), 759–780.

Pierce, L. W. (1974). Rehabilitation in corrections. *A reassessment Federal Probation, 38*(2), 14–19.

Proulx, J., Brien, T., Ciampi, A., Allaire, J. F., McDonald, M., & Chouinard, A. (2004, October). *Treatment attrition in sexual offenders*. Paper presented at the 23rd Annual Research and Treatment Conference of the Association for the Treatment of Sexual Abusers, Albuquerque, NM.

S. (2019). Serving time in two prisons. In *Sexual crime and the experience of imprisonment* (pp. 1–33). Palgrave Macmillan.

Schalast, N., Redies, M., Collins, M., Stacey, J., & Howells, K. (2008). EssenCES, a short questionnaire for assessing the social climate of forensic psychiatric wards. *Criminal Behaviour and Mental Health, 18*(1), 49–58. https://doi.org/10.1002/cbm.677

Schmucker, M., & Lösel, F. (2015). The effects of sexual offender treatment on recidivism: An international meta-analysis of sound quality evaluations. *Journal of Experimental Criminology, 11*(4), 597–630. https://doi.org/10.1007/s11292-015-9241-z

Schwaebe, C. (2005). Learning to pass: Sex offenders' strategies for establishing a viable identity in the prison general population. *International Journal of Offender Therapy and Comparative Criminology, 49*, 614–625. https://doi.org/10.1177/0306624X05275829

Serran, G., Fernandez, Y., Marshall, W. L., & Mann, R. E. (2003). Process issues in treatment: Application to sexual offender programs. *Professional Psychology: Research and Practice, 34*(4), 368.

Smith, P., & Schweitzer, M. (2012). The therapeutic prison. *Journal of Contemporary Criminal Justice, 28*(1), 7–22. https://doi.org/10.1177/1043986211432201

Smith, P., Cullen, F. T., & Latessa, E. J. (2009). Can 14,737 women be wrong? A meta-analysis of the LSI-R and recidivism for female offenders. *Criminology & Public Policy, 8*(1), 183–208.

Stasch, J., Yoon, D., Sauter, J., Hausam, J., & Dahle, K. P. (2018). Prison climate and its role in reducing dynamic risk factors during offender treatment. *International Journal of Offender Therapy and Comparative Criminology, 62*(14), 4609–4621. https://doi.org/10.1177/0306624X18778449

Sykes, G. (1958). *A society of captives: A study of a maximum security prison*. Princeton, NJ: Princeton University Press.

Tate, H., Bladgen, N., & Mann, R. M. (2017). Prisoners' perceptions of care and rehabilitation from prison officers trained as five minute interventionists. HMPPS.

Tewksbury, R. (2012). Stigmatization of sex offenders. *Deviant Behavior, 33*(8), 606–623.

Trotter, C. (1993). *The effective supervision of offenders*. Unpublished PhD Thesis, LaTrobe University, Melbourne.

Van der Helm, P., Stams, G. J., & Van der Laan, P. (2011). Measuring group climate in prison. *The Prison Journal, 91*(2), 158–176. https://doi.org/10.1177/0032885511403595

Van Ginneken, E. F. J. C., Palmen, H., Bosma, A. Q., Nieuwbeerta, P., & Berghuis, M. L. (2018). The life in custody study: The quality of prison life in Dutch prison regimes. *Journal of Criminological Research, Policy and Practice, 4*(4), 253–268. https://doi.org/10.1108/JCRPP-07-2018-0020

Vaswani, N., & Paul, S. (2019). 'It's knowing the right things to say and do': Challenges and opportunities for trauma-informed practice in the prison context. *The Howard Journal of Crime and Justice, 58*(4), 513–534. https://doi.org/10.1111/hojo.12344

Walton, J. S. (2019). The evolutionary basis of belonging: Its relevance to denial of offending and labelling those who offend. *The Journal of Forensic Practice, 21*(4), 202–211. https://doi.org/10.1108/JFP-04-2019-0014

Ward, T., & Brown, M. (2004). The good lives model and conceptual issues in offender rehabilitation. *Psychology, Crime & Law, 10*(3), 243–257.
Ware, J., Frost, A., & Hoy, A. (2010). A review of the use of therapeutic communities with sexual offenders. *International Journal of Offender Therapy and Comparative Criminology, 54*, 721–742.
Ware, J., & Blagden, N. (2016). Responding to categorical denial, refusal, and treatment dropout. The Wiley Handbook on the Theories, Assessment and Treatment of Sexual Offending (pp. 1559–1574). London: Wiley.
Ware, J., & Galouzis, J. (2019). Impact of prison climate on indivduals with sexual convictions: Desistance and rehabilitation. In N.Blagden, B. winder, K. Hocken, R. Livelesley, P. Banyard and H. Elliott (Eds.), *Sexual Crime and the Experience of Imprisonment* (pp. 35–60). London, UK: Palgrave McMillan.
Weaver, B., & McNeill, F. (2015). Lifelines: Desistance, social relations, and reciprocity. *Criminal Justice and Behavior, 42*(1), 95–107. https://doi.org/10.1177/0093854814550031
Williams, L. S., Green, E. L., & Chernoff, W. A. (2019). "There's More to It Than Just a Box Check": Measuring Prison Climate in Three Correctional Facilities. *International journal of offender therapy and comparative criminology, 63*(8), 1354–1383.

12

They Need Somebody, and Not Just Anybody: Help-Seeking Behaviour in Minor-Attracted Persons

Kasia Uzieblo and Minne De Boeck

Over the years, various interventions and treatment programmes have been developed to prevent recidivism in people who have committed a sexual offence (PCSO). However, the common denominator of these approaches is that the individuals who enrol in these programmes, have already committed a sexual offence *and* have been caught. Two problems arise: First, given

We have no known conflict of interest to disclose.

K. Uzieblo (✉)
Van der Hoeven Kliniek, Utrecht, The Netherlands

Free University of Brussels, Brussels, Belgium
e-mail: kuzieblo@dfzs.nl

M. De Boeck
Stop it Now!, Flanders, Belgium

University Forensic Centre, University Hospital Antwerp, Edegem, Belgium

Collaborative Antwerp Psychiatric Research Institute (CAPRI), University of Antwerp, Antwerpen, Belgium

© The Author(s), under exclusive license to Springer Nature Switzerland AG 2022

K. Uzieblo et al. (eds.), *Challenges in the Management of People Convicted of a Sexual Offence*, Palgrave Studies in Risk, Crime and Society,
https://doi.org/10.1007/978-3-030-80212-7_12

that numerous sexual offences go undetected (Delisi et al., 2016), many PCSO, that is, those who are not caught, do not receive professional help for prevention purposes. Second, these programmes are not developed for those who struggle with their own sexual interests towards minors, without having committed child sexual abuse (CSA) or without posing a risk to do so. We have long assumed that these two groups do not experience the necessity to voluntarily seek help. But the enrolment of various programmes in Europe and North America targeting these two groups (see Chap. 16) have taught us otherwise: Many do seek help, *if* help is available. The question then arises as to what the nature and the extent of their help-seeking behaviour is, and what the mechanisms and factors are that prohibit or facilitate their quest for help. These insights will not only support us to facilitate help-seeking behaviours in individuals who struggle with their interests and/or behaviours but will also enable us to further amend prevention strategies.

It is striking that help-seeking behaviour for sexual interests and/or behaviours towards minors has, until recently, received relatively little attention in both research and practice. The aim of the current chapter is to take stock of current knowledge on help-seeking behaviour in minor-attracted persons (MAP) and discuss how this field could move forward. First, we examine the help-seeking process from a conceptual and theoretical viewpoint. Second, we take stock of current empirical knowledge of this process in MAP. Finally, we offer suggestions on how to deepen our understanding of the help-seeking process in these individuals through research and how to make more professional help available to them. But let us first consider the specific target group.

Defining Minor Attraction

Regarding sexual attractions to children, paedophilia is the most-known sexual interest. Paedophilia is commonly defined as a persistent and recurrent sexual interest in prepubescent children (under the age of 13), and is recognized as a paraphilia or deviant sexual interest (American Psychiatric Association, 2013). People may also exhibit a sexual interest in pubescent children who are in early adolescence, usually ages 11/12 to 14 (i.e., hebephilia), and/or in mid-to-late adolescents, usually ages 15 to 18 (i.e., ephebophilia). Large-scale epidemiologic studies are not available (Seto, 2018), but it is estimated that less than 1% of the population meets the DSM 5 criteria for paedophilia (Cantor & McPhail, 2016; Seto, 2018). Although the majority of the adult male population seems to be at one time or another sexually attracted to minors (Seto, 2018), the true prevalence of hebephilia and ephebophilia remains unknown. The term MAP has been increasingly used to refer to adults exhibiting a persistent sexual interest in children or adolescents under the age of consent, which differs from country to country, and thus includes all three aforementioned interests (B4UAct, 2018).

Exhibiting deviant sexual interests, like paedophilia, is considered as a risk factor for sexual (re)offending (Hanson et al., 2015; Mann et al., 2010), but does not necessarily induce sexual deviant behaviour. In fact, it is assumed that many with such interests manage to control or cope with their feelings in a safe and offence-free way (Cantor & McPhail, 2016). Whether MAP commit CSA depends on various interrelated risk factors, including external circumstances, personality traits and social influences (Cantor & McPhail, 2016; Ward & Beech, 2006). Hence, it is important to emphasize that, whereas a subgroup will commit online and/or offline offences, not every MAP will act upon these interests (see, Chap. 9; Cantor & McPhail, 2016). We will therefore apply the terms 'non-offending MAP' and 'offending MAP' to distinguish both groups from each other.

Conceptualizing Help-Seeking Behaviour

Some studies have focused on help-seeking behaviour in MAP; however, a theory of help-seeking that provides a framework for these findings has yet to be developed. In this chapter, we therefore draw from current models for help seeking for other mental health problems in order to elucidate the process of help seeking in MAP. Let us start with a proper conceptualization of the topics of interest: help-seeking behaviour. At face value, its meaning seems self-evident. Dictionary definitions generally describe the behaviour as "the act of looking for or going in search of a relief or cure to fulfil need" (Cornally & Mccarthy, 2011, p. 281). It is however important to note that, although the term is extensively used and the concept intensively studied, and scholars do not univocally agree on its definition. There is no consensus about the specific elements that make up help-seeking behaviour and, therefore, about the elements that should be included in the definition. Notwithstanding these conceptual discussions, consensus can be found on the following elements of help-seeking behaviour. First, help-seeking behaviour is regarded as *a coping strategy* that is adaptive in nature. It entails cognitive and behavioural efforts to regulate emotions and distress, and to manage the problem that is causing these emotions and distress (Rickwood & Thomas, 2012). Second, help-seeking behaviour is not an event that occurs at a single point in time. Instead, it entails *a complex decision-making process* consisting of several stages. Theoretical frameworks describing this process differ in the number of stages delineated in this process and, in the emphasis put on specific components of that process. Most seem to primarily focus on the help-seekers' internal, cognitive processes, whereas some (also) emphasize the relevance of contextual factors and the help-seeking sources.

One framework that takes most of these components into account is the model of Cornally and McCarthy (2011). In this model, the authors delineate the following elements of the help-seeking processes: attributes, antecedents, and consequences. First, they specify three salient characteristics or attributes of help-seeking behaviour. The behaviour is problem focused. Simply put, the individual will not seek help if there is no problem. The external help is viewed as necessary to solve or lessen the problem. The help-seeking behaviour is also intentional in nature. The help-seeker is actively selecting and pursuing a source of help. This implies that help-seeking behaviour should be differentiated from receiving help when help is not sought, which is the case when help is imposed (e.g., mandatory treatment). According to the authors, a final attribute refers to the fact that an interpersonal action is needed to receive help: The help-seeker must disclose the problem. Hence, simply seeking information online or from self-help books is not categorized as help-seeking behaviour in this model. Subsequently, help-seeking behaviour involves three distinct elements, that is, the help-seeker, the problem for which help is sought, and the individual (or body) from whom help is required (Rickwood & Thomas, 2012). These three elements interact with each other, and thus, cannot be considered in isolation.

Second, various antecedents are described as conditions required for help-seeking behaviour to occur. The help-seeking processes obviously starts with problem recognition and problem definition by the person himself/herself. Several factors, including the (perceived) cause, significance, severity, durations, and consequences, determine the ability to and preparedness to acknowledge and define the problem. When an individual acknowledges his/her problem, he subsequently needs to decide whether to seek help. Deciding to seek help entails a rational decision process on its own and is dependent on a wide range of individual characteristics (e.g., fears, knowledge, attitudes, and expectations), motivational factors (e.g., self-efficacy and past experiences with help-seeking behaviour and self-management), and social influences (e.g., influence of significant others, professionals, and society). When the decision to seek help is made, the person then must select the source of help. This can be a formal (e.g., agencies that provide help, including—but not limited to—the criminal justice system or mental health service providers) and/or an informal source (i.e., people in the social networks, including—but not limited to—family members, friends, colleagues, and neighbours).

Finally, the help-seeker obviously desires to solve and/or manage the problem (i.e., the desired consequence). When this goal is achieved, the person will usually experience a sense of well-being, more satisfaction, and/or an improved quality of life. But when the problem remains unresolved, the help-seeker might even experience negative changes. Such dire consequences often lead to feelings of dissatisfaction, stigma, and/or helplessness. The help-seeker might even start resenting the source of help and might become reluctant to seek help from that source, or, even worse, from any source in the future.

Help-Seeking in MAP

In this section, we want to explore current knowledge on the different components of the help-seeking process in offending and non-offending MAP. It is however important to point out that we ran into two problems when examining the literature. First, published research into help-seeking behaviour in MAP remains very limited. Consequently, the current analysis should be regarded as preliminary. Second, several studies in criminal populations do not clearly distinguish offending MAP from other sexual offending groups. Given the limited literature on this topic, a thorough delineation of the target group, that is, offending MAP, was not deemed feasible. Consequently, we will also describe studies examining help-seeking behaviour in PCSO, including offending MAP.

What Are the Reasons for Help-Seeking in MAP?

In practice, we are often confronted with the commonly held assumption that MAP are not capable of any introspection, let alone, of identifying any problematic interests and behaviours. However, there is growing evidence from research and practice indicating that these individuals do struggle with various problems and can identify them. In general, their reasons for help-seeking can be divided into two broad categories: problems related to deviant sexual interests and/or behaviours, and psychosocial problems, often associated with these interests and/or behaviours.

Both offending and non-offending MAP report concerns about their deviant sexual self-regulation, feeling attracted towards minors, and fear of losing control of their own sexual feelings (B4U-ACT, 2011a; Levenson et al., 2017; Piché et al., 2018). Importantly, many have grappled with these deviant fantasies and behaviours for a long time (Piché et al., 2018), starting from early adolescence (B4U-ACT, 2011b; Bailey et al., 2016), before they start contemplating seeking help.

More often, MAP seem to seek help for psychosocial issues that arise from their deviant sexual interests and/or behaviours (B4U-ACT, 2011a, b). They suffer from a wide range of mental problems and disorders, including, but not limited to, depression, anxiety, low self-esteem, drug- and alcohol abuse, and suicidal ideation (B4U-ACT, 2011a, b; Cohen et al., 2018; Levenson & Grady, 2019a; Stevens & Wood, 2019), and they exhibit low levels of psychological well-being and general happiness (Houtepen et al., 2016; Lievesley et al., 2020). In sum, MAP's main aims to seek help are to increase their understanding of their sexual interests, how to deal with their surroundings, to cope with or reduce their attraction to minors, and to learn how to have a fulfilling life (Levenson & Grady, 2019a).

What Keeps MAP from Seeking Help?

MAP are confronted with numerous internal and external obstacles that prohibit them from acting upon a voluntary need for help. We will describe the three most common obstacles described in the literature.

First of all, most MAP feel ashamed of and guilty about their interests (and behaviours), a feeling that is most likely elicited by the stigma associated with deviant sexual interests, and paedophilia in particular (Jahnke, 2018; Van Horn et al., 2015). Individuals exhibiting paedophilia are considered as dangerous, abnormal, amoral, in control of being sexually attracted to children, but not in control of their own sexual desires and urges. People with paedophilia are more fiercely rejected than, for instance, people with antisocial tendencies or people exhibiting sexual sadistic behaviour, even if they have not committed any crime (see for a review, Jahnke, 2018). Experiencing such stigma is considered very stressful, even if one succeeds to avoid discrimination by concealing or suppressing the deviant interests or behaviours (Jahnke et al., 2015; Lievesley et al., 2020). Indeed, stigma and the internalization of stigma are associated with various emotional problems (e.g., low self-esteem and emotion regulation problems) and social problems (e.g., social isolation and loneliness) (Jahnke, 2018; Lievesley et al., 2020). Stigmatization and stereotypical portrayal of MAP as criminals (to be) might evoke low self-efficacy regarding one's control of the feelings and urges towards children and generate a reluctance to seek professional help (B4U-ACT, 2011a, b; Grady et al., 2019; Jahnke, 2018), which might in turn increase the risk of (re-)offending.

Second, fear is also identified as a very important obstacle to seek help in MAP. Many fear negative reactions and are sceptical regarding confidentiality that mental health professionals should adhere to; they assume confidentiality will not be respected and/or they will get into legal trouble (B4UAct, 2011a; Grady et al., 2019; Levenson et al., 2017; Levenson & Grady, 2019a). Notably, such fears are reported not only by individuals living in countries with mandated reporting laws, such as the United States, but also by those living in countries where professional confidentiality laws provide more protection to clients, such as the Netherlands (Van Horn et al., 2015).

Even if they manage to overcome these feelings of shame and fear, various practical obstacles emerge: Many MAP do not know where to go to and whom to turn to. Finding a knowledgeable, affordable professional or someone supportive from their social environment is very challenging (Levenson & Grady, 2019a; Piché et al., 2018). Not being aware of, not having access to adequate professional help, and being confronted to restricted availability of known services prohibit many MAP from seeking help (Houtepen et al., 2016; Van Horn et al., 2015).

From Whom to Seek Help?

In general, people tend to seek informal help more often than formal help for issues like mental health problems (e.g., Brown et al., 2014). However, this is not necessarily true for MAP: Many live quite isolated with few outlets for social support, and the fear of being ostracized by their limited social network prohibits them from addressing their struggles with their network. Empirical evidence for this assumption is however ambiguous with some studies indicating that sought support is more often formal than informal (Levenson et al., 2017), while other studies find the opposite pattern (Beier et al., 2009) or find the reliance on formal and informal sources to be similar (Houtepen et al., 2016). These ambiguous results might of course reflect differences in methodologies but might also reflect differences in the accessibility to adequate professional help within that region, the confidence MAP have in the expertise and the trustworthiness of services, and whether MAP are knowledgeable of formal sources in their region (see e.g., Beier et al., 2009).

Aside from these formal and informal sources of help, a third source of help commonly identified in empirical studies are other individuals with sexual interests in minors. Such (online) sources of help, however, provoke a lot of aversive reactions. Many fear that contacts among like-minded MAP will facilitate CSA; such contacts are commonly seen as a breeding ground for networks of offending MAP in which tips and tricks are being shared on how to abuse children. Although we cannot rule out this possibility entirely, several websites for non-offending MAP, like the English website www.virped.org and the Dutch website www.pedofilie.nl to name a few, explicitly state that all on- and offline behaviour eliciting or justifying CSA is prohibited. The importance of such opportunities to contact like-minded others should not be underestimated; indeed, involvement in self-help groups is found to facilitate recovery from various mental health issues and to improve self-esteem, self-confidence, and quality of life (Markowitz, 2015; Parkman et al., 2015). More specifically, it gives MAP the unique opportunity to be themselves and talk openly about their feelings and struggles. In addition, these contacts might reassure them that there are other MAP who do not want to engage in CSA and that these interests do not imply that they will commit offences one day (Houtepen et al., 2016).

What Help Is Helpful?

When we seek help, we hope to receive support that helps us resolve the problem and/or diminish the negative effects of that problem. Numerous studies on help-seeking, however, only assess whether participants have sought help for their problem, and, thus, start from the underlying assumption that all help is helpful. In practice, many services evaluate their effectiveness only by the number of people who have contacted them, without exploring whether their services managed to provide to the needs of the help-seeker. However, finding helpful assistance for MAP is all but self-evident. It cannot be emphasized enough how important it is to look at the impact of the support on the help-seeker's well-being, satisfaction, and subjective experiences.

Only about half of MAP who have sought formal help rate the services they have received as helpful or very helpful, and about one-third rate the service as not helpful (Levenson et al., 2017; Levenson & Grady, 2019a). Overall, services from professionals who listen and understand them, who are not judgemental, who offer hope and practical solutions for changing thoughts or behaviours, and who acknowledge the whole person and are thus not fixated on sexuality, are considered helpful (Levenson et al., 2017; Levenson & Grady, 2019a). By contrast, confrontations with false or unjustified assumptions expressed by the professional, most commonly questioning the client's intentions and behaviours towards minors and their ability to self-control, and a lack of clinical knowledge on minor attraction keep MAP from seeking further help (B4U-ACT, 2011a; Houtepen et al., 2016; Levenson & Grady, 2019a).

Broadening Theoretical Perspectives on Help-Seeking Behaviour

Although research on help-seeking behaviour in MAP is beginning to gain a foothold in the literature, there are still many gaps in current knowledge. As deciding to seek help entails a rational decision process which is dependent on various characteristics, we argue that decision-making models may guide future research in identifying the factors that influence MAP in taking action.

One of the most prominent decision-making models is the prototype/willingness model (PWM; Gerrard et al., 2008). The PWM identifies two information-processing pathways to behaviour: a deliberative, reasoned path and a social reaction path. This reasoned path describes how positive attitudes towards performing the behaviour and supportive subjective norms (i.e., perceptions of what others are doing) increase one's intention to conduct certain behaviour, which in turn serves as the proximal antecedent to behaviour. By contrast, the social path entails reactive, spontaneous decision-making, influenced by prototypes of people engaging in certain behaviours, with behavioural willingness (i.e., one's openness to behavioural opportunity) as a key determinant of behaviour. Empirical support for the PWM has been established (Todd et al., 2016). Importantly, behavioural willingness seems to be a better predictor of behaviour than reasoned intention when this behaviour is unfamiliar, socially undesirable, or involves emotional processes (see, for an overview, Hammer & Vogel, 2013).

It remains unclear to what extent help-seeking behaviour in MAP is determined by reasoned or reactive processes. Given that seeking help is a novel behaviour for many, is related to stigma, especially a stigma related to disclosing minor attraction, and invokes a lot of fear and discomfort, it can be hypothesized that willingness is the most important determinant of help-seeking behaviour in these individuals (Hammer & Vogel, 2013). However, it can also be argued that in general MAP experience a lack of relevant prototypes, and that therefore their help-seeking behaviour is mostly determined by their own intentions to seek help, rather than by their willingness. Insights into the relevance of both reasoned and reactive decision-making processes are thus needed if we want support services to be better tailored to the factors that have an actual relevance in facilitating help-seeking decisions in MAP.

Is Practice Ready to Work with MAP?

Professionals can draw lessons from the available, albeit still limited, research on help-seeking behaviour in MAP. First, contrary to popular belief, various offending and non-offending MAP experience a need for help and a considerable group acts upon this need. As a field we should therefore create opportunities for them to find adequate low-barrier help. In the last decade, we have witnessed the emergence of several professional initiatives worldwide to guide and support MAP as appropriately as possible. Several anonymous helplines (e.g., Stop it Now!; see Chap. 16) and group-based treatment programmes (e.g., the German Dunkelfeld Project; Beier et al., 2009) aim to provide free and accessible help to MAP. Although we are still awaiting proper evaluations of the efficacy of these projects in terms of helpfulness as perceived by MAP (see also Chap. 16), these initiatives tackle several obstacles that MAP have pointed out in previous research: having easy access to affordable, knowledgeable, and non-judgemental professionals. However, not all MAP know these initiatives (Van Horn et al., 2015), nor do all MAP relate to these initiatives, given that the main aim of these programmes is often to prevent CSA. It is time to explore MAP's position on and experiences with these initiatives and to use these insights to further optimize them. At the same time, professional organizations and self-support groups can join forces where appropriate.

In addition, we should create more openness to MAP in the non-forensic clinical field. Mental health providers who work with forensic clients are assumed to have the necessary expertise and skills to understand and assist MAP. But it is doubtful that MAP will voluntarily turn to forensic services if they do not consider themselves at risk for offending. So, are non-forensic mental health providers willing and able to provide adequate support to MAP? The answer to this question may be disappointing: Research suggests that a substantial number of (future) mental health professionals exhibit poor knowledge about MAP, endorse a negative attitude towards people with paedophilia (Jahnke, 2018), still have many misunderstandings about the relation between MAP and CSA, and are therefore prepared to automatically report MAP to the police (Walker et al., 2021), or simply refuse to work with MAP (Stiels-Glenn, 2010). These problems could be addressed by sensitization campaigns, proper trainings into MAP and other relevant domains, including ethical guidelines, and the development of practice-oriented tools to engage MAP (see Levenson et al., 2020). But it remains to be seen whether such interventions lead to real and lasting changes in attitudes in individuals who exhibit stereotypical and judgemental views of MAP (Levenson & Grady, 2019b; Walker et al., 2021). Moreover, if professionals want to be able to get to the bottom of the MAP's psychosocial problems and offer adequate help, the client must be able to disclose the true underlying reasons for their psychosocial problems and diminished well-being. Being a trustworthy, transparent, knowledgeable, and unjudgemental professional will help create a safe environment for the client to do so. This does not imply that professionals should be blind to possible risk factors for offending behaviour, but it is important to find a balance between helping their client to strive for a good and healthy life and staying attentive to possible risks.

To Conclude

Our willingness to understand the origins, characteristics, and risks of minor attraction has increased exponentially in recent decades. Notwithstanding, there is still an oversimplified and stereotypical thinking about MAP. The strongly held belief that MAP are child abusers and evil by nature makes us all too often close our eyes to the problems with which MAP struggle and makes us turn a deaf ear to their calls for help. It is therefore time that we move beyond current barriers and reach out to these individuals, carefully listen to their needs and worries, and help them to find a way to cope with their problems, with a dual focus on CSA prevention and the client's well-being.

References

American Psychiatric Association. (2013). *Diagnostic and statistical manual of mental disorders* (5th ed.). Author.

B4UAct. (2018). http://www.b4uact.org/know-the-facts/faq/

B4U-ACT. (2011a). Mental Health Care and Professional Literature Survey results. http://www.b4uact.org/research/survey-results/spring-2011-survey/

B4U-ACT. (2011b). Youth, suicidality, and seeking care. Retrieved from http://www.b4uact.org/research/survey-results/youth-suicidality-and- seeking-care/

Bailey, J. M., Bernhard, P. A., & Hsu, K. J. (2016). An internet study of men sexually attracted to children: Correlates of sexual offending against children. *Journal of Abnormal Psychology, 125*(7), 989–1000. https://doi.org/10.1037/abn0000213

Beier, K. M., Ahlers, C. J., Goecker, D., Neutze, J., Mundt, I. A., Hupp, E., & Schaefer, G. A. (2009). Can pedophiles be reached for primary prevention of child sexual abuse? First results of the Berlin prevention project Dunkelfeld (PPD). *The Journal of Forensic Psychiatry & Psychology, 20*, 851–867. https://doi.org/10.1080/14789940903174188

Brown, J. S. L., Evans-Lack, S., Aschan, L., Henderson, M. J., Hatch, S. L., & Hotopf, M. (2014). Seeking informal and formal help for mental health problems in the community: A secondary analysis from a psychiatric morbidity survey in South London. *BMC Psychiatry, 14*, 275. https://doi.org/10.1186/s12888-014-0275-y

Cantor, J. M., & McPhail, I. V. (2016). Non-offending pedophiles. *Current Sexual Health Reports, 8*, 121–128. https://doi.org/10.1007/s11930-016-0076-z

Cohen, L., Ndukwe, N., Yaseen, Z., & Galynker, I. (2018). Comparison of self-identified minor-attracted persons who have and have not successfully refrained from sexual activity with children. *Journal of Sex & Marital Therapy, 44*(3), 217–230.

Cornally, N., & Mccarthy, G. (2011). Help-seeking behaviour: A concept analysis. *International Journal of Nursing Practice, 17*(3), 280–288. https://doi.org/10.1111/j.1440-172X.2011.01936.x

Delisi, M., Caropreso, D. E., Drury, A. J., Elbert, M. J., Evans, J. L., Heinrichs, T., & Tahja, K. M. (2016). The dark figure of sexual offending: New evidence from federal sex offenders. *Journal of Criminal Psychology, 6*(1), 3–15. https://doi.org/10.1108/JCP-12-2015-0030

Gerrard, M., Gibbons, F. X., Houlihan, A. E., Stock, M. L., & Pomery, E. A. (2008). A dual-process approach to health risk decision making: The prototype willingness model. *Developmental Review, 28*(1), 29–61. https://doi.org/10.1016/j.dr.2007.10.001

Grady, M. D., Levenson, J. S., Mesias, G., Kavanagh, S., & Charles, J. (2019). "I can't talk about that": Stigma and fear as barriers to preventive services for minor-attracted persons. *Stigma and Health, 4*(4), 400–410. https://doi.org/10.1037/sah0000154

Hammer, J. H., & Vogel, D. L. (2013). Assessing the utility of the willingness/prototype model in predicting help-seeking decisions. *Journal of Counseling Psychology, 60*(1), 83–97. https://doi.org/10.1037/a0030449

Hanson, R. K., Helmus, L., & Harris, A. J. R. (2015). Assessing the risk and needs of supervised sexual offenders: A prospective study using STABLE-2007, static-99R, and static-2002R. *Criminal Justice and Behavior, 42*(12), 1205–1224. https://doi.org/10.1177/0093854815602094

Houtepen, J. A., Sijtsema, J. J., & Bogaerts, S. (2016). Being sexually attracted to minors: Sexual development, coping with forbidden feelings, and relieving sexual arousal in self- identified pedophiles. *Journal of Sex & Marital Therapy, 42*(1), 48–69. https://doi.org/10.1080/0092623X.2015.1061077

Jahnke, S. (2018). The stigma of paedophilia: Clinical and forensic implications. *European Psychologist, 33*, 144–153. https://doi.org/10.1027/1016-9040/a000325

Jahnke, S., Schmidt, A. F., Geradt, M., & Hoyer, J. (2015). Stigma-related stress and its correlates among men with pedophilic sexual interests. *Archives of*

Sexual Behavior, 44, 2173–2187. https://doi.org/10.1007/s10508-015-0503-7

Levenson, J. S., & Grady, M. D. (2019a). Preventing sexual abuse: Perspectives of minor-attracted persons about seeking help. *Sexual Abuse: Journal of Research and Treatment, 31*(8), 991–1013. https://doi.org/10.1177/1079063218797713

Levenson, J. S., & Grady, M. D. (2019b). "I could never work with those people...": Secondary prevention of child sexual abuse via a brief training for therapists about paedophilia. *Journal of Interpersonal Violence, 34*(20), 4281–4302. https://doi.org/10.1177/0886260519869238

Levenson, J. S., Grady, M. D., & Morin, J. W. (2020). Beyond the "ick factor": Counseling non-offending persons with paedophilia. *Clinical Social Work Journal, 48*(4), 380–388. https://doi.org/10.1007/s10615-019-00712-4

Levenson, J. S., Willis, G. M., & Vicencio, C. P. (2017). Obstacles to help-seeking for sexual offenders: Implications for prevention of sexual abuse. *Journal of Child Sexual Abuse, 26*(2), 99–120. https://doi.org/10.1080/10538712.2016.1276116

Lievesley, R., Harper, C. A., & Elliott, H. (2020). The internalization of social stigma among minor-attracted persons: Implications for treatment. *Archives of Sexual Behavior, 49*(4), 1291–1304. https://doi.org/10.1007/s10508-019-01569-x

Mann, R. E., Hanson, R. K., & Thornton, D. (2010). Assessing risk for sexual recidivism: Some proposals on the nature of psychologically meaningful risk factors. *Sexual Abuse: A Journal of Research and Treatment, 22*(2), 191–217. https://doi.org/10.1177/1079063210366039

Markowitz, F. E. (2015). Involvement in mental health self-help groups and recovery. *Health Sociology Review, 24*(2), 199–212. https://doi.org/10.1080/14461242.2015.1015149

Parkman, T. J., Lloyd, C., & Splisbury, K. (2015). Self-help groups for alcohol dependency: A scoping review. *Journal of Groups in Addiction & Recovery, 10*(2), 102–124. https://doi.org/10.1080/1556035X.2015.1034824

Piché, L., Mathesius, J., Lussier, P., & Schweighofer, A. (2018). Preventative Services for Sexual Offenders. *Sexual Abuse, 30*(1), 63–81. https://doi.org/10.1177/1079063216630749

Rickwood, D., & Thomas, K. (2012). Conceptual measurement framework for help-seeking for mental health problems. *Psychology Research and Behavior Management, 5*, 173–183. https://doi.org/10.2147/PRBM.S38707

Seto, M. C. (2018). *Paedophilia and sexual offending against children: Theory, assessment, and intervention* (2nd ed.). American Psychological Association.
Stevens, E., & Wood, J. (2019). "I despise myself for thinking about them." a thematic analysis of the mental health implications and employed coping mechanisms of self-reported non-offending minor attracted persons. *Journal of Child Sexual Abuse, 28*(8), 968–989. https://doi.org/10.1080/10538712.2019.1657539
Stiels-Glenn, M. (2010). The availability of outpatient psychotherapy for paedophiles in Germany. *Recht & Psychiatrie, 28*(2), 74–80.
Todd, J., Kothe, E., Mullan, B., & Monds, L. (2016). Reasoned versus reactive prediction of behaviour: A meta-analysis of the prototype willingness model. *Health Psychology Review, 10*(1), 1–24. https://doi.org/10.1080/17437199.2014.922895
Van Horn, J., Eisenberg, M., Nicholls, C. M. N., Mulder, J., Webster, S., Paskell, C., Brown, A., Stam, J., Kerr, J., & Jago, N. (2015). Stop it now! A pilot study into the limits and benefits of a free helpline preventing child sexual abuse. *Journal of Child Sexual Abuse, 24*(8), 853–872. https://doi.org/10.1080/10538712.2015.1088914
Walker, A., Butters, R. P., & Nichols, E. (2021). "I would report it even if they have not committed anything": Social service students' attitudes toward minor-attracted people. *Sexual Abuse.* https://doi.org/10.1177/1079063221993480
Ward, T., & Beech, A. (2006). An integrated theory of sexual offending. *Aggression and Violent Behavior, 11*(1), 44–63. https://doi.org/10.1016/j.avb.2005.05.002

13

How to Thrive as a Provider of Treatment to Those Convicted of Sex Offences

Joanna Clarke

The provision of treatment for men convicted of sexual offences really only became a global endeavour in the early 1990s. Prior to that, treatment tended to be localised to sites where there were practitioners who were interested and motivated to address the complex issue of sexual offending. In all likelihood however, these professionals would have been limited in terms of training, and intuitive in the application of their skills, given that the evidence-based concerning efficacy of treatment had yet to be developed. Over the last 30 years that evidence base has grown substantially, with treatment models shared around the world and a broadly consistent approach to intervention.

Whilst the potential for psychological damage to treatment providers was first noted in the early 1990s by Farrenkopf (1992), the research

---

I have no known conflict of interest to disclose.

J. Clarke (✉)
Petros Ltd, York, UK
e-mail: jo@petros.org.uk

© The Author(s), under exclusive license to Springer Nature Switzerland AG 2022

K. Uzieblo et al. (eds.), *Challenges in the Management of People Convicted of a Sexual Offence*, Palgrave Studies in Risk, Crime and Society,
https://doi.org/10.1007/978-3-030-80212-7_13

domain has failed to keep pace with intervention research, in terms of either quantity or quality. In a recent review of the literature by Bach and Demuth (2018), a number of issues were raised which highlight that little has changed in terms of empirical evidence or understanding in the past 20 years (see Clarke, 2004), and what there is lacks the rigour of its contextual counterpart. For example, nearly all the research into the impact on treatment providers

- Focuses on deleterious outcome, such as burnout, vicarious trauma or secondary traumatic stress;
- Is cross-sectional and retrospective in nature;
- Relies on generic and often poorly constructed questionnaires;
- Is descriptive in nature;
- Is overly reliant on self-report;
- Lacks control groups.

What this means in practice is that whilst we might understand how a certain number of providers are feeling at any given time, in response to specific (often unvalidated or generic) questions it tells us little about how or why therapists arrived at the psychological condition they report in the research, how long they have felt that way, what the contributing factors were, what the prognosis is for recovery, what the potential causes may have been, what rewards there might be in their work, or how organisations should best respond to look after their people. Developing an organisational strategy to support staff based on this type of evidence is problematic, because what is unknown is:

- What risk factors are associated with poor outcome and how these might be mitigated;
- What the rewards of the work are and how they might be enhanced;
- How the impact on providers changes over time;
- How treatment providers compare with other professionals working in psychologically challenging fields, for example those working with victims of sexual violence;

- How best to support staff to ensure their skills and experience are not lost;
- The importance of individual differences in terms of protective factors or risk of harm.

Therapeutic work with those convicted of sexual offences is usefully conceptualised as a 'critical occupation'. This term was coined by Paton and Violanti (1996) to capture the critical nature of professions that protect communities (e.g., emergency services), while also recognising the potential for critical impact on the psychological well-being of those undertaking such roles. Work that immerses staff in a world of sexual violence and deviance, with mandated and resistant clients, in often hostile environments (e.g., prisons), exemplifies a critical occupation. Perhaps this is why there has been an arguably overzealous focus on the potential for treatment of men convicted of sexual offences to result in psychological harm to providers. However, Bach and Demuth (2018) conclude that there is actually sufficient evidence to determine that many therapists find satisfaction in their work. This was supported by Clarke (2004), who reported that 96% of survey respondents agreed that their work was the best they had ever been involved in. Focusing only on negative impact has a number of significant consequences; it assumes that it is the content of the work that results in harm, it negates the possibility and therefore promotion of the rewards of the work, and it results in fixation error. In other words, if the costs and the content of the work remain the sole focus of research, organisations will be extremely limited in efforts to promote good psychological health, because the focus is too narrow and excluding of other important variables.

The original critical occupations literature opens up a whole host of other foci for research, and has resulted in the development of a number of models to help support the development of evidence-based strategies to not only identify risks, but also to prevent deleterious outcome for staff in critical roles. Using this literature, Clarke & Roger (2002, 2007, 2008, 2011, 2012, 2013, 2017) developed and empirically tested a model based specifically on the experiences of treatment providers. What follows in this chapter is a brief description of the literature on which the model is based, an explanation of the model, and suggestions about how to utilise it to build an evidence-based strategy specific to your organisation and based exclusively on the needs of treatment providers.

A Brief Description of the Literature

As previously mentioned, the overwhelming assumption about working as a treatment provider in the field of sexual offending, is that it must be psychological harmful. Whilst this is not an unreasonable premise, it has biased the research to such an extent that no other outcome has ever been seriously considered. A vast majority of published work conceptualises the impact of the work in terms of burnout (Maslach, 2003), vicarious trauma McCann & Pearlman, 1990), secondary trauma (Stamm, 1995) or compassion fatigue (Figley & Stamm, 1996). These outcomes are variously investigated the context of client characteristics, therapist demographics or organisational factors. For example, demographics such as age (Clarke & Roger, 2002; Steed & Bicknell, 2001), coping style (Clarke, 2013; Wallace et al., 2010), length of service (Amen, 2003), gender (Clarke, 2004) and trauma history (Clarke & Roger, 2002, 2004, 2013; Moulden & Firestone, 2007) have all been considered as relevant, with equivocal results. To illustrate, younger therapists may be more at risk owing to less life experience in which to contextualise their work. Those with a trauma history may be more vulnerable to re-traumatisation. Organisational factors such as supervision, training and organisational support have also been considered (Clarke & Roger, 2002), along with organisational culture and occupational health (Clarke, 2013; Gist & Woodall, 2000; Paton et al., 2008). Lack of supervision may leave staff uncertain about the efficacy of their working practices, and a culture that is not supportive of treatment, or at odds with it (such as prisons), may leave staff feeling isolated and vulnerable.

While correlations between variables might offer useful insight, without longitudinal research and the inclusion of control groups, little causal inference can be made. It is also essential that the rewards and benefits of therapeutic work with those convicted of sexual offences is also considered (Kadambi & Truscott, 2006). Without an understanding of what connects people with their work and motivates them to continue, any strategy to enhance well-being can only aim to minimise the risk of harm. A comprehensive and holistic approach should also seek to maximise the rewards and support professional (and personal) growth.

The Model of Dynamic Adaptation

Reading the range of literature about impact can overwhelm even the most research savvy reader! It can also feel impenetrable and confusing to organisational leaders who want to ensure that they address the well-being and longevity of their staff in this most complex, but also potentially rewarding, of fields. Fortunately, the multitude of factors identified in the research as relevant, significant and interesting to consider lend themselves well to the formulation of a model (Clarke, 2004), which over the years has been empirically tested (Clarke, 2013) and found to be a helpful evidence base on which to base interventions to enhance the well-being of staff. The Model of Dynamic Adaptation (MDA), described in Fig. 13.1, is a data-driven model that emerged from research involving upwards of 300 UK-based prison and probation staff over a three-year period. Interestingly, a very similar theory-driven model, the Stress Shield Model, developed by Paton et al. (2008), emerged at around the same time. This model was tested with over 500 criminal justice staff across Europe (Latvia, Estonia, Bulgaria, the UK and the Netherlands), in a project managed by the State Probation Service of Latvia and funded by the EU (Clarke, 2013). These two models reinforce the point that it is possible to make sense of the data and the theory to develop a practical and effective infrastructure to protect staff and mitigate the risks of burnout, compassion fatigue and secondary traumatic stress.

The MDA is so called to represent the fact that nothing actually stays the same (i.e., life is dynamic) and that human beings constantly strive to adapt to their circumstances. In essence, this is represented in the model by the arrow that connects positive and negative outcome. Contrary to what the research might suggest on first inspection, not all treatment providers are experiencing compassion fatigue, secondary traumatic stress or burnout all of the time, or at all. Indeed, a bulk of the research suggests

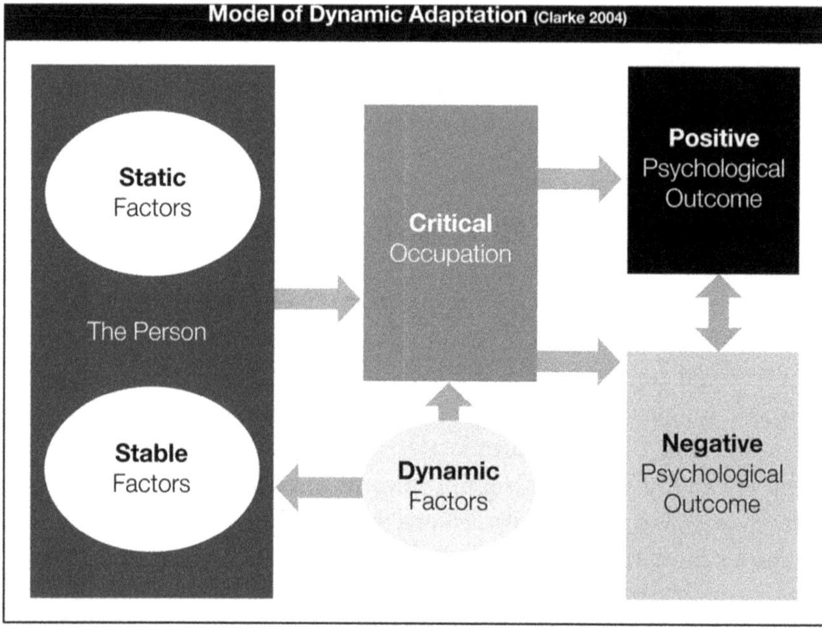

Fig. 13.1 The Model of Dynamic Adaptation (Clarke, 2004)

that it is between a quarter and a third of research respondents that are struggling at any given time. Interestingly, this tends to match the reported prevalence rate of mental ill-health in the general population at any given time, although Ginn and Horder (2012) call that figure into question, arguing it is unclear to what the figure actually refers—lifetime prevalence, yearly prevalence or single point in time prevalence. Examples of positive outcomes might include factors from Kadambi and Truscott's (2006) research, such as professional benefits, influencing offender change and wellness, socially meaningful work and so on. Negative outcomes include all those identified in the literature, such as intrusive thoughts, increased substance use, feelings of guilt, lack of sleep, increased suspicion and cynicism and so on. It is also important to recognise that positive and negative outcomes are not mutually exclusive and that it is quite possible to experience both at the same time.

Ideally, the range of outcomes for treatment providers, from phenomenally good to utterly miserable, should be considered as a continuum, influenced by a whole host of factors, some of which can be controlled and managed and some of which cannot. What the MDA offers is a way of testing what factors influence movement along the continuum and therefore how individuals and organisations can mitigate risk and enhance well-being. For example, conscientiousness, age, gender, coping style, organisational culture, physical work environment and contracted hours have all been found to be significant (Clarke, 2013; Ellerby, 1998; Fox, 2010). Whilst it may be neither feasible nor reasonable to expect all staff to report feeling phenomenally good all of the time, the ultimate organisational goal should be to manage all the recognised factors in order to have a majority of staff in the positive outcome box for a majority of the time.

To make sense of all the possible combinations of factors that influence outcome, the construction of the model drew on the risk prediction literature, already familiar to those in the treatment field, and factors were divided into static, stable and dynamic. In the MDA, static factors refer to features of the individual that either do not change or change very predictably (e.g., age and gender) and stable factors relate to features that can be subject to change, especially as a result of intervention (e.g., coping style and conscientiousness). Dynamic factors refer to those elements in an individual's life that may change unpredictably or frequently and are often outside of individual control (such as the commute to work, changes in circumstances (work or personal) and even the weather. It is important to note that factors from any of the three categories may increase risk or be protective.

The model would not be complete without the inclusion of organisational factors identified in the Critical Occupations literature as often more significant in the prediction of well-being than the operational characteristics of the role (Paton & Violanti, 1996; Hart et al., 1993). Examples include organisational culture (particularly communication, management, workload and empowerment), the physical work environment, contracted hours and the role of colleagues. Colleagues are regularly cited as the most important source of organisational support; experiencing problems with colleagues is also found to be related to maladaptive coping styles and diminished well-being (Uzieblo et al., 2019).

In the context of treating men convicted of sexual offending, Attrill (1995) undertook a unique piece of research to identify what support was considered most beneficial from which colleagues. She found that senior leaders were considered most supportive by treatment providers when they publicly supported treatment, while specialists were thought most helpful when they shared their knowledge. Co-workers' willingness to discuss treatment and cover sessions was most appreciated. This type of evidence can inform comprehensive strategies to enhance well-being.

Each of these groups of factors (static, stable, dynamic and organisational) interplays to suggest where on the continuum of outcomes an individual might be. To illustrate how the model can be used, below are two hypothetical case studies to consider.

Case A

Simeon is a 24-year-old, very high-achieving, psychology graduate. He has committed himself to therapeutic work with men convicted of sexual offending after his uncle was prosecuted for abusing his sister when she was in her early teens and Simeon was 16 years old. Simeon experienced anxiety at university but nonetheless aced his exams. Since graduating, he started work in a community-based treatment programme and excelled in his training. He is considered an outstanding therapist, despite his young years and relative inexperience. His boss is very supportive, and his project is very well resourced.

Simeon lives alone having moved to the area to take up his post. He is socially shy and does not have a big circle of friends. His family are resistant to him working in the field, based on the family history. However, Simeon makes very good use of supervision and is open and responsive to professional support.

Recently, a new man joined Simeon's treatment group who reminds him physically of his uncle.

Case B

Sondra is 50 years old and has two grown up daughters and a loving and supportive partner. She has worked in prisons for 25 years, and began delivering treatment programmes 12 years ago when a colleague suggested she would be excellent at it. Sondra was reluctant at first, especially as her children were young at the time. She recognises both her strengths and vulnerabilities and wanted to be sure she could manage the psychological demands of the work.

Her work environment is harsh, and the prison resources can be patchy. Sometimes it's a struggle to even ensure the group room is available.

Sondra's colleague was right, and Sondra is considered a natural "go to" person among offenders and colleagues alike. However, she is very professional and maintains clear at all times. Early in her career, she worked with a man who had abused a child who was the same age as her youngest daughter at the time. Sondra sought supervision and with help and support worked through the impact on her. The same man has just returned to her treatment group, five years after release, convicted of a very similar offence. Sondra has also just learned that her eldest daughter has just found out that she is unable to have children.

Before considering Simeon and Sondra's individual needs, there are several issues to address when looking at (Table 13.1). For example, do particular factors have a positive or negative impact on well-being? What about factors that aren't supported by empirical evidence, and do some factors hold more weight than others? At this point in time, it is fair to say that the gathering and testing of empirical evidence in this field is in its infancy. Therefore, clinical judgement, anecdotal evidence and theoretically driven conclusions may need to provide a basis for strategic intervention where evidence is absent. For example, the evidence suggests that younger staff may report more deleterious effects and that men are more likely to inhibit emotion. Therefore, as a manager, considering extra support and additional training for younger staff would be prudent. Considering a variety of options for the processing of emotion would also be recommended. Therapeutic writing or decompression sessions with peers might be preferable to therapy or counselling for those who find emotional expression challenging.

As for which issues carry more weight, much will depend on each individual at any given point in time, speaking to the dynamic nature of the model. Some factors, such as a toxic work culture, will always be challenging and should be addressed as a matter of moral and ethical priority. However, it would still be unreasonable to suggest everyone would be affected by it in the same way. Therefore, all factors should remain on the vigilant leader's radar, and the issue of well-being should be a live and regular topic agenda item.

With the above in mind, and based on the information provided, it would be reasonable to conclude that Sondra is likely to be experiencing

Table 13.1 Case study summaries

Factors	Case A: Simeon		Case B: Sondra	
↓	*Risky*	*Protective*	*Risky*	*Protective*
Static	– Age[a] – Gender[a] – Living status – History of family abuse	– Qualifications	– Parent	– Age[a] – Gender[a] – Time in the role[a] – Living status
Stable	Anxiety – Conscientiousness[a] – Shyness – New Case – Lack of personal support	– Emotionally open and responsive – Openness to supervision	– New Case – Daughter's infertility	– Coping style[a] – Ability to maintain boundaries – Openness to supervision
Organisational		– Supportive boss – Well-resourced project[a] – Pleasant physical environment	– Physical work environment[a]	

[a]Empirical evidence available

more positives from work than Simeon at this point in time. It is not possible, based on the limited available research, to state with any certainty which factors outweigh others. Each individual case needs to be considered on its own merits. However, if a number of risk factors are evident, well-being should be a priority, no matter how well someone is performing in their role. So, even though Simeon appears to be an excellent therapist, he also has a number of risk factors that should not be ignored. Appropriate support and working practices for both staff is essential to ensure they thrive in their roles. What that might look like is covered in the next section. It is perhaps this latter point that underpins most strongly why the development of a robust strategy in complex organisations is challenging. Any strategy needs to be robust enough to be applied consistently across a complex infrastructure (treatment programmes rarely run in isolation), whilst flexible enough to accommodate numerous individual differences in terms of personalities and life circumstances. The model comes into its own when considering how to contain such intricacy in an effective way. It is to this that attention will now be turned.

Interventions

Although there is no evidence to draw on directly, it is likely a provable fact that a majority of organisations only take action to minimise damage once the damage has been done. In Fig. 13.2, this is represented by Intervention Point 4, at Negative Psychological Outcome. Such

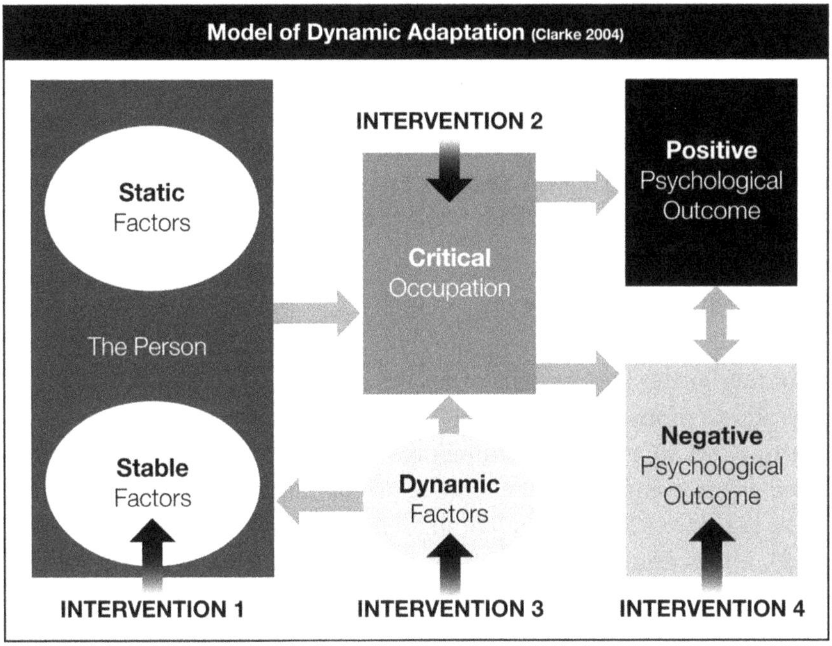

Fig. 13.2 The MDA with intervention points

interventions, for example the provision of therapy, taking time away from treatment or leaving the profession altogether, are known as Tertiary Interventions, ones that seek to reduce the impact of the dysfunctional outcome and promote quality of life through active rehabilitation (Department of Health, 2007). Whilst it is a legal duty of care in most countries to protect staff from harm that may be caused by work, if responding to harm once it has happened is the totality of an organisation's response, it is a very sorry state of affairs. Here are some reasons why:

- It is far more psychologically and economically costly to repair damage than it is to prevent it.
- The qualities associated with effective treatment provision (see Sandhu and Rose (2012) for a review) are largely associated with experience. Losing experienced practitioners may impact on treatment effective.
- The wider organisational impact of damaged staff is rarely, if ever, taken into account.
- The impact on families and communities is rarely, if ever, considered.

It therefore makes economic, psychological, moral and ethical sense to work towards minimising risk of harm to treatment providers. This can be done by instituting primary and secondary measures at both individual and organisational levels that are expressly aimed at preventing harm (primary) or acting very quickly on its causes (secondary).

Primary Interventions

According to the Department of Health (UK, 2007), primary interventions aim to promote good psychological health and require action on its determinants to prevent dysfunctional outcomes. These may be introduced at Intervention Points 1 and 2 on the model. For example, based on the evidence regarding age, coping style and conscientiousness (Clarke, 2013), a selection protocol that considers these factors would be advisable. Further examples might include the following:

- Training to support staff develop effective emotional regulation skills;
- Regular supervision;
- Attention being paid to the physical work environment;
- Addressing organisational issues that may interfere with effective treatment delivery, for example training managers, building communication strategies, empowering staff and ensuring a reasonable workload;
- Wellness action plans;
- Regular reviews;
- Wider organisational training to brief non-treatment focused colleagues on the value of the work;
- Senior leadership briefings to ensure high-level support.

Secondary Interventions

Secondary interventions (both individual and organisational) are those that can detect early any dysfunctional outcome, followed by appropriate intervention (see examples below). So, using Simeon as an example, regular supervision and debriefing may pick up that Simeon is impacted by the new group member who reminds him of his uncle. Perhaps Simeon reports this directly, or the supervisor, who knows Simeon well, notices that he is distracted, more reactive or slightly hostile when discussing that client. This issue may then become a focus of supervision, and a decision may be made to offer Simeon more frequent support, to ensure his co-worker spends more time with that client or that Simeon doesn't work with that client at all. All the examples below should allow for early detection of impact or mitigate the effects of it:

- Regular debriefing;
- Supervision;
- Effective management;
- Mentoring;
- Ongoing training;
- Well-being reviews;
- Role changes that ease demand but maintain involvement in treatment, for example moving from treatment to assessment.

It is worth nothing that primary and secondary interventions tend to be clearer cut at the organisational and individual level. However, when it comes to dynamic factors, which by their very nature are unpredictable and changeable, it is less straightforward. It is here that the flexibility of any strategy is likely to be tested. How the organisation responds to dynamic issues (e.g., family difficulties, house moves, and, even at the time of writing, societal or global events) can influence whether workers barely survive or positively thrive.

Tertiary Interventions

These interventions, as previously described, involve active rehabilitation. It is here that occupational health, therapeutic services, job moves or resignation might need to be considered. To demonstrate the application of a strategy, it is useful to return to Sondra and Simeon and consider what their needs might be given the circumstances described. What is provided in Table 13.2 is not exhaustive or definitive, but to provide examples.

Conclusions

The research as it currently stands is somewhat biased towards deleterious outcome for treatment providers. However, as Bach and Demuth (2018) conclude from their review of the relevant literature, supported by Clarke (2004), there is robust evidence that providers gain considerable satisfaction from their work. The solution to ensuring effective longevity in this most challenging and interesting of fields is knowing how to enhance these areas of satisfaction, whilst reducing the potential for harm. Getting that balance right will undoubtedly make a significant contribution to ensuring the continued effectiveness of treatment for those convicted of sexual offences.

Table 13.2 Case study interventions

Factors	Case A: Simeon		Case B: Sondra	
↓	*Risk factors*	*Intervention*	*Risk factors*	*Intervention*
Static	Age[a] Gender[a] Living status History of family abuse	1 – Selection process that picks up these factors – Mentor 2 – Regular supervision which openly discusses risk factors	– Parent	1 – Awareness of parental status and supervision/ support as needed
Stable	Anxiety Conscientiousness[a] Shy	1 – Training in emotional regulation and resilience (with updates) 2 Specific management to support around levels of conscientiousness and anxiety		1 Working practices that build on existing capacities Regular check-ins
Dynamic	New Case Lack of personal support	1 Discussion of case with supervisor, highlighting issue to monitor 2 Additional mentoring, debriefing	New Case Daughter's infertility	1 Discussion of case with supervisor, highlighting issue to monitor 2 Additional mentoring, debriefing
Organisational		Maintain good physical environment	Physical work environment[a]	1 Assess resource need Work to improve facilities

References

Amen, T. M. (2003). *An investigation of the psychological consequences to sex offender treatment providers*. Unpublished doctoral dissertation. ProQuest Information & Learning.

Attrill, G. (1995). *The dimensions of staff support of the sex offender treatment programme: Why, what, who and how?* Unpublished MSc thesis. University of London.

Bach, M. H., & Demuth, C. (2018). Therapists' experiences in their work with sex offenders and people with pedophilia: A literature review. *Europe's Journal of Psychology, 14*(2), 498–514. https://doi.org/10.5964/ejop.v14i2.1493

Clarke, J. (2008). Promoting professional resilience. In M. C. Clader (Ed.), *Contemporary risk assessment in safeguarding children* (pp. 166–182). Russell House Publishing.

Clarke, J. (2011). Working with sex offenders: Best practice in enhancing practitioner resilience. *Journal of Sexual Aggression, 17*(3), 335–355. https://doi.org/10.1080/13552600.2011.583781

Clarke, J. (2012). The resilient practitioner. In J. Clarke & P. Wilson (Eds.), *Forensic psychology in practice: A practitioner's handbook* (pp. 220–239). Palgrave Macmillan.

Clarke, J. (2013). *Sustaining probation officer resilience in Europe (SPORE): A transnational study.* https://petros.org.uk/wp-content/uploads/2017/11/SPORE_Final_Report1.pdf

Clarke, J. (2017). The resilient organisation. In J. L. Ireland, C. A. Ireland, M. Fisher, & N. Gredecki (Eds.), *The Routledge international handbook of forensic psychology in secure settings* (pp. 236–251). Routledge.

Clarke, J., & Roger, D. (2002). Working therapeutically with sex offenders: The potential impact on the psychological well-being of treatment providers. In L. Falshaw (Ed.), *Issues in forensic psychology, no 3* (pp. 82–106). BPS.

Clarke, J., & Roger, D. (2007). The construction and validation of a scale to assess psychological risk and well-being in sex offender treatment providers. *Legal and Criminological Psychology, 12*(1), 83–100. https://doi.org/10.1348/135532506X93927

Clarke, J. M. (2004). *The psychosocial impact on facilitators of working therapeutically with sex offenders: An experimental study*. Unpublished doctoral dissertation. University of York.

Department of Health. (2007). *Primary, secondary and tertiary prevention.* http://www.dh.gov.uk

Ellerby, L. (1998). *Providing Clinical Services to Sex Offenders: Burnout, Compassion, Fatigue and Moderating Variables*. Unpublished doctoral dissertation. University of Manitoba.

Farrenkopf, T. (1992). What happens to therapists who work with sex offenders? *Journal of Offender Rehabilitation, 18*(3–4), 217–224. https://doi.org/10.1300/J076v18n03_16

Figley, C. R., & Stamm, B. H. (1996). Psychometric review of compassion fatigue self-test. In B. H. Stamm (Ed.), *Measurement of stress, trauma, and adaptation* (pp. 127–130). Sidran Press.

Fox, A., (2010). *Investigating the factors that contribute to staff well-being and professional resilience at a Dangerous and Severe personality Disorder Unit*. Unpublished MSc Thesis. University of York.

Ginn, S., & Horder, J. (2012). "One in four" with a mental health problem: The anatomy of a statistic. *BMJ, 344*, e1302. https://doi.org/10.1136/bmj.e1302

Gist, R., & Woodall, J. (2000). There are no simple solutions to complex problems. In J. M. Violanti, D. Paton, & C. Dunning (Eds.), *Posttraumatic stress intervention: Challenges, issues and perspectives* (pp. 81–96). Charles C. Thomas.

Hart, P. M., Wearing, A. J., & Headey, B. (1993). Assessing police work experiences: Development of the police daily hassles and uplift scales. *Journal of Criminal Justice, 21*(6), 553–572. https://doi.org/10.1016/0047-2352(93)90043-M

Kadambi, M., & Truscott, D. (2006). Concept mapping professionals' perceptions of reward and motive in providing sex offender treatment. *Journal of Offender Rehabilitation, 42*(4), 37–58. https://doi.org/10.1300/J076v42n04_03

Maslach, C. (2003). *Burnout: The cost of caring*. Malor Books.

McCann, I. L., & Pearlman, L. A. (1990). Vicarious traumatization: A framework for understanding the psychological effects of working with victims. *Journal of Traumatic Stress, 3*(1), 131–149. https://doi.org/10.1007/BF00975140

Moulden, H. M., & Firestone, P. (2007). Vicarious traumatization: The impact on therapists who work with sexual offenders. *Trauma, Violence, & Abuse, 8*(1), 67–83. https://doi.org/10.1177/1524838006297729

Paton, D., & Violanti, J. M. (1996). *Traumatic stress in critical occupations: Recognition, consequences and treatment*. Charles C. Thomas.

Paton, D., Violanti, J. M., Johnston, P., Burke, K. J., Clarke, J., & Keenan, D. (2008). Stress shield: A model of police resiliency. *International Journal of Emergency Mental Health, 10*(2), 95–107.

Sandhu, D. K., & Rose, J. (2012). How do therapists contribute to therapeutic change in sex offender treatment: An integration of the literature. *Journal of*

Sexual Aggression, 18(3), 269–283. https://doi.org/10.1080/13552600.2011.566633
Stamm, B. (1995). *Secondary traumatic stress: Self-care issues for clinicians, researchers, and educators*. The Sidran Press.
Steed, L., & Bicknell, J. (2001). Trauma and the counselor: The experience of counselors working with the perpetrators of sexual abuse. *Australasian Journal of Disaster and Trauma Studies, 1*, 2001–2001.
Uzieblo, K., Vertommen, T., Boxstaens, J., & van Dijck, J. P. (2019). How are the Flemish probation officers doing? A study into work-related stress, coping styles, well-being, and quality of life. *Panopticon, 40*(4), 273–296.
Wallace, S. L., Lee, J., & Lee, S. M. (2010). Job stress, coping strategies, and burnout among abuse-specific counselors. *Journal of Employment Counseling, 47*(3), 111–122. https://doi.org/10.1002/j.2161-1920.2010.tb00096.x

Part IV

Community Engagement and Integration of People Exhibiting Deviant Sexual Interests and/or Behaviours

14

Expanding Interventions to Integrate Men Who Have Sexually Offended Back into the Community: Circles of Support and Accountability in Europe

Kieran McCartan, Mechtild Höing, and Riana Taylor

In the other chapters in this edited collection, we have seen authors discuss research and practice demonstrating that working with individuals who have been convicted of a sexual offence can be challenging, in terms of both their engagement with and their understanding of the rehabilitation process. In addition to the individual challenges that each person convicted of a sexual offence has, they also have larger, societal challenges

We have no known conflict of interest to disclose.

K. McCartan (✉)
Department of Criminology, University of the West of England, Bristol, UK
e-mail: kieran.mccartan@uwe.ac.uk

M. Höing
Avans University of Applied Sciences, 's-Hertogenbosch, Netherlands

R. Taylor
Circles UK, Reading, UK

© The Author(s), under exclusive license to Springer Nature Switzerland AG 2022

K. Uzieblo et al. (eds.), *Challenges in the Management of People Convicted of a Sexual Offence*, Palgrave Studies in Risk, Crime and Society,
https://doi.org/10.1007/978-3-030-80212-7_14

as they are viewed negatively by society (Höing et al., 2016), which results in them being ostracised, viewed as a risk, and, therefore, difficult to fully integrate into society (Harris, 2017; Harper et al., 2017). This negative community perspective and attitude can trigger the original risk factors, or create new risk factors, that lead to reoffending (Wilson et al., 2020). It is important to note that although sexual offending involves individuals, it is a community issue (i.e., people who commit sexual offences come from communities and get reintegrated back into communities post-conviction) and therefore communities have a role to play in helping to prevent it and to assist people convicted of a sexual offence desist from future offending. One approach to involve communities in this role is Circles of Support and Accountability (CoSA).

What Are Circles of Support and Accountability?

CoSA are groups of trained community volunteers who support people convicted of a sexual offence to integrate back into the community post-release (Richards et al., 2020). CoSA aims to promote pro-social values, reduce reoffending, promote desistence, and empower communities (Hanvey et al., 2011). CoSA programmes operate on the premise that by providing recently released medium and/or high risk (people convicted of a sexual offence with a circle of four to five volunteers who provide both support and accountability), those people will be better equipped to lead law-abiding lives in the community. The CoSA volunteers are members of the local community and are of a range of ages, genders, occupations, and skills (Hanvey et al., 2011). Each circle is managed by a circle coordinator, who is an experienced and paid criminal justice professional (see Fig. 14.1; for a more detailed logic model of CoSA service delivery, see Elliott & Zajac, 2015). Volunteers report back to the coordinator about the circle and the Core Member (what the person with the conviction for a sexual offence is called in a Circle), and the coordinator may report to statutory authorities (e.g. police and probation) if they are concerned about the Core Members attitudes and/or behaviour.

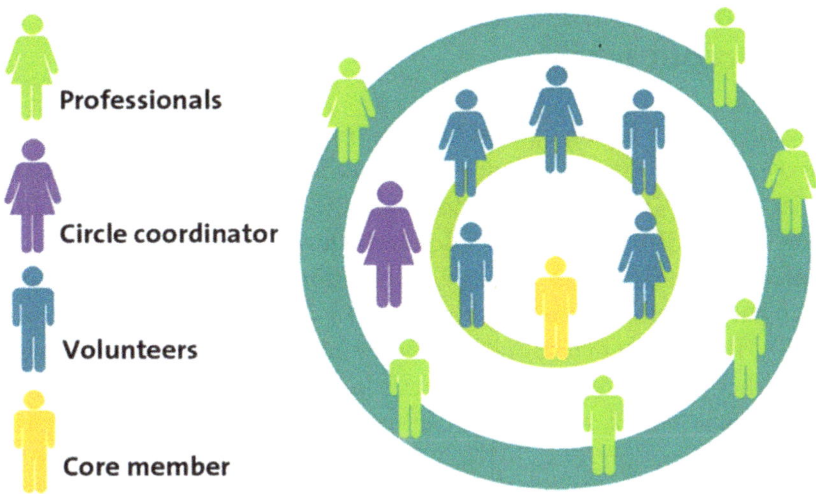

Fig. 14.1 Model of a Circle of Support and Accountability

Since its emergence in Canada in 1994 (Hanvey et al., 2011), CoSA has become a feature of the criminal justice landscape in North America, Europe (including, the UK, Catalonia, the Netherlands, Ireland, Latvia, Belgium, Bulgaria, and Italy), Australia and New Zealand (Richards et al., 2020). CoSA programmes around the globe rely on a variety of operating models, receive funding from a variety of sources, and have varying relationships with the criminal justice system (Richards et al., 2020). For example, in the Netherlands they are funded by the state, whereas in the UK they are funded by both charitable grants and government funding. The original CoSA model from Canada is still the main blueprint version of a circle; however, most countries have now adapted the European version of CoSA—as it is more criminal justice orientated than the grassroots version of CoSA developed and still used in some parts of Canada (i.e., more community orienated, less beaucratic, and less structured) (Hanvey et al., 2011; Höing et al., 2015).

The Evidence Base for Circles of Support and Accountability

Existing research highlights that CoSA assists in the reintegration of people convicted of a sexual offence (Clarke et al., 2017) by providing pro-social support (Fox, 2017; Höing et al., 2013) and by role modelling (McCartan, 2016; Fox, 2017). Research shows that CoSA can reduce reoffending, and therefore reconviction, amongst individuals who have taken part in the intervention as opposed to those who have not (Duwe, 2018). The circle offers Core Members a safe, protected environment, where they are able to seek advice and gain insight into their problematic attitudes and beliefs, so that they can road test their desistance and practice their integration (Fox, 2016). Circles is not a therapy or a treatment; in reality, it is an intervention that parallels statutory working and enables the Core Member to benefit from the "assist and befriend" culture that used to exist in community management (McCartan & Kemshall, 2020). Therefore, the aim, and as the research indicates, the outcomes of CoSA are future facing and inclusive.

The Main Challenges Faced by Providers of Circles of Support and Accountability

CoSA works in the intersection of the different worlds of sanctioning, probation, policing, treatment, and the community (Hanvey et al., 2011; Richards et al., 2020). In this complex field, with diverging views, interests, and responsibilities, where values, policies, and practices can clash, CoSA seeks to cooperate with all as a complementary service that parallels statutory working by adding the unique element of prevention and risk management through social inclusion (Höing & Alards, 2019).

This complementary role is not easy to maintain. In the past decades, many countries have experienced national sexual traumas, in terms of both individuals who have committed high-profile sexual abuses and murders (i.e., such as the Dutroux case in Belgium, Robert M. in the Netherlands) and individuals as high-prolife victims (i.e., the murder of

Sarah Payne in the UK). Such cases shocked the community and shook the justice system (e.g., Belgium: Gies, 2003). National sentiments and legislation became more punitive, and people convicted of a sexual offence are now central to risk management discourses (Simon, 1998; Williams, 2019). While these offences were horrific, they are in fact exceptional. Yet the extensive media coverage of exceptional cases—especially by the more sensationalist press—leads the public to think that all people who commit sexual offences are notorious, untreatable predators (Pickett et al., 2013). When resources are scarce, and the competition for safety and security does not yield equal chances for everyone, populist voices tend to become loud. They simplify the multifaceted issue of sexual offending in the community and promise a simple solution by demanding harsh and punitive measures—which are in fact counterproductive and make societies even more unsafe (Pickett et al., 2013). CoSA projects must withstand such popular punitiveness to offer an alternative solution. In CoSA, the support given to Core Members is not only defined by their medium to high level of risk, but also by their social needs and by the place they seek to claim in the community (Höing & Alards, 2019). To some, this seems like a soft approach, "pampering a sex offender who is feeling lonely", while in fact CoSA volunteers and Core Members are working together in addressing well-known risk factors such as loneliness and general rejection and developing protective factors such as problem-solving skills and adequate coping strategies (Van den Berg et al., 2020; Höing et al., 2013). The challenge that CoSA faces is the reality gap between what they do and what they are perceived as doing (Richards & McCartan, 2018), and the idea that victims and their families are often not supportive of this approach because it is offender-centric, which is not true (Richards et al., 2020).

In such a sociocultural climate, CoSA projects struggle for recognition and funding. While CoSA is one of the most cost-effective preventive approaches in this field (Bitney et al., 2017; Duwe, 2018), the justice system, local authorities, and other funders in many countries hesitate to take on the financial responsibility for this service. Recently in the UK, CoSA was on track to achieve national commissioning which would have significantly opened up its services across England and Wales, but as a result of a review into the prison treatment programmes for people convicted of a sexual offence, which later led to a review of community programmes, it was stated that there was a higher risk of reoffending happening than previously anticipated, and, although it was happening in a different way (i.e., viewing online imagery as opposed to committing a contact sexual offence), it was deemed that current programmes were not working or fit for purpose (Mews et al., 2017). Therefore, the treatment programmes were restructured with Kaizen and Horizon being developed for prisons and the community, and the funding of community services restricted with money being redirected into accommodation rather than CoSA, or related interventions. This, in part, led to a reduction in the overall funding of CoSA and a reduction in service providers from 16 in 2018 to 9 in 2020. In other countries, such as Belgium, CoSA providers have been operating on a local and very small scale for many years now, and their survival is at risk because of funding problems. In small-scale projects, staff is focused on providing CoSA, not having the time and energy for finding the money to expand. There are positive exceptions as well. In the Netherlands, CoSA is provided by the Dutch Probation Service as one of their standard services. After a few years of slow and steady implementation, their CoSA teams have been able to provide a stable, high-quality service for people convicted of a sexual offence under mandatory supervision on a national scale for ten years now (Höing, 2019).

Next to funding, finding volunteers is another constant worry for CoSA providers (Lowe & Willis, 2019; Gilliam et al., 2020). In CoSA projects, volunteers must be willing to engage in a long-term relationship, while all over Europe this type of volunteering is declining in favour of a shorter-term, episodic volunteerism, called "microvolunteering" by some authors (Brudney & Meijs, 2009; Heley et al., 2019). Nevertheless, CoSA projects can count on a substantial potential of interested citizens in European communities. In a European survey, one in eight adult citizens said that they would be interested in becoming a CoSA volunteer if such a project were nearby (Höing et al., 2016).

Finally, keeping core members in a circle can be a challenge too. Since core members enter a circle on a voluntary basis, they may leave the circle at any given moment. In Dutch circles, the 'drop-out' rate (core members leaving the circle prematurely on their own decision) is 23.7% (Höing, 2019), in Canadian circles 19.8% (Chouinard & Riddick, 2015).

Is there a Gap Between Theory and Practice in Circles of Support and Accountability?

Although, CoSA is widely acknowledged by practitioners and experts, they point out that its evidence base is still understudied (Clarke et al., 2017; Uzieblo et al., 2018). The scientific rigour that academics and policymakers want in effectiveness research, for instance the use of Randomised Control Trials (RCTs), is difficult to achieve for COSA providers. The only RCT to date has been carried out in the US (Duwe, 2013, 2018), and a few other studies used matched comparison groups (see Richards et al., 2020, for a more in-depth discussion of this), all of which reflect the overall finding that CoSA works to reduce reoffending compared to doing nothing additional with this population. Most CoSA projects are small scale and have not enough circles to achieve sufficient statistical power in effectiveness research, which means that they often rely on case studies, qualitive research, and descriptive analysis (Richards et al., 2020). The fact that CoSA is parallel to and additional to a variety of professional services (i.e., police and probation) also makes it difficult to identify the unique contribution of COSA to any outcome.

Finally, there is a gap between CoSA theory and research practice regarding the question: What outcome is meaningful and to whom? This question stems from the difference between a utilitarian approach to the management of people convicted of a sexual offence and a more value-driven one (Höing, 2015).

A utilitarian approach, which is mainly taken by statutory agencies: The main goal is effective prevention of further offences and, ultimately, the safeguarding of the community from further risk, which can include, but is not limited to, incapacitation, risk management legislation, and/or treatment. While the main drive is reducing reoffending, there is a recognition that desistance is a journey and that a reduction in offending behaviour is gradual and takes time.

A value-driven approach, which is often taken by community initiatives, which root in the restorative justice movement: The main goal is justice. Justice expresses and reinforces shared values of the community resulting in a moral balance and community cohesiveness, which can include, but is not limited to, retributive sanctioning and/or restorative justice.

CoSA was developed in Canada to be a value-driven approach to a utilitarian problem. However, CoSA is a blend of the two, realised in the overarching principles of 'no more victims' and 'no one is disposable', the latter expressing the importance of community involvement and community cohesion. Outcome in terms of recidivism rates and their psychosocial determinants have been studied by forensic scientists, and show positive results (Clarke et al., 2017). However, reduction of recidivism is not the only goal; the second principle 'no one is disposable' highlights the broader social imperative of CoSA, which is aiming for a society in which both victim and offender needs are acknowledged, met, and reconciled, and, by doing so, a more cohesive and resilient community is the result. CoSA contributions to community cohesion are rarely studied, but this is an important area for future research and development. This requires a more sociological or even ethnographic approach.

How Circles of Support and Accountability Should Move Forward in Future

Traditionally, criminal justice responses to offending behaviour are reactive and punitive, with severe consequences for the person convicted of a sexual offence which are at times overly punitive compared to other offences (i.e., violence, fraud, and gang activity). Governments, policymakers, and the public frame their responses to sexual offending in an increasingly punitive way, with the individual clearly seen to be punished, and as a consequence this can act as a deterrent to others and signal justice for victims. However, the criminal justice landscape is dynamic, and over the 25 years that CoSA has existed for, it has shifted, sometimes for the better (i.e., adaptions in treatment, improvements in risk management) and sometimes for the worse (i.e.,. sex offender registers, public disclosure); CoSA is at a theory, practice, and policy crossroads. The approach has an evidence base that needs expanding in terms of rigour, a theoretical underpinning that needs refining, and a clear route into local and national policy development. CoSA needs to develop an overarching narrative that acknowledges both the rationality of effective prevention and the moral nature of community needs. Such a narrative should be informed by research into reduction of individual recidivism of core members as well as research into the broader impact on the local community, such as upskilling public knowledge on sexual abuse, an understanding of the role of community integration, as well as improvements in safeguarding.

Theory and Policy Adaption

The main theoretical underpinnings, language, and rationale of CoSA have not changed in its 25-year existence, but there has been some expansion of the model (see below). The criminal justice field has become more multi–disciplinary in nature over the last 25 years with a greater emphasis on the individual's journey to, though, and away from offending. The biggest shifts in criminological thinking in general, and sexual offending specifically, have seen the incorporation of desistance theory, the use of person first language, the recognition of the impact of past trauma in the lives of people who commit offences, and a growing recognition that a holistic approach to rehabilitation is needed (McCartan, 2020). Although, these changes have occurred most strongly at a policy and academic level, while practice is catching up in terms of thinking, if not application. A health–social justice narrative is emerging amongst professionals and policymakers internationally, but it's important to recognise that this is a bit of a 'postcode lottery' with different countries and regions at different stages in this journey of recognition. This growing recognition that health–social justice is needed in order to reduce reoffending, we need to work with the individual in a co-ordinated way that responds to their social, health, wellbeing, and psychological needs. All which CoSA does, but it needs to synchronise its language with that of current policy and practice.

Practice Adaption

Since the first CoSA in 1994 in Canada, the model was implemented internationally with the trend to keep the core CoSA model for people who have been convicted of a sexual offence but to broaden its application to different groups within this cohort (i.e., adolescents, people with learning difficulties, people who have downloaded Child Sexual Abuse Material) (Richards et al., 2020). Adaptations to the CoSA model have primarily been driven by professional and community responses to specific Core Member needs, but also by funding issues. The CoSA model is premised on collaboration with statutory agencies and has traditionally been funded (at least in part and initially) through government funding in many of the countries where CoSA exists. However, this funding has been unpredictable in recent years which also contributed to the development of pragmatic adaptations to the model to enable CoSA Providers to access additional funding streams as most funders want to temporarily support innovation rather than provide structural funding for business as usual. The following are examples of recent adaptations:

- **Prison-based Circles**: Prison-based Circles were developed and implemented in Minnesota, USA, in 2008 (Duwe, 2013). The circle starts with the Core Member while they are still in prison, a few weeks prior to release, and then the provision continues with them as they transition into the community. In the UK, this approach was first adopted by HMP Whatton in 2014, and since then was rolled out to a few other prisons in the UK.
- **Youth circles**: A CoSA programme was implemented in the UK in 2018 for Young People who have been convicted for a sexual offence. The programme follows the CoSA methodology but in addition takes

a safeguarding and trauma informed approach to meet the specific needs of children (Circles UK, 2018).

As CoSA is a form of reintegrative shaming (i.e., using public shaming in a positive way to enable prosocial reintegration) (Braithwaite, 1989), it means that the model has the possibility of being adapted, beyond the remit of only working with people convicted of a sexual offence, to other populations.

In Vermont, USA, CoSA is used for a range of other high-risk offenders, not only people with convictions for sexual offending, including people convicted of violent offences (Fox, 2017).

- As part of the Transforming Care programme, one Circles provider is piloting whether the CoSA approach can be used to support people (mostly female) who have had lengthy stays in a secure hospital facility and who have been assessed as posing a risk of harm to others and self.
- A CoSA programme for lower-risk people who have accessed Child Sexual Exploitation Material, called Circles Reboot, has also been implemented. This is the first time in the UK that the CoSA methodology is being used for lower-risk people.

Adaptations of the CoSA model are positive developments and suggest that CoSA may offer benefits beyond its original conceptualisation. However, it is important that any adaptation continues to uphold the principles, aims and integrity of the model and is fully evaluated, so that the original CoSA model can continue and be upheld in the face of innovation.

A European Vision for Circles of Support and Accountability

CoSA provision in Europe started in the UK through an adaptation of the Canadian CoSA model in 2001 (Hanvey et al., 2011). This led to a growing interest in CoSA in other European countries and informed discussions between the UK, the Netherlands, and Belgium, which resulted in a joint application for a grant from the Daphne III programme of the European Commission to support the international implementation of CoSA throughout Europe. This grant co-financed the introduction of CoSA in Belgium, some pilot Circles in the Netherlands, and the further development of Circles standards into a European Handbook. The project success led to a second EU-funded project (Circles4EU), which aimed at the further dissemination of CoSA throughout Europe. Three project partners initiated a CoSA pilot (in Catalonia, Latvia, and Bulgaria), and three partners prepared to adopt CoSA in France, Ireland, and Hungary. The European Handbook was updated (Höing et al., 2015). When the project ended, CoSA provision was continued and sustained in most countries but funding became increasingly difficult. There was also no funding to continue the Circles4EU collaboration.

In late 2017, discussions focused on the need to build on the positive foundation that was established through the Circles4EU project. A group from the UK, the Netherlands, Belgium, and Catalonia was tasked to explore the possibility of creating an overarching association that would support European CoSA providers and promote CoSA as a successful response to reducing sexual reoffending throughout Europe. As a result, the Circles Europe Association (i.e., CirclesEurope) was set up and formally registered in June 2018 in the Netherlands (www.circleseurope.eu). The association has the following objectives:

- To provide and share guidance with members to enable the development and strengthening of the CoSA model.
- To help other countries set up the CoSA model.
- To protect the intellectual property rights of material developed by Circles Europe members.
- To assist and support research and evaluation of Circles Europe, as well as its members.
- To secure research, evaluation, and implementation funding through the exchange of knowledge and expertise.
- To engage and cooperate with other relevant professional associations and agencies.

Association members from 12 organisations participate in three working groups (research, service development, and governance, quality assurance and membership) to enable country representation and sharing of good practice. Examples of work done by the subgroups include research into the international response of CoSA Providers to the COVID-19 pandemic, devising a self-assessment checklist for Providers against which they can assess the quality of their provision and organising a successful mini-conference to share new developments in CoSA.

Conclusion

The current criminal justice landscape is challenging at the best of times, regardless of Covid-19, with punitive sociopolitical attitudes towards the imprisonment and treatment of people convicted of sexual offences, a problematic media discourse that simultaneously sexualises and demonises sexual abuse, and a limited pool of funding to support research and development in the field. All of this means that although there is support for its effectiveness and a growing interest in CoSA across Europe (and beyond), there are still challenges to its implementation and sustainability. As CoSA moves forward from its current conceptualisation and application, it is important that it takes stock of the changing financial and sociopolitical climate, so that it can effectively immerse itself in the emerging discourses of service user engagement and (risk) management of people with convictions for sexual offences. Therefore, we must ask, is it the role of CoSA to adapt its theory, practice, and policies to fit new societal drivers (i.e., the health–social justice paradigm) or is it more that CoSA needs to reassure that it is fit for purpose and find other ways to raise its current Profile? People who commit sexual abuse come from communities and return to communities, which means that communities must be part of the solution and CoSA enables them to do that.

References

Bitney, K., Drake, E., Grice, J., Hirsch, M. & Lee, S. (2017). *The effectiveness of re-entry programs for incarcerated persons: findings for the Washington Statewide Re-entry Council*. Document Number 17-05-1901. Washington State Institute for Public Policy.

Braithwaite, J. (1989). *Crime. Shame and reintegration*. Cambridge.

Brudney, J. L., & Meijs, L. C. (2009). It ain't natural: Toward a new (natural) resource conceptualization for volunteer management. *Nonprofit and Voluntary Sector Quarterly, 38*(4), 564–581. https://doi.org/10.1177/0899764009333828

Chouinard, J., & Riddick, C. (2015). An evaluation of the Circles of Support and Accountability demonstration project: Final report. Ottawa: Church Council on Justice and Corrections.

Circles, U. K. (2018). *Youth Circles operating model*. Circles UK.

Clarke, M., Brown, S., & Völlm, B. (2017). Circles of support and accountability for sex offenders: A systematic review of outcomes. *Sexual Abuse, 29*(5), 446–478. https://doi.org/10.1177/1079063215603691

Duwe, G. (2013). Can Circles of support and accountability (CoSA) work in the United States? Preliminary results from a randomized experiment in Minnesota. *Sexual Abuse: A Journal of Research and Treatment, 25*(2), 143–165. https://doi.org/10.1177/1079063212453942

Duwe, G. (2018). Can circles of support and accountability (CoSA) significantly reduce sexual recidivism? Results from a randomized controlled trial in Minnesota. *Journal of Experimental Criminology, 14*(4), 463–484. https://doi.org/10.1007/s11292-018-9325-7

Elliott, I. A., & Zajac, G. (2015). The implementation of Circles of support and accountability in the United States. *Aggression and Violent Behavior, 25*, 113–123. https://doi.org/10.1016/j.avb.2015.07.014

Fox, K. J. (2016). Contextualizing the policy and pragmatics of reintegrating sex offenders. *Sexual Abuse: A Journal of Research & Treatment*, 1–23. https://doi.org/10.1177/1079063215574711

Fox, K. J. (2017). Civic commitment: Promoting desistance through community integration. *Punishment & Society, 18*, 68–94. https://doi.org/10.1177/1462474515623102

Gies, L. (2003). Up, close, and personal: The discursive transformation of judicial politics in post-Dutroux Belgium. *International Journal for the Semiotics of Law, 16*(3), 259–284. https://doi.org/10.1023/B:SELA.0000004593.72050.3e

Gilliam, M., Novak, M., Northcutt Bohmert, M., & Duwe, G. (2020). Desires and desirability of volunteers in CoSA programs. *Sexual Abuse*. https://doi.org/10.1177/1079063220912454

Hanvey, S., Philpot, T., & Wilson, C. (2011). *A community based approach to the reduction of sexual reoffending*. Jessica Kingsley.

Harper, C. A., Hogue, T. E., & Bartels, R. M. (2017). Attitudes towards sexual offenders: What do we know, and why are they important? *Aggression and Violent Behavior, 34*, 201–213. https://doi.org/10.1016/j.avb.2017.01.011

Harris, D. A. (2017). *Desistance from sexual offending: Narratives of retirement, regulation, and recovery*. Palgrave Macmillan.

Heley, J., Yarker, S., & Jones, L. (2019). Volunteering in the bath? The rise of microvolunteering and implications for policy. *Policy Studies*, 1–14. https://doi.org/10.1080/01442872.2019.1645324

Höing, M. (2015). *Empowering circles. Circles of support and accountability*. Unpublished dissertation. Tilburg University, School of Behavioural Studies.

Höing, M. (2019). *10 Jaar COSA. Onderzoeksrapportage ten behoeve van het 2e Lustrum* [10 years cosa. Research report for the 2nd lustrum] Reclassering Nederland. Download available via: mechtildhoing.nl/publicaties.

Höing, M., & Alards, A. (2019). Circles of support and accountability. Een social netwerk voor zedendelinquenten. *Justitiele verkenningen, 45*(3), 61–77.

Höing, M., Bogaerts, S., & Vogelvang, B. (2013). Circles of support and accountability: How and why they work for sex offenders. *Journal of Forensic Psychology Practice, 13*(4), 267–295. https://doi.org/10.1080/15228932.2013.808526

Höing, M., Hare Duke, L., & Völlm, B. (2015). *European handbook. Circles4EU*. Avans University of Applied Sciences. Center for Public Safety and Criminal Justice.

Höing, M. A., Petrina, R., Hare Duke, L., Völlm, B., & Vogelvang, B. (2016). Community support for sex offender rehabilitation in Europe. *European Journal of Criminology, 13*(4), 491–516. https://doi.org/10.1177/1477370816633259

Lowe, G., & Willis, G. (2019). Looking inside a circle: Volunteer experiences of circles of support and accountability. *Psychiatry, Psychology and Law, 26*(1), 129–149. https://doi.org/10.1080/13218719.2018.1485521

McCartan, K., & Kemshall, H. (2020). The potential role of recovery capital in stopping sexual offending: Lessons from Circles of support and accountability to enrich practice. *Irish Probation Journal.*

McCartan, K. F. (2016). *Circles of support and accountability: Cabinet office—Social action fund evaluation: Final report.* http://eprints.uwe.ac.uk/28279/7/CoSA%20Social%20Action%20Fund%20-%20Full%20version%20final.pdf

McCartan, K. F. (2020). *Trauma-informed practice.* HM Inspectorate of Probation. Academic Insights 2020/05.

Mews, A., Di Bella, L., & Purver, M. (2017). *Impact evaluation of the prison-based core sex offender treatment programme.* Ministry of Justice Analytical Series.

Pickett, J. T., Mancini, C., & Mears, D. P. (2013). Vulnerable victims, monstrous offenders, and unmanageable risk: Explaining public opinion on the social control of sex crime. *Criminology, Criminal Justice, Law & Society, 51*(3), 729–759. https://doi.org/10.1111/1745-9125.12018

Richards, K., Death, J., & McCartan, K. (2020). *Community-based approaches to sexual offender reintegration.* ANROWS.

Richards, K., & McCartan, K. (2018). Public views about reintegrating child sex offenders via Circles of support and accountability (CoSA): A qualitative analysis. *Deviant Behavior: An Interdisciplinary Journal, 39*(3), 400–416. https://doi.org/10.1080/01639625.2017.1304800

Simon, J. (1998). Managing the monstrous: Sex offenders and the new penology. *Psychology, Public Policy, and Law, 4*(1–2), 452. https://doi.org/10.1037/1076-8971.4.1-2.452

Uzieblo, K., Merckx, L., & Vertommen, T. (2018). What lessons can Belgium learn from a quarter century of Circles of support and accountability (CoSA)? A reflection on the effectiveness and the underlying principles of CoSA. *Panopticon, 39*(6), 489–506.

Van den Berg, J., Smid, W., Kossakowski, J., Borsboom, D., Janssen, E., & Gijs, L. (2020). The application of network analysis to dynamic risk factors in adult male sex offenders. *Clinical Psychological Science, 8*(3), 539–554. https://doi.org/10.1177/2167702620901720

Williams, M. (2019). The Sex Offender Reintegration Crisis. Viewpoints Radio. Accessed on 29-09-2021 via https://viewpointsradio.org/the-sex-offender-reintegration-crisis/.

Wilson, R. J., Sandler, J. C., & McCartan, K. (2020). Community dynamic risk management of persons who have sexually offended. In J. Proulx, F. Cortoni, L. A. Craig, & E. J. Letourneau (Eds.), *The Wiley handbook on what works with sexual offenders: Contemporary perspectives in theory, assessment, treatment and prevention* (pp. 247–263). Wiley. Chapter 14.

15

Desistance Narratives in Men Who Have Committed Sexual Offences

Lucile de Kruijff and Arjan Blokland

Contrary to popular perceptions, desistance from sexual offences is common and most individuals who commit sexual offences stop doing so at one point or another (Jennings et al., 2015). Understanding the reasons and processes by which they do so may provide valuable insights that can be used to aid others in reaching this goal, and help reduce future sexual victimization. This chapter will take a narrative approach and review theory and research that views desistance as resulting from agentic actions that are linked to fundamental changes in self-perception.

We have no known conflict of interest to disclose.

L. de Kruijff
NSCR, Amsterdam, Netherlands
e-mail: ldekruijff@redcross.nl

A. Blokland (✉)
Leiden University, Leiden, Netherlands

Aalborg University, Aalborg, Denmark
e-mail: ablokland@nscr.nl

© The Author(s), under exclusive license to Springer Nature Switzerland AG 2022

K. Uzieblo et al. (eds.), *Challenges in the Management of People Convicted of a Sexual Offence*, Palgrave Studies in Risk, Crime and Society,
https://doi.org/10.1007/978-3-030-80212-7_15

Desistance from crime is commonly understood as the causal process of ending a period of criminal involvement resulting in a continued state of non-offending (Farral & Calverley, 2006). Those seeking to explain desistance from commonplace crime, like burglary, violence, and drug dealing, argue that desistance primarily occurs in reaction to transitions to conventional adult roles, and the daily obligations, societal expectations and changes in routine activities and associations that come with them (Laub & Sampson, 2003). Stable employment, a good marriage, and becoming a parent are said to function as 'turning points', markedly altering the course of the offender's criminal trajectory, and contributing to the initiation and maintenance of a crime-free life.

This approach however is increasingly criticized for not adequately explaining why such transitions would even happen to those criminally involved—how does one acquire stable employment if one is not seeking a job?—and when they do, why active offenders would be interested in pursuing these conventional roles and be susceptible to the controlling forces inherent to them (Paternoster & Bachman, 2017). In response, desistance theories stressing *human agency* have been put forth (Giordano et al., 2002; Maruna, 2001; Paternoster & Bushway, 2009). Though a notably fuzzy concept, agency is commonly understood as the human capacity to choose and to act upon these choices (Emirbayer & Mische, 1998). Rather than being a passive recipient of whatever events and transitions take place in their lives, agentic theories of desistance argue that individuals actively engage with their social environment, both in choosing their response to a given transition and by intentionally pursuing some transitions rather than others.

As people identify themselves and others by their choices and behaviours, agentic action is closely tied to the individuals' identity and self-perception (Korsgaard, 2009). Agency theories of desistance have indeed emphasized past, present, and future perceptions of the self as drivers of agentic action (Giordano et al., 2002; Paternoster & Bushway, 2009). They have also highlighted the narratives by which these perceptions are integrated in a single coherent identity relating actors to their actions

(Maruna, 2001). Narrative identity refers to the internalized and continuously developing story of the self that individuals construct to make sense and meaning out of their life (McAdams, 2018). The individuals' life story integrates a selective reconstruction of the past with weighted anticipations of imagined futures, to explain to the self and others who the person is, how he or she came to be, and where his or her life might be going (McAdams, 2011). Smaller stories involving the self as an employee, as a father, or as an (ex)offender, feed into the overarching life narrative that defines the person. To construct their life narrative, individuals make use of the cultural scripts or storylines that are available to them to imbue meaning to their experiences and actions (McLean & Syed, 2016).

Current State of Affairs

Theory

Rather than focusing on the individual's reaction to life course transitions, Giordano et al. (2002, 2007) propose a desistance theory that focuses on the 'up front' work performed by the individuals themselves. Their *cognitive transformation theory* states that for the process of desistance to take hold, the individual first needs to be open to change and willing to engage with their environment in ways that would support and sustain a crime-free life. To induce desistance, individuals need to start envisioning what Giordano and colleagues call a 'replacement self', a more or less concrete image of their future conventional self to provide a goal and purpose to their agency. Rather than 'turning points', life course transitions are seen as providing 'hooks for change' that the individual may use as launching pads for 'agentic moves' toward desistance. The desistance process is said to reach completion when the individual begins to see offending behaviour as out of keeping with their newly acquired identity.

In their *identity theory of desistance*, Paternoster and colleagues (Paternoster & Bushway, 2009; Paternoster et al., 2015) argue that, more so than by what is desired, agentic choice in desistance is influenced by what the individual seeks to avoid. Fear of what one might become can be a powerful motivator for change. Especially when individuals face hurdles, hopes of a better life may quickly fade, whereas fears of detrimental outcomes become even more real. The identity theory of desistance furthermore argues that individuals become more susceptible for behavioural change when they grow increasingly discontent with their current behaviour due to continued lack of success or mounting negative experiences. Especially, hitting 'rock bottom', going through an intensely negative experience that elevates the feared future from a mere possibility to a sure outcome, may prompt individuals to initiate the desistance process. Life course transitions are seen as neither necessary nor sufficient to maintain a crime-free life but may be part of the road map to increase the divergence of the present with the feared future self.

Finally, the focus of the theory suggested by Maruna (2001) is on bridging the gap between the past and the present. Offenders willing to desist cannot simply knife off their past and pretend it didn't happen (Maruna & Roy, 2007). Instead, they need a convincing storyline to explain to themselves and others why they behaved the way they did, and also why ending their criminal involvement is not 'out of character' for them. To do so, individuals make use of cultural scripts—socially accepted storylines that offer individuals the opportunity to narrate their desistance—while at the same time maintain continuity in their self-narrative. In much of the Western world, this script is one of *redemption* in which past behaviour is attributed to external circumstances clouding the 'real self', but in which the individual—often with the help of an outside force—is able to overcome these circumstances and begin to act in ways that are in line with who that person really is. Ex-offenders may even 'make good out of the bad' and find purpose in their past transgressions, as they put them in a position better able to help others and make amends for their earlier wrongdoings.

Despite their differences, the desistance theories of Giordano, Paternoster, and Maruna can be reconciled by viewing agentic choice as simultaneously driven by imagined futures—both desired and feared—as well as informed by past experiences (Emirbayer & Mische, 1998). Sculpting a viable replacement self-entails constructing a narrative putting this future within reach of the present self. This narrative, in turn, can only be persuasive when it connects to past behaviours in ways that grant the individual a convincing level of temporal integrity.

Research

Three dimensions of doing desistance work are commonly identified. *Act desistance* entails the behavioural change from offending to non-offending (Maruna & Farral, 2004; Nugent & Schinkel, 2016). As act desistance does not change the way individuals view their past behaviour, the risk of relapse remains high and permanent change is unlikely. *Identity desistance* refers to the shift in identity needed to render a particular offending behaviour incompatible with the present self (Maruna & Farral, 2004; Nugent & Schinkel, 2016). The enactment of conventional roles can serve as hooks for change and aid in the realization of the replacement self (Healy, 2014). Identity desistance can scaffold a continued state of non-offending as it stops the individual from seeing offending as a behavioural option, even when opportunity presents itself. Finally, *relational desistance* refers to others starting to accept and interact with the individual based on the individual's changed or changing identity (McNeil, 2016). Relational desistance is pivotal for individuals to be able to fully express their desired identity and distance themselves from feared outcomes. Both identity desistance and relational desistance are facilitated by self-narratives that follow culturally accepted storylines. Whereas identity desistance is primarily about convincing one's self and others that change is possible and attainable, relational desistance is about encouraging others to act accordingly.

Only a small body of literature has focused on the desistance narratives of men convicted of sexual offences. The characteristics of these studies, as well as their main findings are summarized in Table 15.1. While these studies differ in the points highlighted, the contours of some more general conclusions are slowly becoming apparent.

Whereas some studies report narratives that involve reconciling past behaviour with present self-perceptions—for example, Harris' (2017) 'recovered' men, and the men interviewed by Richards et al. (2020)—the

Table 15.1 Overview of studies on desistance narratives of men convicted of sexual offenses

Publications	Sample size	Sample type	Main findings
Harris (2014, 2016, 2017)	73	Men convicted of sexual offenses (64% recruited via outpatient sex offender treatment programme; 36% referred for civil commitment and released between 1976 and 1991. Of all men, 81% had child victims.	*Recovered* men (30%) successfully reconstructed their identity and had begun to rebuild their lives. *Retired* men (21%) distinguished their old and their new self based on psychological maturation. *Regulated* men (49%) refrained from reoffending mostly out of fear of its consequences.
Farmer et al. (2015, 2016), McAlinden et al. (2017)	32	Men convicted of a sexual offense against a child victim (78% whose last conviction for a sexual offense was over 5 years ago, and 22% whose last conviction was within 12 months preceding the interview).	*Desisting* men (78%), whose last conviction was over 5 years ago, emphasized situational aspects and voiced future directed agency. Conventional roles offered hooks for change. The narratives of the comparison men (22%) generally lacked agency and direction.
Kras (2014, 2019), Kras and Blasko (2016)	28	Men convicted of a sexual offense, of which 64% had child victims, and were released back in the community for 3 years	*Desisters* (no reoffending) (18%) emphasized external factors and situations. *General persisters* (non-sexual reoffense) (25%) likewise attempted to negotiate the sex offender stigma. *Sexual persisters* (reimprisonment for sexual condition violation) (57%) voiced acceptance of their sexual deviance as an integral part of their self-narrative.

(*continued*)

Table 15.1 (continued)

Publications	Sample size	Sample type	Main findings
De Kruijff and Berckmoes (2018), De Kruijff et al. (in preparation)	25	Men convicted of a sexual offense against a child victim, who had been released back in the community for a period of 7 months to 8 years.	Agency was directed at behavioural rather than identity change. Relinquishing control served to regain trust and societal integration.
Victor (2014), Victor and Waldram (2015)	18	Men convicted of a sexual offense, of whom 61% participated in a COSA programme.	Narratives reflect different stages in self-appraisal, moving from shame and confusion, through growth and self-improvement, to self-acceptance.
Hulley (2016a, 2016b, 2017)	15	Men convicted for a sexual offense against a child victim, who had been released back in the community for a period of 1 to 15 years	*Substantive desisters* (67%) were able to reconstruct their identity and rebuild their lives. *Formal desisters* (33%) lacked identity change but nevertheless refrained from reoffending.
Richards et al. (2020)	11	Men convicted of a serious sexual offense—that is, a violent sexual offense or a sexual offense with a child victim—who participated in a Cultural Mentoring Programme	Narratives generally followed a redemption script and voiced future directed agency and generativity.

desistance narrative of most of the men interviewed in these studies does not seem to follow a redemption script. The redemption script implies a discrepancy between the individual's past, criminal self, and the individual's present, conventional self that then needs to be overcome. Most men interviewed however rejected the sexual offender label, wholly or at least partly, acquitting them of the need for a convincing story to explain any identity change. Instead, many men emphasized situational aspects that led to them committing their offence and stressed that their offending was best understood as an aberration rather than a proof of character (Farmer et al., 2015; Kras & Blasko, 2016).

Instead of redemption, the narratives of many men convicted of sexual offences appear to be best characterized by a lack of identity work, and their agency directed at behavioural change rather than at attaining a desired future self—for example, Harris' (2017) 'regulated' men and Hulley's (2016a) 'formal desisters'. These men abided the restrictions imposed upon them, or at least held up the appearance of doing so, based on the perceived negative consequences of continued offending. Rather than identity desistance, these men thus displayed act desistance only. Still, despite only showing act desistance, some had been in the community—and were presumably crime-free—for prolonged periods of time (De Kruijff & Berckmoes, 2018; Hulley 2016a).

A desire for relational desistance did figure in the desistance narrative of many men convicted of sexual offences. Regaining employment and restoring or forging relationships were key to many in rebuilding their life upon release from custody and reclaim a sense of purpose in life (Farmer et al., 2015). While denouncing the sex offender label, the interviewed men also seemed to be aware that they somehow had to win back the trust of others to reclaim their place in society. To signal their trustworthiness, they invoked self-raised barriers—like actively avoiding opportunities for offending or creating tangible reminders of the pains of imprisonment or the lessons learned during therapy—or offered others a chance to co-supervise their behaviour (De Kruijff & Berckmoes, 2018; Hulley, 2016a). Hence, though their agency was primarily directed towards act desistance, their narrative also seemed to seek relational desistance, without (the need for) identity desistance.

Treatment and Supervision

Findings on the role of therapy and supervision in the above-mentioned studies on desistance from sexual offending are mixed. Some men reported the usefulness of the techniques and skills they learned during therapy in monitoring their own actions and desires and maintaining crime-free (Farmer et al., 2015), especially when therapy focused on the individual's behaviour rather than on the individual himself (De Kruijff & Berckmoes, 2018). Others however, resented the routines and obligations that defined their surveilled existence and struggled with the 'risk narrative' that was handed to them (Harris, 2017). The latter felt that treatment providers were encouraging them to internalize the sex offender label and were cautious to give the 'right' answers during treatment interactions, such as not to negatively affect the treatment provider's risk assessment (Hulley, 2016b).

The role of supervision, if mentioned at all, seemed to depend heavily on how the relationship with the probation officer was experienced (Hulley, 2016b). Those who had received practical assistance in their efforts to actualize their desired conventional life, like housing or employment, spoke most positive about their probation officer. Those who experienced monitoring rather than assistance were more negative about their supervision. Adding to the complexity of the association between supervision and relapse however, Kras (2019) finds that men who reflected positively on their relationship with their parole officer were more instead of less likely to recidivate than those who described this relation in more negative terms. It could be that men evaluating the relation with their parole officer more positively were consequently more likely to disclose any subsequent transgressions. This finding may however also be illustrative of the tight rope supervisors must walk when exercising their discretionary powers between gaining trust by being lenient and straining the client–practitioner relationship by being strict.

Policy

All interviewees experienced drastic consequences of their offending. Especially for men with no prior criminal justice contacts, imprisonment is experienced as a low point in their lives, and a powerful deterrent for future offending (Hulley, 2016a). Those who sexually victimized children rank low in the prison hierarchy, and many men report feeling unsafe during their detention. Procedures that render their offence history public knowledge within the prison community not only evoke feelings of unsafety but also limit men's ability to distance themselves from the sex offender label and as such interfere with the conditions their desistance journey seems to require. Similarly, policies that in effect continuously remind both these men and their social surroundings of their sex offender status—like publicly accessible sex offender registries—may complicate their return to a conventional life and as such unintendedly hinder their desistance.

Many men who were interviewed also report difficulties in obtaining salaried employment following their conviction, especially in jurisdictions where disclosure of criminal records is commonplace. This is experienced as frustrating, especially by those that held paid jobs prior to their arrest. Based on the available studies however, there seems no clear association between unemployment and sexual recidivism. While some men appear to accept that they will never find paid work again, others seem to compensate their loss of formal employment by various types of self-employment or take up ancillary activities that help them uphold their self-image as active individuals (Farmer et al., 2015).

What is Needed and Why?

Theory

Central to agency theories of desistance is the individual's shift in identity from criminal to conventional. These theories implicitly assume that at one point offending is so central to the individual's life that it comes to define the person, and that desistance therefore requires more than just discontinued behaviour. For men committing sexual offences, and especially for those victimizing children, this seems very different. The 'sex offender' status became their master status only after they were arrested. Many men subsequently reject the sex offender label, and reasons for doing so appear both actual and functional. Actual, because many of those interviewed appeared not to be enmeshed in blatantly criminal lifestyles. They reported stable employment prior to their arrest—some even held esteemed societal positions and were clergymen or high-ranked military officers—and had friends and families that respected and trusted them (De Kruijff & Berckmoes, 2018; Harris, 2015; Hulley, 2016a). In fact, their positions of trust often facilitated the settings in which the abuse could take place (Farmer et al., 2015). Rather than a fundamental shift in identity, these men seem to experience the stigma they are confronted with as a temporary and exogenous interruption of their otherwise stable and conventional self-image. More so than building a replacement self, these men's agentic moves seem to reflect efforts at rebuilding their 'ordinary life' in the new context of being labeled a 'sex offender'. As such, their narratives question the central position identity desistance takes in desistance theories emphasizing agency.

Rejection of the sex offender identity may also be functional given the evocative power and strong negative associations presently attached to that label. By fully embracing the sex offender identity, these men would risk creating a gap between them and society that is simply too broad to bridge with the cultural scripts presently available (De Kruijff & Berckmoes, 2018). Societal sentiments towards men sexually victimizing children gravitate towards exclusion rather than inclusion. Denouncing the sex offender label may function to keep this 'othering' within limits, such as to leave relational desistance open as a viable option.

The men interviewed subsequently vary in the ways they chose to deal with the consequences of being labelled in their daily lives and in the ways this label impacts their desistance. Some may not feel the need to re-establish personal relationships and social bonds, either because they had few to begin with or because these conventional ties endured the period of turmoil following their arrest. These men may simply decide to refrain from future offending in light of the direct costs associated with repeated arrest and imprisonment. Others who did experience the severance of ties may seek to restore what they once had. Still others might withdraw from society altogether and show strategies signalling resigned helplessness. They seem to see their feared future no longer as something that can be avoided, but rather as something that has already materialized. Somewhat surprisingly, all these strategies seem to be able to support prolonged periods of non-offending. Extant theories of desistance which emphasize 'up front work' and changes in narrated identity, therefore, seem to fall short of providing a full explanation of the desistance process of men convicted of sexual offences.

Research

The empirical foundation on which the desistance from sexual offending literature rests is still narrow, and studies share a number of limitations.

First, the vast majority of interviewees are middle-aged men convicted of sexually victimizing a child, limiting the generalizability of the findings. Often, this was due to selective sample attrition. Unwillingness of young men and men victimizing adults to participate in the studies limits the representativeness of the extant findings. Sexual offences against adults, for instance, are more often part of a broader criminal repertoire than are sexual offences against children. To the extent that individuals sexually victimizing adults are more enmeshed in an antisocial lifestyle than are those victimizing children (Lussier et al., 2005; but see, Spaan et al., 2020), their desistance narratives might resemble those found in the general offending population more closely. Though less prevalent in forensic populations than men, women convicted of sexual offences might employ different narrative strategies and scripts to narrate their desistance journey, also warranting future research.

Second, most interviewed men had gone through extensive therapy. Possibly, some of the men keeping up appearances by simply regurgitating the narrative handed to them during therapy, rather than providing an authentic account of their desistance journey (Hudson, 2005). For others however, therapy may have genuinely provided the narrative needed to reconcile the past with the present and enable desistance. Researchers have addressed this issue by probing interviewees on the authenticity of their narrative and by taking into account nonverbal cues that might signal recitation rather than lived experience (De Kruijff & Berkmoes, 2018). Future research might seek to compare the narratives of those who received therapy with those who did not.

Finally, all extant studies are cross-sectional and retrospective in nature, asking interviewees about their desistance during just one occasion and 'after the fact'. To the extent that the self is best understood as a continuous work in progress, longitudinal, prospective studies are crucial to capture the dynamics of desistance (Farral et al., 2014). Those studies comparing men at different intervals after their last known sexual offence indeed suggest that the desistance narratives of men convicted of sexual offences change over time (Farmer et al., 2015; Victor, 2014).

Treatment and Supervision

Act, identity, and relational desistance likely reflect different dimensions of the desistance process, rather than subsequent steps (Nugent & Schinkel, 2016). Therapy should therefore aim to simultaneously attend to all three, rather than withhold attention for relational desistance until all criteria of identity desistance are met. The trust that is an essential element of conventional social ties may make individuals feel empowered and able to retake control of their own destiny. Subsequently meeting the obligations and expectations that come with these conventional ties will not only help (re)shape and consolidate these men's conventional self but will also act as signals of trustworthiness to their social environment. When the offender's social environment is unavailable, unwilling, or unable to provide for social ties, institutionalized ties, like Circles of Support and Accountability, may provide for an effective alternative.

Policy

The absence of a rigorous comparison of the long-term success of identity desistance versus mere act desistance precludes making concrete policy recommendations at this point. Some have warned that strict sex offender policies may serve to widen the gap between 'us' and 'them', and as such knife off opportunities for those convicted of sexual offences to reconcile their criminal past and conventional present self (Maruna, 2018). On the other hand, many men convicted of sexual offences appear to be deterred by these same strict measures and consciously choose to avoid the consequential damages of reoffending. To the extent that relational desistance facilitates continued abstinence from sexual offending—either with or without identity desistance—policymakers may however be advised to seek to facilitate the social reintegration of men convicted of sexual offences. One simple way to do so would be to provide the public with factual information about sex offender recidivism to outweigh public prejudice based on ill-informed folk wisdom on the dangerousness and criminal persistence of men who committed a sexual offence (Harris, 2017).

Conclusion

Desistance narratives of men convicted of sexual offences against children were found to orbit around act desistance and relational desistance more so than around identity desistance. Men's narratives tend to emphasize their conscious decision to refrain from future sexual offending as well as a desire for social inclusion. In the absence of accepted cultural scripts bridging the gap between the past and current self, identification as a sex offender, even in the past, is typically avoided (De Kruijff & Berckmoes, 2018). Denial of the sex offender label may serve as a productive stigma management strategy, rather than be the product of distorted cognitions (Waldram, 2010), especially during the first stages of desistance. Treatment efforts could benefit by aiming at increasing men's responsibility for their future behaviours, rather than for their past transgressions (Farmer et al., 2016; Maruna & Mann, 2006). Informing the public about the empirical realities of (relatively low) sexual recidivism may provide the foundation for a societal discourse that provides narrative scripts through which relational desistance of men convicted of sexual offences can be realized and future victimization can be avoided.

References

De Kruijff, L. & Berckmoes, L. (2018). Narratieven van mannen veroordeeld voor zedenmisdrijven tegen minderjarigen in België. Panopticon, 39, 5, 435–454.

De Kruijff, L., Hendriks, J. & Blokland, A. (in preparation) Desistance narratives of Belgian men convicted of sexual offenses against children: a behavioral script.

Emirbayer, M., & Mische, A. (1998). What is agency? *American Journal of Sociology, 103*(4), 962–1023. https://doi.org/10.1086/231294

Farmer, M., McAllinden, A.-M., & Maruna, S. (2015). Understanding desistance from sexual offending: A thematic review of research findings. *Probation Journal, 62*(4), 320–335. https://doi.org/10.1177/0264550515600545

Farmer, M., McAllinden, A.-M., & Maruna, S. (2016). Sex offending and situational motivation: Findings from a qualitative analysis of desistance from sexual offending. *International Journal of Offender Therapy and Comparative Criminology, 60*(15), 1756–1775. https://doi.org/10.1177/0306624X16668175

Farral, S., & Calverley, A. (2006). *Understanding desistance from crime. Theoretical Directions in resettlement and rehabilitation*. Open University Press.

Farral, S., Hunter, B., Sharpe, G., & Calverley, A. (2014). *Criminal careers in transition. The social context of desistance from crime*. Oxford University Press.

Giordano, P. C., Cernkovich, S. A., & Rudolph, J. L. (2002). Gender, crime and desistance: Toward a theory of cognitive transformation. *American Journal of Sociology, 107*(4), 990–1164. https://doi.org/10.1086/343191

Giordano, P. C., Schroeder, R. D., & Cernkovich, S. A. (2007). Emotions and crime over the life-course: A neo-Median perspective on continuity and change. *American Journal of Sociology, 112*(6), 1603–1661. https://doi.org/10.1086/512710

Harris, D. A. (2014). Desistance from sexual offending: Findings from 21 life history narratives. *Journal of Interpersonal Violence, 29*(9), 1554–1578. https://doi.org/10.1177/0886260513511532

Harris, D. A. (2015). Desistance from sexual offending: Behavioral change *without* cognitive transformation. *Journal of Interpersonal Violence, 32*(20), 3049–3070. https://doi.org/10.1177/0886260515596537

Harris, D. A. (2016). A descriptive model of desistance from sexual offending: Examining the narratives of men released from custody. *International Journal of Offender Therapy and Comparative Criminology, 60*(15), 1717–1737. https://doi.org/10.1177/0306624X16668176

Harris, D. A. (2017). *Desistance from sexual offending. Narratives of retirement, regulation and recovery*. Palgrave Macmillan.

Healy, D. (2014). Becoming a desister: Exploring the role of agency, coping and imagination in the construction of the new self. *British Journal of Criminology, 54*(5), 873–891. https://doi.org/10.1093/bjc/azu048

Hudson, K. (2005). *Offending identities; Sex offenders' perspectives on their treatment and management.* Willan Publishing.

Hulley, J. L. (2016a). *"My history is not my destiny": Exploring Desistance in Adult Male Child Sex Offenders* (Unpublished Doctoral Dissertation). University of Sheffield.

Hulley, J. L. (2016b). "While this does not in any way excuse my conduct …": The role of treatment and neutralizations in desistance from sexual offending. *International Journal of Offender Therapy and Comparative Criminology, 60*(15), 1776–1790. https://doi.org/10.1177/0306624X16668177

Hulley, J. L. (2017). Desistance from sexual offending and risk management. In H. Kemshall & K. McCartan (Eds.), *Contemporary sex offender risk management, Vol. II* (pp. 175–204). Palgrave Macmillan.

Jennings, W. G., Piquero, A. R., Zimring, F. E., & Reingle, J. M. (2015). Assessing the continuity of sex offending over the life course. Evidence from two large birth cohort studies. In A. Blokland & P. Lussier (Eds.), *Sex offenders: A criminal career approach* (pp. 129–142). Wiley Blackwell.

Korsgaard, C. M. (2009). *Self-Constitution. Agency, identity, and integrity.* Oxford University Press.

Kras, K. R. (2014). *Redemption or condemnation? A long-term follow-up of the desistance patterns of sex offenders* (Unpublished Doctoral dissertation). University of Missouri, St. Louis.

Kras, K. R. (2019). Can social support overcome the individual and structural challenges of being a sex offender? Assessing the social support-recidivism link. *International Journal of Offender Therapy and Comparative Criminology, 63*(1), 32–54. https://doi.org/10.1177/0306624X18784191

Kras, K. R., & Blasko, B. L. (2016). Pathways to desistance among men convicted of sexual offenses: Linking post hoc accounts of offending behavior and outcomes. *International Journal of Offender Therapy and Comparative Criminology, 60*(15), 1738–1755. https://doi.org/10.1177/0306624X16668178

Laub, J. H., & Sampson, R. J. (2003). *Shared beginnings, divergent lives: Delinquent boys to age 70.* Harvard University Press.

Lussier, P., LeBlanc, M., & Proulx, J. (2005). The generality of criminal behavior: A confirmatory factor analysis of the criminal activity of sex offenders in adulthood. *Journal of Criminal Justice, 33*(2), 177–189. https://doi.org/10.1016/j.jcrimjus.2004.12.009

Maruna, S. (2001). *Making good. How ex-convicts reform and rebuild their lives*. American Psychological Association.

Maruna, S. (2018). *There are no words: Sex offending and the search for a redemption narrative*. Paper presented at the 2018 annual meeting of the European Society of Criminology, Sarajevo, Bosnia & Herzegovina.

Maruna, S., & Farral, S. (2004). Desistance from crime: A theoretical reformulation. *Kölner Zietschrift für Soziologie und Sozialpsychologie, 43*, 171–194.

Maruna, S., & Mann, R. E. (2006). A fundamental attribution error? Rethinking cognitive distortions. *Legal and Criminal Psychology, 11*(2), 155–177. https://doi.org/10.1348/135532506X114608

Maruna, S., & Roy, K. (2007). Amputation or reconstruction? Notes on the concept of "knifing off" and desistance from crime. *Journal of Contemporary Criminal Justice, 23*(1), 104–124. https://doi.org/10.1177/1043986206298951

McAdams, D. P. (2011). Narrative identity. In S. J. Schwartz, K. Luyckx, & V. L. Vignoles (Eds.), *Handbook of identity theory and research* (pp. 99–115). Springer.

McAdams, D. P. (2018). Narrative identity: What is it? What does it do? How do you measure it? *Imagination, Cognition and Personality: Consciousness in Theory, Research and Clinical Practice, 37*(3), 359–372. https://doi.org/10.1177/0276236618756704

McAllinden, A.-M., Farmer, M., & Maruna, S. (2017). Desistance from sexual offending: Do the mainstream theories apply? *Criminology & Criminal Justice, 17*(3), 266–283. https://doi.org/10.1177/1748895816670201

McLean, K. C., & Syed, M. (2016). Personal, master, and alternative narratives: an integrative framework for understanding identity development in context. *Human Development, 58*(6), 318–349. https://doi.org/10.1159/000445817

McNeil, F. (2016). Desistance and criminal justice in Scotland. In: Croall, H., Mooney, G. & Munro, R. (eds) Crime, Justice and Society in Scotland. London: Routledge, pp. 200–216.

Nugent, B., & Schinkel, M. (2016). The pains of desistance. *Criminology & Criminal Justice, 16*(5), 568–584. https://doi.org/10.1177/1748895816634812

Paternoster, R., & Bachman, R. (2017). Human agency; The missing element in theories of desistance. In A. Blokland & V. van der Geest (Eds.), *The Routledge international handbook of life-course criminology* (pp. 29–42). Routledge.

Paternoster, R., Bachman, R., Bushway, S., Kerrison, E., & O'Connell, D. (2015). Human agency and explanations of criminal desistance: Arguments for a rational choice theory. *Journal of Developmental and Life Course Criminology, 1*(3), 209–235. https://doi.org/10.1007/s40865-015-0013-2

Paternoster, R., & Bushway, S. (2009). Desistance and the feared self: Toward an identity theory of desistance. *Journal of Criminal Law and Criminology, 99*(4), 1103–1156. http://www.jstor.org/stable/20685067

Richards, K., Death, J., & McCartan, K. (2020). Toward redemption: Aboriginal and/or Torres Strait Islander men's narratives of desistance from sexual offending. Victims & Offenders, 15(6), 810–833.

Spaan, P., Blokland, A., De Blander, R., Robert, L., Maes, E., Blom, M., & Wartna, B. (2020). Differentiating individuals convicted of sexual offenses: A two-country latent class analysis. *Sexual Abuse, 32*(4), 423–451. https://doi.org/10.1177/1079063219893370

Victor, J. (2014). *"I'm better now": Sexual Offender Narratives of Moral Habilitation* (Unpublished Doctoral Dissertation). University of Saskatchewan.

Victor, J., & Waldram, J. B. (2015). Moral habilitation and the new normal. In L. Presser & S. Sandberg (Eds.), *Narrative criminology: Understanding stories of crime* (pp. 96–121). New York University Press.

Waldram, J. B. (2010). Moral agency, cognitive distortion, and narrative strategy in the rehabilitation of sexual offenders. *Ethos, 38*, 251–274. https://doi.org/10.1111/j.1548-1352.2010.01144.x

16

Moving Forward in Offender-Oriented Prevention: The Stop It Now! Prevention Project from an International Perspective

Minne De Boeck, Jenny Coleman, Jill Van Dijk, and Donald Findlater

Over recent years, many countries have been rocked by major scandals involving child sexual abuse (CSA) in a variety of organisational, institutional, and other contexts. The Dutroux affair in Belgium, the Robert M. case in the Netherlands, and Jimmy Savile in the United Kingdom, all sparked public outrage. CSA in specific institutions, such as in church, sport, youth movements, and high-profile schools, made the

All authors are employees of the Stop it Now! projects.

M. De Boeck (✉)
Stop it Now!, Flanders, Belgium

University Forensic Centre, University Hospital Antwerp, Edegem, Belgium

Collaborative Antwerp Psychiatric Research Institute (CAPRI), University Antwerp, Antwerpen, Belgium
e-mail: Minne.DeBoeck@uza.be

J. Coleman
Stop it Now!, Northampton, MA, USA

© The Author(s), under exclusive license to Springer Nature Switzerland AG 2022

K. Uzieblo et al. (eds.), *Challenges in the Management of People Convicted of a Sexual Offence*, Palgrave Studies in Risk, Crime and Society,
https://doi.org/10.1007/978-3-030-80212-7_16

indignation even greater. The World Health Organisation (WHO) and the Council of Europe identifies CSA as a priority health problem because of its massive presence. The WHO (2017) estimates that one in five girls (20%) and slightly fewer than one in ten boys (8%) experience sexual harm and/or abuse by the age of 18, and a meta-analysis of 55 studies from 24 countries revealed prevalence rates of 13% for girls and 6% for boys experiencing contact sexual abuse before the age of 18 (Barth et al., 2013). Regarding (online) child sexual exploitation, the International Labour Organisation (2015) estimated that 1.8 million children are victimised worldwide every year. It is widely recognised that many cases go unreported (80–90%) (Tabachnick, 2013) due to a range of factors, including feelings of shame and fear that victims often experience and because young victims are sometimes unaware of the abuse as a result of the offender's grooming process (Assini-Meytin et al., 2020; Lalor & McElvaney, 2010, Maniglio, 2009). Even when reported, only a minority of alleged perpetrators are convicted (Longfield, 2015). Research reveals that many victims of CSA suffer many adverse—and often long-term—physical and psychological consequences, including dissociation, anxiety, and post-traumatic stress disorder (Cutajar et al., 2010; Felitti & Anda, 2009; Hardner et al., 2017). In conclusion, CSA is a major global public health problem with many adverse health consequences resulting in significant personal and economic cost to individuals and to society. For all these reasons, we believe it is time to shift from a criminal justice approach to a public health approach with a larger focus on prevention rather than on response.

Over recent decades, several initiatives to prevent CSA have been designed and implemented; many of these focus on increasing the resistance and resilience of children as potential victims. However, research shows that child victim–oriented prevention (e.g., sex education in schoolgirls) has its limitations and on its own does not appear to actually reduce CSA (Bolen, 2003; Laws & O'Donohue, 2016). In their seminal publication, "Preventing Child Sexual Abuse", Smallbone et al. (2008) argue for a combination of preventive interventions and approaches from

J. Van Dijk
Stop it Now!, Amsterdam, The Netherlands

D. Findlater
Stop it Now!, UK and Ireland, Bromsgrove, UK

different perspectives, thus addressing the diversity of the phenomenon, with offender-oriented prevention as a necessary component. Other scholars also argue the importance of offender-oriented prevention (Assini-Meytin et al., 2020; Butchart et al., 2006; Finkelhor, 2009). Offender-oriented prevention focuses on those who are at risk of offending, to prevent CSA prior to the behaviour, as well as on child abusers to prevent recidivism. This also means that pre-offending behaviours, as for example grooming, are included in these prevention efforts. Some preventive initiatives have already responded to this need, such as the CSA prevention project 'Stop it Now!'. Stop it Now! offers confidential help, support, and advice via a helpline, as well as chat and email service to individuals who have committed CSA or who are at (potential) risk to do so,[1] and sensitises society to the importance of offender-oriented prevention to effectively prevent CSA. In this chapter, we will outline the problem of CSA through literature review and descriptive analysis, describe how CSA can be approached preventatively using a comprehensive framework, and demonstrate how preventive initiatives such as the Stop it Now! projects set up around the world (the United States, the United Kingdom, the Netherlands and Flanders, Belgium) fit in this framework and contribute to such prevention. We will present a case study to illustrate how Stop it Now! Helplines work and how prevention can be achieved and conclude with common challenges to formulate some suggestions to move forward in offender-oriented prevention.

The Prevention of CSA in a Conceptual Framework

CSA as a Public Health Problem

Given the scale, social costs, and significant psychological, physical, and social consequences for the victims, CSA should be seen as a public health problem (Letourneau et al., 2014; McCartan, et al. 2018), requiring a

[1] Although we prefer person-first language, 'perpetrator/potential perpetrator' terminology will be used for efficiency in subsequent paragraphs. In addition, this terminology is used in the framework for the prevention of CSA developed by Smallbone et al. (2008).

public health approach (Butchart et al., 2006). A public health approach focuses not only on the identified possible causes and consequences of a problem at an individual level but also on the causes and consequences of—and for—society more broadly. Consequently, responsibility for tackling the problem is not only held by the individuals involved but also by other actors who may not seem, or may not see themselves, as responsible. Within the public health approach, prevention considers the emergence of a problem and identifies the elements that increase or decrease the likeliness of it occuring. By addressing the general and specific risk and protective factors of the problem, a public health approach seeks to achieve maximum benefit for the maximum number of people. Its concern is for the care and safety of the whole population (Rattray et al., 2002; WHO, 2017). For example, the prevention of heart disease will purposefully target smoking and diet across society as factors relevant to risk, and not only address smokers or people with obesity. A current experience for us all is Covid-19—where in many countries individuals with suspected Covid-19 and individuals with increased health vulnerabilities were required to isolate themselves, whilst at the same time the entire society was required to behave differently (e.g., stay at home, not socialise, and not attend work unless essential), all to avoid the spread of the virus. In similar fashion, the prevention of CSA needs a focus on those individuals who have perpetrated or are at risk to perpetrate CSA, those individuals who have been harmed or are seen to be at elevated risk for harm, and, crucially, on the actions society can take to prevent harm, including creating a healthy social climate with respectful attitudes and views on sexuality and the rights of children (Casey & Lindhorst, 2009; Mian & Collin-Vézina, 2017). This approach to CSA is fundamentally different from a reactive criminal justice approach which, for many years and in many countries, has achieved the main focus as a result of emotional responses and policy resistence for public health interventions with longer-term effects and less measurable objectives (Letourneau et al., 2014).

Towards a Comprehensive Framework for the Prevention of CSA

In their book, "Preventing Child Sexual Abuse", Smallbone et al. (2008) provide a comprehensive framework for target audiences and interventions to deliver a public health approach to CSA as described above. According to this framework, preventive activities are divided into several stages, based on timing and audience. First of all, the primary, secondary, and tertiary prevention level are split up in this framework. Although their definitions often differ in literature, in this chapter we use, as Smallbone and colleagues, the understanding that: (1) *primary prevention* is aimed at the *general population* (including subsets of that population) with the purpose of preventing CSA *before* it occurs; (2) *secondary prevention* also aims to prevent abuse *before* it takes place, but focuses on specific groups *at risk*, such as people with deviant sexual interests or children who are regarded as being at risk of abuse (e.g. vulnerable family situation, lack of general and mental health support, and increased personal stressors such as economic insecurity); (3) *tertiary prevention* takes place *after* the abuse occurs and is aimed at preventing further CSA by focusing on targetted individuals (Knack et al., 2019; Smallbone et al., 2008). In many countries, there is disproportionate attention to tertiary prevention of CSA, with primary and secondary prevention receiving insufficient attention. Additionally, current prevention initiatives often focus only on the individual level, rather than on the wider socio-ecological context of those directly involved within relationships, communities, and wider society (Brown, 2005; Seto, 2012; Tabachnick, 2013). To meet this need, the prevention framework of Smallbone and colleagues also emphasises different orientation targets for each prevention level: (1) offender-oriented prevention specifically targeted on the person who has perpetrated or might be at risk; (2) victim-oriented prevention, which targets the child who may be vulnerable to abuse or who has been abused; (3) community-oriented prevention, which targets the ecological context in which each of these individuals lives; (4) situation-oriented prevention, which targets the situation or places of risk. These different levels and orientations create 12 focal points for preventive action (see Table 16.1) (Smallbone et al., 2008). All prevention initiatives concerning CSA can be placed within this framework. By doing so, important shortcomings in provision can be exposed. Some scholars also describe a quaternary level, which is about reducing the negative impact of overcriminalisation on men convicted of a sexual offence to ensure the interventions themselves do not cause harm (McCartan et al., 2020). However, in this chapter we will focus on the three prevention levels as described in the framework.

As mentioned, various authors emphasise the need for greater attention to offender-oriented prevention. This chapter, therefore, will concentrate on those specific activities of Stop it Now!—directed towards those with the potential to offend or to facilitate desistance in those who have already offended. There are additional offender-oriented projects in other nations (e.g., Prevention Project Dunkelfeld in Germany, Preventell in Sweden, etc.); however, this chapter focuses on the family of Stop it Now! projects currently operating.

Offender-Oriented Prevention in Action: Stop it Now!

Different country-based Stop it Now! projects will be outlined with their specific interventions and applied to the framework for CSA prevention (see listed interventions in Table 16.1). In this way we aim to provide insight into how Stop it Now! contributes to the prevention of CSA and what the main common challenges are. In addition, the work of the Stop it Now! helplines will be clarified by a case study containing specific interventions mentioned in the description of the helplines.

Stop it Now! from an International Perspective

Stop it Now! believes that CSA is a preventable social problem that is best approached from a public health perspective, where all adults have a responsibility for prevention. The mission, therefore, involves the mobilisation of adults, families, and communities to take protective actions before harm occurs. Its overarching aim is to prevent CSA through three areas of activity: (1) raising adults' awareness of CSA and the need for prevention; (2) encouraging adults worried about their own sexual

Table 16.1 Framework prevention child sexual abuse

	Primary prevention (before abuse)	Secondary prevention (before abuse)	Tertiary prevention (after abuse)
(Potential) perpetrators	• Healthy sexual education	• Helpline support for (potential) offenders • Self-help tool for people with sexual deviant interests (e.g., Get Support)	• Helpline support for offenders • Self-help tool for CSEM users (e.g., Get Help) • Psycho-educational courses CSEM users (e.g., Inform Plus) • Psycho-educational courses youth CSEM users (e.g., Inform YP) • Treatment of offenders
(Potential) victims	• Education about relationships, respect, consent, sex education		
Situations and places	• Family safety plan	• Trainings to caregivers (e.g., Circles of Safety)	• Safety planning
Communities/ families	• Tools for general society, researchers, families… (e.g., Upstream) • Relationships and Sex education • Awareness courses communities (e.g., Parents Protect) • Lectures, workshops, trainings…	• Helpline support for social environment of (potential) offenders • Trainings to caregivers (e.g., Circles of Safety) • Awareness courses schools (e.g., Parents Protect) • Psycho-educational courses families (e.g., Inform) • Manual for discussing concerns (e.g., Let's talk)	• Helpline support for social environment of offenders • Safety planning • Psycho-educational courses families of offenders (e.g., Inform) • Support groups for relatives • Manual for discussing concerns (e.g., Let's talk)

Based on and with permission from: Smallbone et al. (2008)

feelings or behaviour or those worried about others, to seek help, and (3) helping adults to challenge or change behaviour. In this way, Stop it Now! seeks to prevent CSA at the primary, secondary, and tertiary levels. To accomplish this, one fundamental component of Stop it Now! is the provision of a confidential helpline for everyone concerned to prevent CSA.

A primary target audience for the Stop it Now! helpline are adults and youth who are worried about their own sexual feelings or behaviour towards minors. By leaving room for dialogue for this target group and by supporting the search for help for (potential) perpetrators, harmful and abusive behaviours can be avoided. The helpline also offers support to those who are worried about the feelings or behaviour of someone in their family, social or work environment. After all, the taboo and stigma surrounding CSA and paedophilia means that the threshold to seek help and support is high for them as well. Finally, the helpline is available for professionals who have questions or want information or advice—for example, social workers, mental health professionals, and teachers. The helpline offers anonymous, confidential information, advice, guidance, and support, and, when necessary, it facilitates the step to suitable long-term treatment or other help. Helpline staff come from a range of backgrounds in mental health, criminal justice, sexology, and related fields, with additional expertise in the prevention of CSA and (potential) offender treatment.

Stop it Now! was founded in 1992 in the United States (US) by a survivor of CSA, swiftly becoming a model for other Stop it Now! projects developed in Europe. The first European Stop it Now! was established in 2002 in the United Kingdom and Ireland (UK&I), followed in 2012 by Stop it Now! Netherlands (NL). As the most recent initiative, Stop it Now! Flanders (FL), Belgium, was set up in 2017.

United States

Stop it Now! US is recognised as having developed one of the first CSA perpetration prevention models globally. They introduced a new shift in focus regarding CSA prevention; addressing those responsible for sexually abusing children accountable instead of previous prevention messages and programmes that focus on teaching children how to protect themselves and not be sexually abused.

In 1992, Stop it Now! US created public service messaging to reach adults who might be at risk for sexually abusing a child, or who were already engaged in illegal and/or harmful behaviours and developed a free and confidential helpline to offer information about treatment and safety planning for themselves. The US Helpline also became a resource for bystanders to reach out for information and support if they suspected a child was being abused or was vulnerable to abuse, or if they were worried about the potentially harmful sexual behaviours of an adult they knew. Ever since, they have responded to 27,000 inquiries across multiple access points (email, phone, chat, social media). A study from 2019 looked at the US! Helpline over a period of five years, 12% of inquiries came from people looking help for their own at-risk and abusive behaviours, and 70% of inquiries were from bystanders knowing the person abusing or at-risk to abuse. The remaining inquiries were by bystanders seeking to respond to a child's recent disclosure of abuse, professional's questions about CSA prevention and survivors. Of those inquiries specifically about one's own behaviours, 51% of these inquiry types were asking for help before a child was sexually abused (Grant et al., 2019). The Stop it Now! US website, a public education resource, gains over 100,000 visits monthly and provides a platform for tools and resources that can be shared within families, youth serving organisations, researchers, and communities at large. 'Circles of Safety', a training series based on the guidebook, 'Let's Talk', is offered internationally and addresses the need for healthy sexual education and safety planning in families, and to bring prevention conversations and tools into primary relationships.

Due to media reports of CSA in high profile, out of the home cases, the public's awareness about CSA has increased. However, the denial that CSA can happen in one's own family persists. While addressing CSA concerns in any environment, Stop it Now! US most often addresses CSA in families, between relatives and friends and in their homes. In 2019, 72% of the US Helpline's inquiries were about concerns of CSA in the home. Recognising that the vast majority of CSA occurs in intimate settings, the US helpline's current initiatives prioritise the development and dissemination of resources that promote the earliest possible intervention in these most intimate environments. Current initiatives include new campaigns to reach more adults with concerns about their sexual interests and behaviours, by reaching out to online communities to bring awareness of self-help and treatment resources and offering enhanced helpline follow-up services.

United Kingdom and Ireland

Stop it Now! UK&I was established in 2002 by the Lucy Faithfull Foundation (LFF), an NGO specialising in work to respond to and prevent CSA. The campaigning work of Stop it Now! UK&I involves media promotion, dissemination of publicity materials, and public discussions to promote greater awareness and understanding of CSA and of how to prevent it and respond. Other activities aim more directly at protecting children and reducing the risk posed by those with sexual thoughts, feelings, and behaviour towards them.

The core of Stop it Now! UK&I is a confidential helpline, delivered by telephone, email, and chat. The helpline acts as a stand-alone service but also as a gateway to other resources and services provided by LFF and other agencies. Since the helpline was established, they have responded to 93,789 inquiries. In 2019, 47% of these contacts were concerned about their own sexual thoughts or behaviour towards children; 28% were concerned about someone in their close environment (family, friends); and 9% as a concerned professional. Other main contacts were from parents and carers concerned about a child or young person's sexual behaviour or signs of being sexually abused or groomed; and adult survivors of CSA.

Since 2015, two aspects have prompted significant developments in the UK & I project. The first was a growing recognition of the rapidly escalating social problem of viewing and sharing child sexual exploitation material (CSEM)[2] online, with the National Crime Agency estimating some 80,000 people were regular users of this material in 2018. The

[2] We prefer not to use the term 'child pornography', which fails to convey the illegal and abusive nature its content. The abbreviation CSEM is used to refer to viewing and sharing sexual images of under 18s, online sexual grooming, live streaming, and coercing and blackmailing children for sexual purposes. CSEM also has limitations because this often excludes eroticised images of teenagers or much self-generated material. CSEM has been used because it is common in the scientific literature and it simplifies the text.

second was that a significant number of callers were not able to get through to the line due to it being busy. In response, Stop it Now! UK&I developed a large-scale (social) media campaign to promote desistance and prevention, from online CSEM offending, supported by online self-help programmes, like 'Get Help', to provide initial or substantive interventions to assist in individual journeys of desistance. Stop it Now!'Get Help' includes self-help and advice coupled with exercises and activities to promote continued engagement and learning. The site includes additional content for friends and family with concerns about CSEM behaviour in a loved one; as well as for professionals. The site is receiving on average 4,314 visits every month—mostly from anonymous users (over 60%) concerned about their own behaviour. The site is used by Stop it Now! US and in translated versions in the Netherlands and in Flanders. In addition to 'Get Help', a parallel resource, 'Get Support', provides information and support for people troubled by their sexual thoughts about children and young people.

A range of different services are funded and delivered in the different principalities that comprise the United Kingdom—Scotland, Wales, Northern Ireland, and England. For example, in Wales, these activities include the delivery of 'Parents Protect!' awareness-raising courses in schools and communities to ensure parents and caregivers are best placed to protect the children in their care. In Scotland, 'Upstream' is an online version of these primary prevention resources and information, similar to 'Parents Protect!'. In addition, colleagues in Scotland are delivering secondary and tertiary prevention services within a senior school setting for young people who have come to attention for concerning sexual behaviour, both online and offline. In all parts of the United Kingdom, psycho-educational courses are provided for people who have been arrested for committing online abuse offences (Inform Plus), for their families/partners (Inform), and for young people involved in online sexual offences (Inform YP).

The Netherlands

Stop it Now! NL was set up in 2012 as part of the Dutch Bureau of Expertise on Online Child Abuse, and therefore is a national, government-funded foundation whose mission is to prevent CSA. Stop it Now! NL differentiates three types of people concerned about themselves: contact offenders, downloaders of CSEM, and people with sexual feelings towards minors. This differentiation is essential in the provision of relevant services to those affected but also in helping the public better understand the different risks and interventions required for these populations. Stop it Now! NL plays an active role in educating the public about (the difference between) paedophilia and (online) CSA, as to promote greater awareness, decrease stigma, and increase the quality of preventive measures. They do this through conducting research, giving lectures, conducting workshops, and providing general information, to, for example, healthcare institutions or general practitioners.

The core of its work is provision of a helpline which is anonymous, confidential, and free, with key target groups being identical to the Stop It Now! projects previously described. Its main goal is to provide non-judgemental help and advice through a telephone and email service. Since 2012, the NL helpline has had 3,494 contacts by phone and email. Last year 58% of these contacts were people concerned about their own sexual thoughts or behaviour towards minors, most of them were concerned about downloading CSEM. From the callers and emailers Stop it Now! reached, 21% were from people concerned about someone close to them, that is, a family member, a friend, or a colleague. Approximately 10% of calls and emails came from professionals and the remaining 11% were from people posing general questions.

Stop it Now! NL collaborates with 'De Waag', the largest centre for outpatient forensic psychiatry in the Netherlands, specialised in the treatment of clients who exhibit transgressive and/or criminal behaviour. Since the NL helpline does not offer long-term treatment, clients in need of further psychological help are referred to De Waag, or to other (forensic) healthcare organisations. In total, since the founding of Stop it Now NL, 397 persons were referred for a call appointment with one of their therapists, of which almost 50% eventually enrolled in treatment programmes. Stop it Now! NL has also, in collaboration with Stop it Now! FL, translated and developed the online self-help tool 'Get Help' for CSEM downloaders from Stop it Now! UK. The Dutch 'Get Help' was taken into use in late 2018. Finally, Stop it Now! NL offers a support group programme which focuses on relatives of people who are concerned about their sexual feelings or behaviours towards minors or who have engaged in sexual acts concerning minors.

Flanders, Belgium

Stop it Now! FL was founded in 2017 by the University Forensic Centre, the Flemish reference centre regarding the guidance and treatment of sex offenders, in cooperation with I.T.E.R., an outpatient specialised treatment centre for people with deviant sexual interests and/or behaviour.[3] Stop it Now! FL aims to sensitise society about the need for prevention through media campaigns and communication, by providing education and training for law enforcement, universities, and caregivers. They are also involved in several research projects about minor-attracted persons and the prevention of CSA.

Their core business is offering support through an anonymous, confidential, and free helpline, which is accessed by phone, email, and chat. The helpline offers low barrier support, and when there is a need for long-term help, the helpline refers to the specialised outpatient treatment centres for deviant sexual interests or behaviour in Flanders. Since the helpline was set up in 2017, they have answered slightly more than 1500 unique inquiries. Slightly over 10% of the persons contacting the helpline were referred to long-term treatment. Last year 55% contacted the helpline because they were worried about their own sexual thoughts or behaviour, 24% because they were concerned about someone in their close environment (family, friends, colleagues, etc.) and 10% as a concerned professional. Among people who worried about themselves, most were concerned about their sexual feelings towards minors; approximately 30% were concerned about downloading CSEM; and 14% were contact offenders with concerns about the future. The Stop it Now! FL website has gained over 60,000 visits in the first three years and provides a platform for the tools and resources they developed for their target audiences.

[3] I.T.E.R. Brussels: impulscontrole, terugvalpreventie, empathietraining, en responsabilisering.

Through its work so far, the FL helpline observed that it is often distressing for relatives, friends, and even professionals when they discover someone in their social environment is experiencing pedophilic feelings or demonstrates concerning sexual behaviour towards minors. Mostly, they do not know how to express their concerns. Nevertheless, the fact that any concerns are discussable can make a significant difference to those who are experiencing sexual interest in minors. Therefore, Stop it Now! FL has developed 'Let's talk', a manual which can be used when providing support to acquaintances and discussing concerns with the person about whom one is concerned. Next to that, to anticipate the massive increase in CSEM cases given by police and justice but also because of the high demand for help from downloaders on the helpline, the online self-help tool for CSEM users 'Get-Help' is offered. This tool is widely used by individuals as well as those providing therapy for this target audience. The online self-help tool has gained more than 13,000 visits in NL and FL in the first two years of its existence.

Stop it Now! Flanders is funded by the Flemish government, which means they only serve help in Dutch. In a small country like Belgium with 11 million inhabitants, where they speak three languages (i.e., Flemish, French, and German), this is problematic. After all, Stop it Now! Flanders can only offer help for more or less half of the Belgian population. Because CSA does not stop at the border of a region, it is necessary to develop a Belgian Stop it Now! helpline which is also accessible in the other national languages.

A Stop it Now! Case Study

To illustrate the work of these Stop it Now! projects and the help they offer on the helpline and via online resources, we share an anonymised case study below. Some referred interventions in the case may be mentioned already in the discussion of the Stop it Now! projects above.

Adult Concerned about His Own Online Behaviour

Robert (aged 54) called the Stop it Now! helpline to seek help to stop viewing CSEM online. A year ago, Robert's addiction to legal adult pornography had escalated to involve the viewing of CSEM. At this point, Robert became concerned about his behaviour and sought help. He began to work through the 'Get Help' tool, which—alongside support from his wife—helped him to stop viewing illegal images for a short time. However, during a stressful period in his life, he returned to viewing adult pornography and then illegal images, which led him to calling the helpline again. During his first call, he described his behaviour as 'disgusting' and discussed the seriousness of it. He also reflected on his motivation to stop viewing these images as they cause harm to children. Stop it Now! provided some advice and support on the helpline.

How did Stop it Now! advise and support Robert?

- Robert was given positive feedback for taking steps to address his behaviour;
- The operator discussed with Robert the seriousness of his behaviour, and strongly advised him to follow the advice given to him in order to manage his online viewing;
- The operator also described the legal implications of viewing CSEM;
- Robert was advised to go back to, and work through, the 'Get Help'[4] online tool;
- It was recommended that Robert has another honest conversation with his wife about his online behaviour and, with her support, to set up parameters around his internet use[5];
- Robert was advised to pass on details of the helpline to his wife so the helpline can support her if she wants this;
- Robert was encouraged to look after himself and identify activities which will decrease his levels of stress, in order to prevent another relapse;
- Robert was encouraged to continue to call the Stop It Now! helpline for ongoing support;
- It was also suggested that Robert consider the option for long-term outpatient treatment.

What was the outcome in Robert's case?

Robert chose not to engage with the long-term outpatient treatment, but he continued to call the helpline for a number of months as well as

(*continued*)

[4] www.get-help.stopitnow.org.uk; stoppenismogelijk.eu

[5] Specifically, it was suggested that all devices are password protected and internet browser restrictions put in place.

(continued)

accessing 'Get-Help' for support to remain offence free. During follow-up in three calls, Robert stated that he had not accessed CSEM or adult pornography since his first call to the helpline. Robert was actively avoiding any trigger situations which might prompt him to begin viewing adult pornography as he was aware this could escalate into illegal behaviour. For example, Robert indicated that a combination of being home alone, stressed, and ruminating on negative events have in the past led him to pornography. Operators discussed the importance of identifying safe replacement activities to keep him both interested and busy (mindfulness and antique collection). Robert reported that his calls to the helpline had reinforced the fact that the images he previously viewed were images of real children being harmed and served to motivate him to stop his behaviour. He expressed his gratitude and relief to the helpline for providing him a place to talk openly and receive help for his behaviour.

Common Challenges: Moving Forward with Offender-Oriented Prevention

These different country-based Stop it Now! projects are dealing with several challenges, such as the growing problem of (online) CSA, the difficultues with confidentiality and funding insecurity. Regarding international findings, the problem of CSEM is intensively growing and despite several initiatives, many children are still not safe, even in their own homes. Global crises—like COVID-19—painfully exposed the problem of CSA in families and prompted the significant increase in online sexual abuse. The helplines need to develop and deploy a range of initiatives to tackle these problems; discourage at-risk groups and motivate perpetrators to change behaviour.

Another challenge is that the rules of mandatory reporting and professional confidentiality differ from country to country and from state to state. Often helplines are under pressure from government authorities to report cases of child abuse, even when dealing with abuse in the past when there is no immediate danger (e.g., downloading CSEM). Professional confidentiality is however important. It makes it much easier to provide help for offenders and makes helplines for people who are worried about their feelings or behaviour much more accessible. After all, fear of legal consequences that might result through the lack of confidentiality acts as a further barrier (Assini-Meytin et al., 2020; Levenson & Grady, 2018). This is why all Stop it Now! helplines must be given the mandate by society to provide preventive help, even if this means they provide assistance to offenders of whom the authorities are unaware. Although from a criminal justice perspective this may feel like impunity, from a public health point of view it is essential to provide support for this previously unreached target group.

A third and final concern is that the sustained growth and development of the Stop it Now! helplines require sustained funding. However, these Stop it Now! projects still have to deal with national differences in—often uncertain—funding and public (policy) perceptions of prevention (McCartan et al., 2020). Because of frequently mistaken perceptions and myths surrounding CSA, these offender-oriented prevention projects still need to prove and profile themselves in order to gain recognition. Social awareness and correct imaging about CSA and how to prevent it are essential to move forward in these challenges. Also shared research about the psycho-social well-being and help-seeking behaviour of the target audience of offender-oriented prevention projects can achieve even more accessible and substantial help, with the goal of improved prevention. In response to these research results, more targeted resources can be employed to further support the target audience and to address the problems at the primary and the secondary level.

Discussion: Stop it Now! in the Framework of CSA

However large (and growing) the number of contacts received by the Stop It Now! helplines is, it is vital to achieve more than anecdotal evidence that their work is effective in preventing CSA. The CSA prevention framework describes 12 focal points for preventive action. As mentioned, effective prevention requires initiatives on every level, with all perspectives targeted. Although prevention projects like Stop it Now! initially embarked on offender-oriented prevention, the descriptions of the Stop it Now! projects and the application of their specific projects to the framework of Smallbone and colleagues (in Table 16.1) demonstrate that they influence many more levels than only the offender-oriented one. In addition, the most recent published research undertaken on Stop it Now! UK & I and NL by the National Centre for Social Research (2014) concluded: "Both helplines can *contribute to tackling child sexual abuse by helping people who* have sexual thoughts, feelings or behaviour towards children to understand and manage their behaviour, and by assisting all users to be informed about how to protect children and young people from risk of harm" (p. 3).

However, the broader activities of primary and secondary prevention are, as with similar activities by other organisations globally, demonstrating promising results in offering efficient confidential informed service, reducing isolation and misinformation (Beier et al., 2009; Van Horn et al., 2015; Grant et al., 2019), evaluation and objectivating effectivity is still limited (Spittal et al., 2015). It is essential to be aware that prevention projects—such as Stop it Now!—need sufficient resources to continue to fulfil and expand their prevention mission. as Also, partnerships with victim-, community-, or situation-oriented prevention initiatives, to fulfil the framework, can ensure an efficient and comprehensive approach of CSA prevention. Further investment of time and resources is needed to develop and further shape prevention initiatives, as well as to organise research with achievable targets, quality evaluation, and objective results.

Conclusion

Given the scale of CSA and the large number of hidden cases, it is clear that a criminal justice approach will only address a fraction of the problem. And the problem is still growing, with online CSA growing and evolving faster than ever. Nevertheless, there is still much skepticism about preventive help from the public health perspective and for offender-oriented prevention approaches. The future security of Stop it Now! remains uncertain. It is hard to prove its effectiveness and cost-effectiveness in the short term, but the evidence of utility is growing. Public and political attitudes must be changed to help the shift from a criminal justice response to CSA to a stronger focus on a public health prevention focus. Projects like Stop it Now! can have a significant impact and help achieve this shift.

References

Assini-Meytin, L. C., Fix, R. L., & Letourneau, E. J. (2020). Child sexual abuse: The need for a perpetration prevention focus. *Journal of child sexual abuse, 29*(1), 22–40. https://doi.org/10.1080/10538712.2019.1703232

Barth, J., Bermetz, L., Heim, E., Trelle, S., & Tonia, T. (2013). The current prevalence of child sexual abuse worldwide: A systematic review and meta-analysis. *International Journal of Public Health, 58*(3), 469–483. https://doi.org/10.1007/s00038-012-0426-1

Beier, K. M., Ahlers, C. J., Goecker, D., Neutze, J., Mundt, I. A., Hupp, E., & Schaefer, G. A. (2009). Can pedophiles be reached for primary prevention of child sexual abuse? First results of the Berlin Prevention Project Dunkelfeld (PPD). *The Journal of Forensic Psychiatry & Psychology, 20*(6), 851–867. https://doi.org/10.1080/14789940903174188

Bolen, R. (2003). Child sexual abuse: Prevention or promotion? *Social Work, 48*(2), 174–185. https://doi.org/10.1093/sw/48.2.174

Brown, S. (2005). *Treating sex offenders: An introduction to sex offender treatment programmes*. Routledge.

Butchart, A., Harvey, A. P., Mian, M., & Furniss, T. (2006). *Preventing child maltreatment: A guide to taking action and generating evidence*. World Health Organization.

Casey, E. A., & Lindhorst, T. P. (2009). Toward a multi-level, ecological approach to the primary prevention of sexual assault: Prevention in peer and community contexts. *Trauma, Violence, & Abuse*, 91–114. https://doi.org/10.1177/1524838009334129

Cutajar, M. C., Mullen, P. E., Ogloff, J. R., Thomas, S. D., Wells, D. L., & Spataro, J. (2010). Psychopathology in a large cohort of sexually abused children followed up to 43 years. *Child Abuse & Neglect, 34*(11), 813–822. https://doi.org/10.1016/j.chiabu.2010.04.004

Felitti, V., & Anda, R. (2009). The relationship of adverse childhood experiences to adult medical disease, psychiatric disorders, and sexual behavior: Implications for healthcare. In R. Lanius & E. Vermetten (Eds.), *The hidden epidemic: The impact of early life trauma on health and disease* (pp. 77–87). Cambridge University Press.

Finkelhor, D. (2009). The prevention of childhood sexual abuse. *The Future of Children, 19*(2), 169–194. https://doi.org/10.1353/foc.0.0035
Grant, B. J., Shields, R. T., Tabachnick, J., & Coleman, J. (2019). "I Didn't Know Where To Go": An examination of Stop It Now!'s sexual abuse prevention helpline. *Journal of Interpersonal Violence, 34*(20), 4225–4253. https://doi.org/10.1177/0886260519869237
Hardner, K., Wolf, M. R., & Rinfrette, E. S. (2017). Examining the relationship between higher educational attainment, trauma symptoms, and internalizing behaviors in child sexual abuse survivors. *Child Abuse & Neglect, 86*, 375–383. https://doi.org/10.1016/j.chiabu.2017.10.007
International Labour Organisation. (2015). *Commercial sexual exploitation and trafficking of children "in a nutshell": A resource for Pacific Island countries*. ILO. https://www.ilo.org/wcmsp5/groups/public/%2D%2D-asia/%2D%2D-ro-bangkok/%2D%2D-ilo-suva/documents/publication/wcms_494314.pdf
Knack, N., Winder, B., Murphy, L., & Fedoroff, J. P. (2019). Primary and secondary prevention of child sexual abuse. *International Review of Psychiatry, 31*(2), 181–194. https://doi.org/10.1080/09540261.2018.1541872
Lalor, K., & McElvaney, R. (2010). Overview of the nature and extent of child sexual abuse in Europe. In K. Lalor & R. McElvaney (Eds.), *Council of Europe: Protecting children from sexual violence—A comprehensive approach* (pp. 13–43). Council of Europe.
Laws, D. R., & O'Donohue, W. (2016). *Treatment of sex offenders: Strengths and weaknesses in assessment and intervention*. Springer.
Letourneau, E., Eaton, W., Bass, J., Berlin, F., & Moore, S. (2014). The need for a comprehensive public health approach to preventing child sexual abuse. *Public Health Reports, 129*(3), 222–228. https://doi.org/10.1177/003335491412900303
Levenson, J. S., & Grady, M. D. (2018). Preventing sexual abuse: Perspectives of minor-attracted persons about seeking help. *Sexual Abuse, 31*, 991–1013. https://doi.org/10.1177/79063218797713
Longfield, A. (2015). *Protecting children from harm: A critical assessment of child sexual abuse in the family network in england and priorities for action*. Children's Commissioner. https://www.childrenscommissioner.gov.uk/wp-content/uploads/2017/06/Protecting-children-from-harm-executive-summary_0.pdf
Maniglio, R. (2009). The impact of child sexual abuse on health: A systematic review of reviews. *Clinical Psychology Review, 29*(7), 647–657. https://doi.org/10.1016/j.cpr.2009.08.003

McCartan, K., Uzieblo, K., & Smid, W. J. (2020). Professionals' understandings of and attitudes to the prevention of sexual abuse: An international exploratory study. *International Journal of Offender Therapy and Comparative Criminology*, 1–17. https://doi.org/10.1177/0306624X20919706

McCartan, K. F., Merdian, H. L., Perkins, D. E., & Kettleborough, D. (2018). Ethics and issues of secondary prevention efforts in child sexual abuse. *International Journal of Offender Therapy and Comparative Criminology, 9*, 2548–2566. https://doi.org/10.1177/0306624X17723951

Mian, M., & Collin-Vézina, D. (2017). Adopting a public health approach to addressing child sexual abuse and exploitation. *Child Abuse & Neglect, 66*, 152–154. https://doi.org/10.1016/j.chiabu.2017.02.035

NatCen Social Research. (2014). *A public health approach to tackling child sexual abuse: Research on Stop it Now! UK and Ireland and Stop it Now! Netherlands*. NatCen. https://www.natcen.ac.uk/media/329130/overview-of-study_complete-web.pdf

Rattray, T., Brunner, W., & Freestone, J. (2002). *Prevention*. Cchealth. https://cchealth.org/prevention/spectrum/pdf/new_spectrum_of_prevention.pdf

Seto, M. (2012). Is pedophilia a sexual orientation? *Archives of Sexual Behavior, 41*(1), 231–236. https://doi.org/10.1007/s10508-011-9882-6

Smallbone, S., Marshall, W., & Wortley, R. (2008). *Preventing child sexual abuse: Evidence, policy and practice*. Willan Publishing.

Spittal, M. J., Fedyszyn, I., Middleton, A., Bassilios, B., Gunn, J., Woodward, A., & Pirkis, J. (2015). Frequent callers to crisis helplines: Who are they and why do they call? *Australian & New Zealand Journal of Psychiatry, 49*(1), 54–64. https://doi.org/10.1177/0004867414541154

Tabachnick, J. (2013). Why prevention? Why now? *International Journal of Behavioral Consultation and Therapy, 8*(3–4), 55–61. https://doi.org/10.1037/h0100984

Van Horn, J., Eisenberg, M., Nicholls, C., Mulder, J., Webster, S., Paskell, C., Brown, A., Stam, J., Kerr, J., & Jago, N. (2015). Stop it Now! A pilot study into the limits and benefits of a free helpline preventing child sexual abuse. *Journal of Child Sexual Abuse, 24*(8), 853–872. https://doi.org/10.1080/10538712.2015.1088914

World Health Organization (WHO). (2017). *Responding to children and adolescents who have been sexually abused: WHO clinical guidelines*. World Health Organization. https://apps.who.int/iris/bitstream/handle/10665/259270/9789241550147-eng.pdf;jsessionid=2CEB1F2EBF6402F8EDC080184126A399?sequence=1

Part V

Future Directions for the Field of Sexual Abuse

17

The Relevance of Professional Organisations in the Prevention and Treatment of Sexual Violence

Marije Keulen-de Vos, Kasia Uzieblo, Minne De Boeck, Sarah Brown, and Carla Maria Xella

Professional organisations or associations are non-profit bodies established by a group of professionals to unite people of a certain occupation or interest (Moskovskaya et al., 2013). They play a variety of roles in the development of any field. First, they provide up-to-date and extensive professional knowledge through formal networks (i.e., conferences, workshops, blogposts and publications), or informal networks such as committee

We have no known conflict of interest to disclose.

M. K.-d. Vos (✉)
Research department, Forensic Psychiatric Centre de Rooyse Wissel, Venray, The Netherlands

Radboud University Nijmegen, Behavioural Science Institute, Nijmegen, The Netherlands
e-mail: MKeulen-deVos@derooysewissel.nl

© The Author(s), under exclusive license to Springer Nature Switzerland AG 2022

K. Uzieblo et al. (eds.), *Challenges in the Management of People Convicted of a Sexual Offence*, Palgrave Studies in Risk, Crime and Society,
https://doi.org/10.1007/978-3-030-80212-7_17

membership (Rusaw, 1995). By doing so, they meet educational needs (e.g., enable continuing education (CE) credits) and shape professional development (Berger, 2014). Second, associations serve a social function in providing a network of support and enhancing professional identity by giving members a sense of belonging to a certain profession or network (Markova et al., 2013). Third, professional organisations provide normative frameworks for enacting knowledge in practice by, for example, providing a professional code of ethics and practice guidelines (Hager, 2014; Rusaw, 1995). Finally, organisations and their members may be a catalyst for change because they can influence public opinion and policymaking. Examples of professional associations can be found, among others, in nursing, medicine, law and psychology. Within the field of psychology, several organisations or societies have been established around a particular topic

K. Uzieblo
Van der Hoeven Kliniek, Utrecht, The Netherlands

Free University of Brussels, Brussels, Belgium

M. De Boeck
Stop it Now!, Flanders, Belgium

University Forensic Centre, University Hospital Antwerp, Edegem, Belgium

Collaborative Antwerp Psychiatric Research Institute (CAPRI), University Antwerp, Antwerpen, Belgium

S. Brown
Faculty of Arts, Business and Law, Law School, University of Sunshine Coast, Sippy Downs, QLD, Australia

Faculty of Health and Applied Sciences (HAS), University of the West of England, Bristol, UK

National Organisation for the Treatment of Abuse (NOTA), UK and Republic of Ireland, London, UK

C. M. Xella
Centro Italiano per la Promozione della Mediazione (CIPM), Lazio, Italy
CoNTRAS-TI, Rome, Italy

(e.g., the International Society for Research on Impulsivity and Society on the Scientific Study of Psychopathy), or specialty, such as the intersection between law and psychology (e.g., the International Academy of Law and Mental Health) and forensic psychology (e.g., the International Association of Forensic Mental Health Services).

A topic within forensic psychology that receives increasing (inter) national news coverage is sexual violence due to high-profile cases of sexual misconduct in institutions (e.g., sport and church) and on college and university campuses, as well as cases of sexual homicide, online child sexual exploitation materials (CSEM) and human trafficking. Sexual violence is an international issue that knows no borders. Researchers, practitioners and policymakers constantly have to improve their knowledge base on sexual violence, on those who engage in sexual violence and their victims, as well as on how to prevent and respond to it. Although we are not always on the same page in terms of research, practice, policy and evidence, there is an increased recognition that policies and practices for the evaluation, treatment and management of individuals who have engaged in sexually violent behaviour should be evidenced based and collaboratively developed. This field has evolved from working in silos to developing (inter)national partnerships and collaborations to prevent sexual violence. One of the main goals of (inter)national organisations is to support and promote the exchange of knowledge and information about the opportunities to prevent sexual violence. In the current social climate where expert advice is often being rejected for personal ideology or where scientific evidence is considered "fake", professional organisations help us to stand together and unify efforts to incorporate research and adhere to practice standards. As professionals working in the guidance and treatment of individuals convicted of sexual offences, we still struggle to get the topic—and its funding—on the political agenda. Moreover, we are regularly confronted with social and public rejection because society often has a distorted view of what treatment of individuals convicted of sexual offences entails and find it hard to understand that there is investment of time and resources in these individuals, because our most vulnerable groups are affected by the problem. Professional organisations can contribute to raising awareness and society's perception of this issue, as well as join forces to address the importance of investing in prevention and treatment.

The Association for Treatment of Sexual Abusers (ATSA) is one of the largest international organisations within this field but you also have more local branches. In this chapter, we highlight three local professional organisations in Europe that aim to support the prevention of sexual violence by enhancing evidence-based public policy and knowledge on supervision and treatment of individuals who have sexually offended. We provide an overview of their origin, aims and activities, followed by a reflection on their (future) role in practice, policy and research.

Professional Organisations on Sexual Violence: Three Examples

In this section, we introduce three local professional organisations with membership primarily based in five European countries (Belgium, Italy, the Netherlands, Republic of Ireland and United Kingdom).

National Organisation for the Treatment of Sexual Abuse (NOTA; the UK and the Republic of Ireland)

The National Organisation for the Treatment of Abuse grew from a regional network in the North West of England, and has been a registered professional organisation since 1991. NOTA has regional branches in Scotland, Wales, Northern Ireland, the Republic of Ireland and many branches in England; each branch has an elected executive committee. Membership is open to any professional involved in work with, or related to, sexual violence. NOTA's member base consists of practioners, managers, policymakers and academics. It is an international organisation but primarily has members from the United Kingdom (UK) and the Republic of Ireland. The organisation's objectives are to advance education for professionals working with, or providing services for, people who have committed a sexual offence, to promote research into treatment for individuals who have sexually offended, and to promote research into the skills associated with the professionals who work with them.

NOTA hosts an annual international professional conference and regional conferences across the United Kingdom and Republic of Ireland. In addition, the organisation offers national and regional training events, a regular newsletter, bulletin board, blog and a triannual journal (i.e., *Journal of Sexual Aggression*) to disseminate professional knowledge. Members can also join a number of standing committees that focus on prevention, research, membership, policy and practice. NOTA is the only national organisation in the United Kingdom and the Republic of Ireland that focuses specifically on all forms of sexual violence. It has close ties with other organisations and centres such as the National Probation Service, the Prison Service, the Center of Expertise for Child Sexual Abuse, Stop-It-Now, and Circles of Support and Accountability (CoSA). The organisation also has links with similar international networks (e.g., NL-ATSA, CoNTRAS-TI, IATSO, and ATSA) and universities.

Dutch (Speaking) Affiliate Organisation of ATSA (NL-ATSA, the Netherlands and Belgium)

In 1993, the Dutch Association of Forensic Sexology was founded to enhance the treatment of individuals who were convicted of a sexual offence. In 2014, this association transitioned to an international chapter of ATSA for members from the Netherlands and Flanders (Belgium, i.e. Dutch-speaking persons), and the name was changed to “NL-ATSA” to reflect this modification. Membership is open to any Dutch/Flemish professionals involved in work with, or related to, sexual violence. Currently, the member base consists mainly of academics, practioners, forensic therapists and professionals from probation services. Initially, NL-ATSA aimed to disseminate knowledge from North America with regard to treatment and management of sexual violence to a professional audience in the Netherlands and Flanders who work with individuals convicted of a sexual offence and to bring European knowledge to North America. This is why they decided to become a chapter of the international ATSA. In 2020, due to administrative reasons, NL-ATSA became an affiliate organisation of ATSA instead of being a chapter. Over time, the organisation also started inspiring and facilitating prevention and scientific research within this field. In this way, NL-ATSA is dedicated to the prevention of sex abuse. They focus on primary and secondary prevention by means of information and assistance to the society as a whole and people at risk of offending and people at risk to be victimised. In addition, NL-ATSA wants to facilitate tertiary prevention by means of offering training, workshops to offer practioners necessary skills and knowledge on risk assessment and treatment. Furthermore, NL-ATSA promotes collaborations between Dutch and Flemish practitioners and academics, and facilitates connections between fields or disciplines, such as (forensic) psychology, criminology and sexology. Correspondingly, NL-ATSA has formed close connections to other European organisations with similar aims. NL-ATSA organises international conferences and hosts two symposia on a yearly basis. In addition, board members disseminate professional knowledge through newsletters, blogposts, social media and publications. Members can join standing committees on prevention, (risk) assessment, treatment and research. The purpose of these committees is to disseminate up-to-date information on current research and evidence-based best practices in their topic. In this way, as well as by organising networking events, NL-ATSA aims to bring the Ducth-speaking professional network in the prevention of sexual abuse togheter. NL-ATSA has close ties with other universities and organisations like the Dutch National Probation Service, specialised outpatient and inpatient treatment centres, and specific prevention projects focusing on child sexual abuse, like Stop-it-Now! Flanders and the Netherlands.

National Coordination of Treatment and Research about Sexual Offending—Italian Experiences

CoNTRAS-TI is an acronym for *Coordinamento Nazionale Trattamento e Ricerca sull'Aggressione Sessuale—Testimonianze Italiane*; in English: the National Coordination of Treatment and Research about Sexual Offending—Italian Experiences. The acronym can be translated to "pathways to stop", referring to sexual violence. The association was established on October 13, 2017. Its foundation was the result of a considerable effort by some non-profit associations to gather professionals, researchers and public officers all over the country involved in the management of those who have committed sexual offences, as in Italy. Projects for treatment for sexual violence primarily depends on personal initiatives which are often discontinued due to a lack of coordination. In addition, there is a lack of continuity between prison care and rehabilitation in the community. In October 2018, CoNTRAS-TI became an affiliate organisation of ATSA. CoNTRAS-TI has three aims: first, to build a network for the prevention of sexual abuse by developing scientific research and treatment practice based on clinical evidence and international guidelines; second, to promote new strategies and practices to influence national decision-making and policies regarding monitoring, assessment, treatment and re-entry into the community of individuals convicted for sexual offences; finally, to encourage the development of a culture of prevention, to make the early identification of high-risk situations possible and to facilitate access to community resources. Furthermore, the association aims to change the approach to sexual abuse, from mere punishment and stigmatisation of the abusers to treatment and rehabilitation. In order to achieve these goals, CoNTRAS-TI collaborates with other international associations operating with similar scientific and clinical purposes. They also organise national conferences.

In this section, three local professional European organisations were discussed. NOTA is the oldest organisation (est. 1991), whereas CoNTRAS-TI is the most recent. NL-ATSA recently celebrated its first lustrum. They all share the aims to prevent sexual abuse, advance practice, disseminate knowledge and provide a professional network among those working with individuals convicted for sexual offences or indivuals at risk. NOTA, NL-ATSA and CoNTRAS-TI are in close contact with each other to improve prevention, treatment and rehabilitation of individuals who have sexually offended. Over the years, several countries have expressed interest in developing similar organisations. Hence, we expect to see an increase in the number of organisations in Europe and (hopefully) elsewhere.

Relevance and Challenges of Professional Organisations on Sexual Violence

Professional organisations are of all ages. Guilds and guild-like institutions were introduced in the Middle Ages as permanent, generally local organisations of people in the same profession or trade, or a combination of the same professions, recognised by the local, provincial or central government (Lucassen et al., 2008). They progressed into early modern Europe, the Industrial Revolution and our current modern age, and played a central role in the organisation of political, social and economic life. Professional organisations are still relevant today, also in the field of medicine and (forensic) psychology. Over the last decades and especially thanks to the #METOO movement, there has been greater recognition of specific forms and contexts of sexual victimisation. Therefore, professional organisations that focus on sexual violence are more important than ever before. There are four primary "chains" of activity for these professional organisations (see also Box 17.1).

A first key activity is to improve the understanding of the scale and nature of sexual violence, and to provide sector-wide access to scientific and best-practices evidence on the prevention of sexual violence, treatment and rehabilitation of those who have sexually offended. In a way, professional organisations are a hub of information. Scientific research is not easily conducted and not easily exchanged to media and society. With regard to research, we know that countries need to deal with national differences in funding and public policy perceptions of prevention

Box 17.1 Activities of Professional Organisations

1. Understanding sexual violence and improving sector-wide access to evidence on prevention of sexual violence, and treatment and rehabilitation of individuals who have sexually offended
2. Influencing evidence-based public opinion and policy
3. Engaging and developing practice with those who work directly with people at risk for sexual offending or who have sexually offended
4. Improving the effectiveness of interventions to stop or prevent sexual violence

(McCartan et al., 2020). Research funding on prevention and treatment services is often limited, and research budgets are usually insufficient. Many countries do not have large agencies that specifically subsidise research in forensic psychology in general and research on sexual violence specifically. Professional organisations could bridge this gap by subsidising small-scale and local research, as well as bringing professionals together to join forces in the field.

Another barrier in scientific knowledge exchange is that much research is offered behind journal paywalls. Systematic collaboration between professional organisations by, for example, linking websites or knowledge platforms might subsequently aid in improving sector-wide access to evidence on the prevention of sexual violence, as well as providing information on the treatment and rehabilitation of individuals who have sexually offended. But it is a challenge to provide sector-wide information when member numbers are small and access to documentation is typically available for members only. Being a member of a professional organisation is not yet common practice in every country/institution/discipline or membership fee is considered too high an additional and unnecessary cost; after all, (potential) members often have to deal with financial uncertanties in their profession themselves. This reluctance however elicits a vicious circle: Professional organisations need membership fees to disseminate knowledge and tools, but if membership numbers remain limited, the organisations' reach is limited. A general, related, challenge for professional organisations is to stay financially viable. Organisations are often financially dependent on members and the income that organisations generate from training and conferences. If member numbers decrease or stall, or conferences are cancelled, less funds are available to host events and invest in research and practice development. After all, also (potential) members are often suffering from funding problems or have to deal with financial uncertanties in their profession.

A second key goal is to inform public opinion and policy. There are many misconceptions and myths about sexual offences and individuals who have sexually offended. For example, many people think that most individuals who have sexually offended will sexually reoffend (Harper et al., 2017), whereas reconviction data suggests that this is not the case (Hanson et al., 2018). These misconceptions can strongly influence public opinion and policymaking. Typically, laws and policies are also reactive and developed in response to nationally traumatic, well-publicised crimes instead of being based on research and professional insights, and a long-term vision towards sexual violence. These policies and laws need to prevent sexual violence but, from a rehabilitative perspective, simultaneously minimise harm to perpetrators. Negative consequences like social isolation, lack of employment and housing hamper well-being and may in fact increase risk for reoffending (Hudson & Ward, 1997; Lindsay, 2011; Parton & Day, 2002). Another challenge is that policymaking sometimes involves a process of reasoning backwards (e.g., this is the desired policy, what can support this) or is driven by an emotional perspective, whether or not under the influence of victim's interests, media or societal uproar. As a result, policymakers may be less sensitive to scientific advice or ask experts to provide facts that support the policy instead of drawing a conclusion based on the empirical evidence. Many professional organisations support the development of evidence/knowledge-based laws and policies, and work to educate and advise policymakers. As such, a professional organisation can be a catalyst for change. It can prove, however, to be a challenge to inform the community effectively and correctly. Professional organisations need to invest resources in connecting with stakeholders active in policy agenda; we need to meet politicians, charities and other bodies that have a stake in sexual violence policy and be more visible in public policy debates and seminars.

The third chain of activity is to engage and develop practice with those who work directly with people at risk for sexual offending or who have sexually offended. Relatedly, the fourth key activity is to objectivate and improve the effectiveness of interventions to stop or prevent sexual violence. Effective treatment is important in preventing victimisation. Many professional organisations support the use of research-based and evidence-informed treatment known to reduce the likelihood of someone sexually offending. They encourage those involved in addressing sexual violence to adopt practices consistent with the best available evidence and to adapt their approaches as new research and insights emerge. Many organisations offer practice guidelines for various perpetrators (e.g., adults, juveniles and internet offenders) and actively support research assessing the effectiveness of services. Practitioners are often well aware of the wealth of academic research available, often taking part in the interviews and fieldwork feeding into research projects and are purported to be the key audience for the findings. But the reality is that it is notoriously difficult to translate academic research findings into digestible guidance, useable tools and practical application. To be effective, communication needs to reach people with the information that they need and in a form that they can use (Fischhoff, 2013). Sometimes research protocols are not easily adaptable to real life; in other instances, researchers have difficulty in translating their work. These factors are barriers to effective practice and effective communication. It is a major task and challenge for professional organisations to overcome these barriers. Ideally, they should be intermediaries between science and professionals or government agencies and need to identify what information is most relevant to decisions that people face and design a communication plan to fill the gaps between what professionals and policymakers do know and need to know.

To Conclude

Professional organisations on sexual violence aim to prevent sexual victimisation through effective and evidence-based prevention, offender treatment and rehabilitation. Organisations that are based in one country have the advantage over international organisations that they can familiarise themselves with a nation's public policy, legal stance and societal conventions, and tap into regional differences. They are better able to have their ears on the ground so that they can tailor communication and resources. Obviously, there remains a lot to do. In the future, organisations like NOTA, NL-ATSA and CoNTRAS-TI will continue to collaborate and join activities (e.g., organise conferences, joint board meetings and network events) with each other and other organisations (e.g., ATSA and IATSO) and will actively reach out and help other countries to establish similar organisations. If more organisations are established in Europe, we can join forces to maximise our societal footprint on sexual violence prevention and inspire each other in combatting this massive public health problem.

References

Berger, J. I. (2014). Role of professional development associations in the future of our field. *Adult Learning, 25*(1), 31–33. https://doi.org/10.1177/1045159513510149

Fischhoff, B. (2013). The science of science communication. *PNAS, 110*(3), 14033–14039. https://doi.org/10.1073/pnas.1213273110

Hager, M. A. (2014). Engagement Motivations in Professional Associations. *Nonprofit and Voluntary Sector Quarterly, 43*(S2) https://doi.org/10.1177/0899764013502582

Hanson, K. R., Harris, A. J. R., Letourneau, E., & Helmus, L. M. (2018). Reductions in risk based on time offense-free in the community: Once a sexual offender, not always a sexual offender. *Psychology, Public Policy, and Law, 24*(1), 48–63. https://doi.org/10.1037/law000013

Harper, C. A., Hogue, T. E., & Bartels, R. M. (2017). Attitudes towards sexual offenders: What do we know, and why are they important? *Aggression and Violent Behavior, 34*, 201–213. https://doi.org/10.1016/j.avb.2017.01.011

Hudson, S. M., & Ward, T. (1997). Intimacy, loneliness, and attachment style in sexual offenders. *Journal of Interpersonal Violence, 12*(3), 323–339. https://doi.org/10.1177/088626097012003001

Lindsay, W. R. (2011). Theoretical perspectives and their practical application for assessment and treatment of sexual offenders with an intellectual disability. In D. P. Boer, R. Eher, L. A. Craig, M. H. Miner, & F. Pfäfflin (Eds.), *International perspectives on the assessment and treatment of sexual abusers* (pp. 215–233). Wiley-Blackwell.

Lucassen, J. M. W. G., de Moor, T., & Luiten van Zanden, J. (2008). The return of the guilds: towards a global history of the guilds in pre-industrial times. *International Review of Social History, 53*(16), 5–18. https://doi.org/10.1017/S0020859008003581.

Markova, G., Ford, R. C., Dickson, D. R., & Bohn, T. M. (2013). Professional associations and members' benefits. *Nonprofit Management & Leadership, 23*(4), 83–96. https://doi.org/10.1002/nml

McCartan, K., Uzieblo, K., & Smid, W. J. (2020). Professionals' understandings of and attitudes to the prevention of sexual abuse: An international exploratory study. *International Journal of Offender Therapy and Comparative Criminology*, 1–17. https://doi.org/10.1177/0306624X20919706

Moskovskaya, A. A., Oberemko, O. A., Silaeva, V. L., Popova, I. P., Nazarova, I. B., Peshkova, O. A., & Chernysheva, M. V. (2013). *Development of professional associations in Russia: a research into institutional framework, self-regula-*

tion activity, and barriers to professionalization. National Research University Higher School of Economics. WORKING PAPERS SERIES: SOCIOLOGY WP BRP 26/SOC/2013

Parton, F., & Day, A. (2002). Empathy, intimacy, loneliness and locus of control in child sex offenders: A comparison between familial and non-familial child sex offenders. *Journal of Sexual Abuse, 11*(2), 41–57. https://doi.org/10.1300/J070v11n02_03

Rusaw, A. C. (1995). Learning by association: Professional associations as learning agents. *Human Resource Development Quarterly, 6*(2), 215–226. https://doi.org/10.1002/hrdq.3920060209

18

Translating the Sexual Abuse Evidence Base into Effective Policy and Practice

Kieran McCartan

The current edited collection identifies and reinforces the complex multidisciplinary, and multi-agency, nature of preventing as well as responding to sexual offending. The book has highlighted that there is not a "one size fits all" approach to working with individuals convicted of a sexual offence either in their rehabilitation and integration back into the community or on their desistance pathway. Therefore, if we cannot take a blanket approach to rehabilitation, then why do we think that we can take a blanket approach to the policies that direct practice in order to reduce reoffending, protect communities, and safeguard society? We cannot! But the reality is that that is exactly what we try to do. In the field of

I have no known conflict of interest to disclose.

K. McCartan (✉)
Department of Criminology, University of the West of England, Bristol, UK
e-mail: kieran.mccartan@uwe.ac.uk

© The Author(s), under exclusive license to Springer Nature Switzerland AG 2022

K. Uzieblo et al. (eds.), *Challenges in the Management of People Convicted of a Sexual Offence*, Palgrave Studies in Risk, Crime and Society,
https://doi.org/10.1007/978-3-030-80212-7_18

sexual offending, as in other areas of criminal justice (Wilson & Petersilia, 2011), we develop cross-reaching risk management policies that lack nuance and are not adaptive to the individual needs of the client (Beauregard & Lieb, 2011; Kemshall, 2017), which is problematic and challenging. This final chapter of the edited collection will draw together ideas from across the book to show how our sexual offence policies are problematic, often insufficiently evidence-based; therefore, having the potential to create more harm than good (Kras et al., 2019). The chapter will highlight that sexual offending policy is mainly based upon impulsive, reactionary policymaking and instead argues that we need a much more thoughtful, reflective approach (Beauregard & Lieb, 2011; Tabachnick & McCartan, 2017). The author will use ideas from the decision-making literature (Kahneman, 2011; Evans & Stanovich, 2013) to indicate that we need to use both parts of the dual process model (i.e., thinking, fast and slow) to have more rounded and fit for purpose sexual offence policies. The chapter will finish on evolving international trends in sexual offence–related policymaking, including the new recommendations on the assessment, treatment, and integration of people convicted of a sexual offence back into the community.

Overview of Evidence-based Practice in the Field of Sexual Abuse

The edited collection has covered a range of topics including sexual offending behaviours and its aetiology (Chaps. 1, 2, 3, and 4), assessment of people convicted of a sexual offence (Chaps. 5, 6, 7, and 8), their treatment and rehabilitation (Chaps. 9, 10, 11, 12, and 13), (risk) management (Chaps. 14 and 15), community integration (Chap. 14), and how this can potentially feed into the prevention of sexual offending (Chap. 16). In doing so, the collection has highlighted that sexual offending is complex and nuanced, that there is no simple cause, and that we need to understand each individual's risk (i.e., *what aspects of the individuals' lives makes it more likely that they will (re-)offend*) and protective factors (i.e., *what aspects of the individuals' lives makes it less likely that they will (re-)*

offend). Which becomes a challenge when we start to develop policy around this group, as policy is often direct, easy to translate, and un-nuanced (Beauregard & Lieb, 2011; Tabachnick & McCartan, 2017; Cairney, 2020). Developing sexual offence–related policy means that we need to balance the opinion of the public at large, politicians, professionals (including, criminal justice professional lawyers, social care providers and therapists), and activists/advocates (including, victims, and clients/service users and their support networks), all of whom have differing degrees of power, control, and input into the process (Wilson, 2011; Cairney, 2020). Developing effective sexual offending policies can be, and is, as challenging as working with the people who have committed the offences themselves.

The Policy Development Process

Policy formation is challenging at the best of times; it is often a mixture of political ideology and evidence (Cairney, 2020). However, sometimes the ideology can outweigh the evidence, which is often the case with criminal justice–related policy in general and sexual offence–related policy in particular (Beauregard & Lieb, 2011). This results in policies that are not fit for purpose, cause more harm than good, and even potentially increase the likelihood of reoffending. The sexual offending policy landscape is filled with examples, from sexual offender registration, the disclosure of sexual offender information, the use of the polygraph, housing policies, and longer incarceration (for contemporary and a more in-depth discussion of these issues and more, please see, Laws & O'Donohue, 2016, and, Proulx et al., 2020). Therefore, although punitive policies are popular in the sociopolitical arena (Harper et al., 2017; Socia et al., 2019), they are not fit for purpose in practice as they often negatively impact the desistance pathway (Harris, 2017). Interestingly, these policies are often maintained and developed without regard to the evidence base which begs the question of why they were created and if they were always destined to fail? It is important to note that while there are geographical differences in the development and implementation of sexual offence policies, they exist internationally, to greater or lesser extent (see

Special edition of Sex Offender Treatment, McCartan et al., 2019, for more detail) and are often driven by similar causal factors (i.e., high-profile cases, public outcries, etc.). Some countries have a more evidence-based approach than others (e.g., approaches in the UK and Canada are more evidenced based than the US) in some policies, but no country is completely evidence based with ideology influencing policy and practice. Therefore, the question needs to be asked: How are sexual offence policies in the main created? (See Fig. 18.1.)

Policy development often starts with a "problem" that needs to be resolved and the speed with which it needs to be solved becomes important factors in the process. Good policy development involves a clear, cohesive, and integrated pathway with different interested and relevant

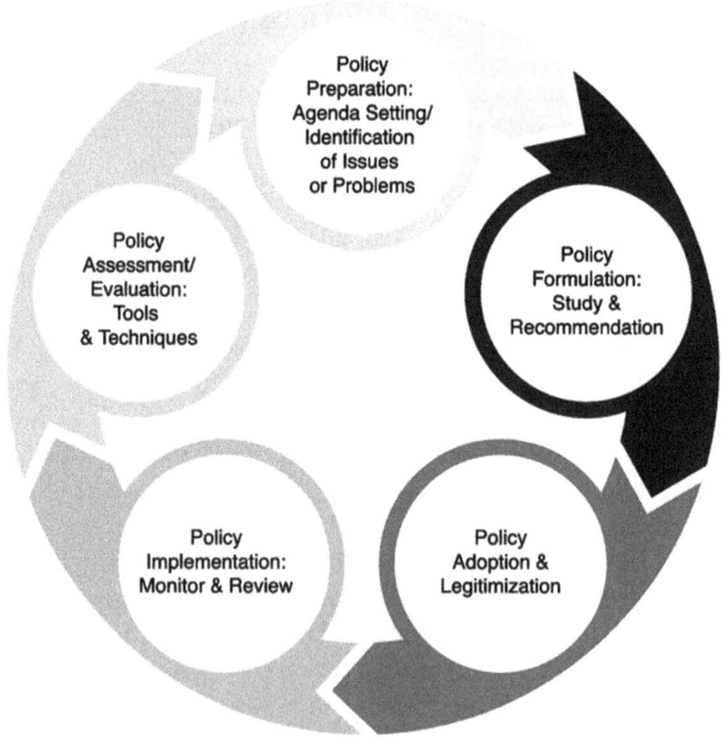

Fig. 18.1 The policymaking process as described by Moonesar (2016)

parties feeding into it (Cairney, 2020). Policy creation is a process that is moved through at different speeds depending on the nature of the problem, the outside influences, and the need to produce an outcome. Different political standpoints view policy development in different ways (for instance, moderate governments tend to be driven by the evidence base and pursue "slow" policy development, whereas extremist governments tend to be ideologically driven and pursue "fast" policy development), all of which influence the process and outcome of the policy that's developed (for more information, please see Cairney, 2020, for a good introduction). Which means that the public, political, media, and professional climate that the policy is being developed in matters. This is especially the case for criminal justice policy. Criminal justice policy, after a period of liberalism in the 1990s and early 2000s, is moving back towards the putative arena that it operated in during the 1970s and 1980s (Kemshall, 2017). Politically the reason for this shift back is the increase in right wing, conservative, governments globally which tend to be more punitive than left wing, or liberal, ones (Millman, 2018). We are seeing an increase in more restrictive policies, cuts to funding, and criminal justice organisations (i.e., police, prisons, and probation) being expected to do more with less. However, it is not all negative as we are seeing increase in multiagency working (Pycroft & Gough, 2019), the development of trauma-informed practice (McCartan, 2020), and a preventive, public health-based approach (Akers et al., 2013) starting to emerge. Hence, if perspectives on people who commit sexual offences, and the reason why they commit these offences, are starting to change towards a more nuanced understanding (see all previous chapters of this book for evidence of this), then how do we correct public policy to make sure it is in line with adapted professional practice? How do we enable politicians and policymakers to think outside of the box while at same time not feel exposed, or that they are ruining their re-election potential? We need broad-based societal, cultural shifts that are simultaneously top-down and bottom-up, which is not easy.

Policy Development in Respect to Sexual Offending: Thinking Slow vs Thinking Fast

In his book, Kahneman (2011) discusses the two main approaches to thinking, and therefore decision-making, in human life. He states that there are two systems of the mind, and therefore decision-making systems, a fast one (automatic, intuitive) and a slow one (reflective, complex). This reflects cognitive psychological research on dual process theory (Evans & Stanovich, 2013); see Table 18.1.

It is important to understand cognitive decision-making to fully realise how public policy is developed, as we are social creatures and all aspects of our sociopolitical lives are constructed (see Andrews, 2012, for a good introduction to the concept). This means that the policies that govern the punishment, rehabilitation, reintegration, and risk management of

Table 18.1 Dual-process model of cognition (Evans & Stanovich, 2013)

Type 1 process (intuitive)	Type 2 process (reflective)
Defining features	
Does not require working memory Autonomous	*Requires working memory Cognitive decoupling; mental simulation*
Typical correlates	
Fast	Slow
High capacity	Capacity limited
Parallel	Serial
Nonconscious	Conscious
Biased responses	Normative responses
Contextualized	Abstract
Automatic	Controlled
Associative	Rule-based
Experience-based decision making	Consequential decision making
Independent of cognitive ability	Correlated with cognitive ability
System 1 (old mind)	**System 2 (new mind)**
Evolved early	Evolved late
Similar to animal cognition	Distinctively human
Implicit knowledge	Explicit knowledge
Basic emotions	Complex emotions

Note. Italicized attributes are the proposed defining characteristics in the current article. Authors proposing two systems include the features attributed to Type 1 and 2 processing but may also include the additional features named people convicted of a sexual offence are constructed in a sociopolitical vacuum; therefore, by changing the parameters of that vacuum, we can change the way that these policies are developed and rolled out. Policy development needs to be a balancing act between the intuitive and the reflective, so that rounded policy can be developed and refined; but often it is not. What we often see is a clear divide between fast and slow policies.

Thinking "fast" uses existing ideological frameworks, is uncomplicated, and reinforces pre-existing biases; therefore, it's easy and flawed; for instance, "all crime is a result of personal, rational choice and therefore punishment acts as a deterrence". Generally speaking, policy development in the arena of sexual offending, and criminal justice in general, is often as a result of impulsive or "knee-jerk" reactions to rare high-profile cases and accompanying community outcry (i.e., the murder of eight-year-old Sarah Payne by Roy Whiting, an individual previously convicted of a sexual offence in the UK), and therefore is created quite quickly (Beauregard & Lieb, 2011), an example of "thinking fast" (Kahneman, 2011) or intuitive processing (Evans & Stanovich, 2013). It is the policy equivalent of an autonomous response or our "fight or flight" response. This can create issues as the policies are often not fully thought through, there can be loopholes, and there may be deficiencies in the capability of practice to implement these changes. However, these reactionary or thinking fast policies fill a sociopolitical void and demonstrate that the government is acting "swiftly" around high-profile cases, and is, therefore, "tough on crime"; but the collateral consequences can be massive and far-reaching (Wilson & Petersilia, 2011; Cairney, 2020). A clear example of this is the development and roll-out of the registration and public disclosure (notification) of information related to people who have committed a sexual offence in the US. Research has demonstrated that the policies have not been well thought through, do not align to the evidence base, and cause more harm than good for the individuals impacted by them and their extended families, which can include stigmatisation, housing issues, employment issues, socio-economic deprivation, mental health, and well-being problems, as well as potential reincarceration (McCartan & Gotch, 2020). However, publicly and politically they are a success and supported (Harris & Socia, 2016; Pickett et al., 2013) as they reinforce notions of punitiveness, naming and shaming, and the ostracisation of people convicted of these offences from society (Frenzel et al., 2014). This is problematic as goes against the strengths-based approach, results in labelling, despair, isolation, and increased capacity for reoffending (Harris, 2017; McCartan et al., 2019).

If "thinking fast" results in the development of problematic policies, the counterargument is that policy development needs to be more thoughtful, more reflective, and a case of "thinking slow". This approach is critical and nuanced, it is challenging and results in different ways of working, and, therefore, it's harder and more complex, for instance, "Crime is a product of social-economic conditions and inequality therefore to prevent crime we have change the fundamental building blocks of society". This approach has its benefits as it means that the policy that is developed is more thoughtful, that there has been more expert and consultative input, and that the policies are less likely to fail; however, it takes longer and is more costly (financially and politically). Slow policy development often does not happen in respect to sexual offending, but when it does, it can challenge and alter problematic practices for the better. A good example of this approach is the one that the UK government took to develop the sexual offender's register (Kemshall et al., 2010). In the UK, the register was developed over a ten-year period, based on existing research and incorporating new pilot research, the government at the time wanted to build something that was fit for purpose (Kemshall et al., 2010). While they looked to the US for their inspiration, they did not simply replicate what they had done; rather, they made it bespoke for the UK's purposes (Kemshall et al., 2010). For instance, after looking at the research, and consulting with experts, on the public disclosure of information on people convicted of a sexual offence, the UK dropped that aspect of the legislation (Kemshall et al., 2010), as have most other countries that have adopted registration policies (Thomas, 2016; McCartan & Gotch, 2020). The development of the registration scheme in the UK (Kemshall et al., 2010) and in New Zealand (McCartan & Laws, 2018) are both examples of "thinking slow" and the development of a piece of reflective public policy. While we may want to see more policies developed in this way, it is becoming more challenging in the current public policy arena, with less time, space, and funding being given to develop policy. We are seeing a shift in language from evidence based (i.e., *policy directly based on research and practice evidence*) to evidence informed (i.e., *policy influenced by research and practice evidence, but it does not necessarily align to it 100%*), which is problematic as evidence informed is a movable feast and, therefore, more challenging to hold to governments to account.

Developing a New Way of Policymaking, "Thinking Fast and Slow"?

What is really needed is a bridge between the two, "thinking fast and slow simultaneously". We need to be able to develop and produce quick evidence-based responses to policy challenges based on clear existing research ("fast" policy), which is then followed by review and refinement processes ("slow" policy"). This may seem like a challenge as policy is a reaction to need, but it is not. Regarding sexual offence policy development, a lot of the variables change (i.e., gender of perpetrator, gender, and age of victim, etc.), while the overarching narratives do not (i.e., sexual offence, risk management failures, re-offending, desistance, etc.). This means that several policy issues (e.g., treatment, housing, registration, and community reintegration) can be identified with existing research and evidence collated, with knowledge gaps being identified as well as researched, resulting in a "slow" ongoing process of policy development and review. Thus, supplying the evidence base that is needed for your "fast" response enables the development of informed reactionary public policy. A parallel process of slow and fast policy develops, while ideal rarely happens; instead, we often engage in the "fast" while ignoring the "slow". Policymakers and governments do not always review, reconsider, and test policy post implementation. This is the important part. We recognise that no policy is ever perfect, but in doing so we have to make sure that it is refined and redeveloped so that it is fit for purpose; therefore, policies need to be able to evolve, radically shift, or even die. Public policy is a process and not an end point; but in criminal justice policy, this is exactly what happens: policies are created quickly, not reviewed, not changed, left to stagnate, and only re-examined if there is a problem with them (Beauregard & Lieb, 2011; Tabachnick & McCartan, 2017).

Best practice, therefore, should be the development of an ongoing, independent review procedure where all polices are examined across a breath of criteria every five years or so. If we can get into this cycle as a matter of course it means that the development of new policies will be thoughtful and considered as their will be an eye towards revision, justification, and definable outcomes. A clear example of this process is the registration and notification policy in the UK where it went through a slow, reflective process, taking ten years to develop, and then it has not been reviewed again since, despite evidence that its underused and not fit for purpose (Hoggett et al., 2020). Good policy needs a clear development life cycle (Cairney, 2020), but unfortunately the development of sexual offending policy does not include that.

When Fast Meets Slow, New Emerging Areas of Policy

In recent years, there has been a slow but steady move to the incorporation of a multidisciplinary approach to understanding and developing policy regarding people convicted of a sexual offence (Pycroft & Gough, 2019). In the main, the field of sexual offending policy is still punitive, but now we are starting to see new ideas based on the evidence base emerging. One of the clearest examples of this is the emergence and use of public health, health, and well-being research feeding into criminal justice policy development, for instance the inclusion of child sexual abuse prevention strategies and bystander intervention training in colleges (Brown, 2017; Tabachnick & McCartan, 2017). Interestingly, these new ideas are not new and have been used in other parts of the criminology field previously like drug policy and youth offending policy, for instance recovery capital (McCartan & Kemshall, 2020), but not in respect to interpersonal violence, especially sexual offending. Sexual offending is a multidisciplinary issue that takes and needs, a multi-agency approach, and therefore any policies that are created around it need to be developed in this way. We have started to see joined-up policy following on from joined-up practice, a bottom-up approach whereby experts and professionals inform the creation of new policies based on good practice. This has resulted in the increased use of first-person language in policy, practice, and research (Willis & Letourneau, 2018; Travers et al., 2020), a growing recognition of the role of past trauma in the lives of people who sexually offend as well as how professionals can effectively recognise this (Janssen, 2018), the importance of life-course criminology and desistance (Blokland & van der Geest, 2015), harm reduction (McCartan & Kemshall, 2020), and a deeper understanding of the role that mental health plays in the offending pathway (Thornton et al., 2017). As a result, we had seen a more nuanced depiction of the person who has committed the offence and recognition that responding to sexual offending needs a developmental, health-based, life-course approach (Tabachnick & McCartan, 2017). We are starting to see the continued development of clear research and practice lines around different types of people who commit sexual abuse (i.e., paedophilia, individuals who offend only in online environments, rapists, etc.), so as to emphasise their nuances in respect to mental health, well-being, and psychosocial development and, therefore, create bespoke prevention and rehabilitation interventions (see, for an in-depth discussion of these issues, Laws & O'Donohue, 2016, and Proulx et al., 2020). It is about harm reduction and self-management, as much as it is about state sanction risk management. This is accompanied by the recognition that more resources and support need to be provided to people with a criminal conviction, especially those who are high need and high risk, to enable them to live an offence-free life. However, with this realisation comes the recognition that this will be expensive, time consuming, and resource intensive. Also, that no programme has 100% success rate and that sometimes it is about accepting the risk of reoffending and finding additional ways to support and risk management the individual. The biggest shift that has happened in the development of the new emerging policy directions related to sexual offending is the recognition that sexual offending can be prevented and that we need to look at new ways to stop first time offending (i.e., primary and secondary prevention) and reoffending (i.e., tertiary and quaternary prevention) (Brown, 2017; Tabachnick & McCartan, 2017). This policy shift indicates that "slow" policy development can, and does, occur but that it takes time and needs to be protected from the negative impact of "fast" policy development.

Current Policy Development in Europe

Currently across Europe, and more broadly afield, there is no coherent policy or framework for preventing sexual abuse and/or managing people who have been convicted of a sexual offence, which means that there are widely disparate practices (see special edition of Sex Offender Treatment, 2018, and McCartan et al., 2020, for a more in-depth discussion). While it is important to recognise the need to see the person who has committed a sexual offence as an individual, what it does mean is that there are few shared values, which need to be built on, a range of good practices that are poorly shared, and a lot of "fast" policy in practice. Recently, in response to this, the Council of Europe decided to develop a series of recommendations, on the assessment, treatment, and management of people accused or convicted of a sexual offence (Council for Penological Co-operation, 2020). The aim of the recommendations is for each of the 47 countries in the Council of Europe to have similar values and criteria and to consider the same good practices so that they can make the informed, evidence-based "slow" policies in this area. The recommendations include guidance on a structured approach to assessment, treatment, interventions, staff training, community management, and media relations, and developing an evidence base in prison as well as in probation for people accused or convicted of a sexual offence. In doing so, the recommendations emphasise the importance of a service user approach, staff understanding and knowledge, that rehabilitation (either as a psychological treatment or as an intervention) should be offered and that a non-offending lifestyle is the end goal of working with this client group. It is hoped that these guidelines will help frame the evolution of "slow" policy development across the Council of Europe and provide a platform for thoughtful, and engaged, "fast" policy when it needs to happen.

Conclusion

The current chapter has highlighted some of the challenges that we face in the development of effective sexual offence related policy. It indicates that although poor, knee-jerk policies may be the norm, they are not best practice, and we need to keep developing a body of thoughtful nuanced policies. The chapter has looked at policymaking through the frame of "thinking, fast and slow" and suggested that we need to develop a policy framework that allows us to do both in a proactive way, rather than as it is currently; we do one or the other retrospectively.

References

Akers, T. A., Potter, R. H., & Hill, C. V. (2013). *Epidemiological criminology: A public health approach to crime and violence*. John Wiley & Sons.

Andrews, T. (2012). What is social constructionism? *The Grounded Theory Review, 11*(1), 39–46.

Beauregard, E., & Lieb, R. (2011). Sex offenders and sex offender policy. In J. Q. Wilson & J. Petersilia (Eds.), *Crime & public policy* (pp. 345–367). Oxford University Press.

Blokland, A., & van der Geest, V. (2015). Life-course transitions and desistance in sex offenders: An event history analysis. In A. Blokland & P. Lussier (Eds.), *Sex offenders: A criminal career approach* (pp. 257–288). Wiley-Blackwell.

Brown, J. (2017). Public health, prevention, & risk management. In K. McCartan & H. Kemshall (Eds.), *Contemporary sex offender risk management, Volume I* (pp. 35–60). Palgrave Macmillan.

Cairney, P. (2020). *Understanding public policy: Theories and issues* (2nd ed.). Red Globe Press.

Council for Penological Co-operation. (2020). Terms of reference valid from: 1 January 2020 until 31 December 2021. Official memo. https://rm.coe.int/adopted-tor-pc-cp-2020-2021-eng/168098e921

Evans, J. S. B. T., & Stanovich, K. E. (2013). Dual-process theories of higher cognition: Advancing the debate. *Perspectives on Psychological Science, 8*(3), 223–241. https://doi.org/10.1177/1745691612460685

Frenzel, E. D., Bowen, K. N., Spraitz, J. D., Bowers, J. H., & Phaneuf, S. (2014). Understanding collateral consequences of registry laws: An examination of the perceptions of sex offender registrants. *Justice Policy Journal, 11*(*2*), 1–22.

Harper, C. A., Hogue, T. E., & Bartels, R. M. (2017). Attitudes towards sexual offenders: What do we know, and why are they important? *Aggression and Violent Behavior, 34*, 201–213. https://doi.org/10.1016/j.avb.2017.01.011

Harris, A. J., & Socia, K. M. (2016). What's in a name? Evaluating the effects of the "Sex Offender" Label on public opinions and beliefs. *Sexual Abuse, 28*(7), 660–678. https://doi.org/10.1177/1079063214564391

Harris, D. A. (2017). *Desistance from sexual offending: Narratives of retirement, regulation and recovery*. Palgrave Macmillan.

Hoggett J, McCartan K, & O'Sullivan J. (2020). Risk, discretion, accountability and control: Police perceptions of sex offender risk management policy in England and Wales. *Criminology & Criminal Justice, 20*(4), 433–450.

Janssen, E. (2018). *Integrating trauma informed care into the treatment of adult male sex offenders: A systematic review.* Retrieved from Sophia, the St. Catherine University repository website: https://sophia.stkate.edu/msw_papers/826Janssen

Kahneman, D. (2011). *Thinking, fast and slow*. Penguin.

Kemshall, H. (2017). The historical evolution of sex offender risk management. In K. McCartan & H. Kemshall (Eds.), *Contemporary sex offender risk management, Volume I* (pp. 1–34). Palgrave Macmillan.

Kemshall, H., Wood, J., & Westwood, S. (2010). *Child Sex offender review (CSOR): Public disclosure pilots, a process evaluation*. Home Office.

Kras, K. R., Morgan, M., Pleggenkuhle, B., & Huebner, B. M. (2019). Compounded stigmatization: Collateral consequences of a sex offence conviction. In B. M. Huebner & N. A. Frost (Eds.), *Handbook on the consequences of sentencing and punishment decisions*. Routledge.

Laws, R., & O'Donohue, W. (2016). *Treatment of sex offenders: Strengths and weaknesses in assessment and intervention*. Springer International Publishing.

McCartan, K., & Kemshall, H. (2020). The potential role of recovery capital in stopping sexual offending: Lessons from circles of support and accountability to enrich practice. *Irish Probation Journal, 17*, 87–106.

McCartan, K., Uzieblo, K., & Smid, W. J. (2020). Professionals' understandings of and attitudes to the prevention of sexual abuse: An international exploratory study. *International Journal of Offender Therapy and Comparative Criminology.* Online First. https://doi.org/10.1177/0306624X20919706

McCartan, K. F. (2018). Special issue: International approaches to sex offender risk assessment and management. *Sexual Offender Treatment, 13*(1/2). http://www.sexual-offender-treatment.org/sot-1-2-2018.html

McCartan, K. F. (2020). *Trauma-informed practice*. HM Inspectorate of Probation. Academic Insights 2020/05.

McCartan, K. F., & Gotch, K. (2020). International approaches to the management of perpetrators of sexual harm policy: Preventative, practical, or political? In J. Proulx, F. Cortoni, L. A. Craig, & E. J. Letourneau (Eds.), *The Wiley handbook on what works with sexual offenders: Contemporary perspectives in theory, assessment, treatment and prevention* (pp. 441–454). Wiley-Blackwell.

McCartan, K. F., Harris, D. A., & Prescott, D. S. (2019). Seen and not heard: The service user's experience through the justice system of individuals convicted of sexual offenses. *International Journal of Offender Therapy and Comparative Criminology*. Online First. https://doi.org/10.1177/0306624X19851671

McCartan, K. F., & Laws, M. (2018). Risk assessment and management of perpetrators of sexual abuse in New Zealand. *Sexual Offender Treatment, 13*(1/2). http://www.sexual-offender-treatment.org/174.html

Millman, N. (2018). Why are right-wing populists winning everywhere? *The Week*. https://theweek.com/articles/804453/why-are-rightwing-populists-winning-everywhere

Moonesar, I. A. (2016). UAE health professionals policy involvement on maternal and child health. In *Conference: Oxford Women's Heath Symposium 2016*. Oxford University. https://www.researchgate.net/publication/299028243_UAE_Health_Professionals_Policy_Involvement_on_Maternal_and_Child_Health

Pickett, J. T., Mancini, C., & Mears, D. P. (2013). Vulnerable victims, monstrous offenders, and unmanageable risk: explaining public opinion on the social control of sex crime. *Criminology, 51*(3), 729–759. https://doi.org/10.1111/1745-9125.12018

Proulx, J., Cortoni, F., Craig, L. A., & Letourneau, E. J. (2020). *The Wiley handbook on what works with sexual offenders: Contemporary perspectives in theory, assessment, treatment and prevention*. Wiley-Blackwell.

Pycroft, A., & Gough, D. (2019). *Multi-agency working in criminal justice: Theory, policy and practice* (2nd ed.). Polity Press.

Socia, K. M., Rydberg, J., & Dum, C. P. (2019). Punitive attitudes toward individuals convicted of sex offenses: A vignette study. *Justice Quarterly*. Online first. https://doi.org/10.1080/07418825.2019.1683218

Tabachnick, J., & McCartan, K. (2017). Sexual harm, public education, and risk management. In K. McCartan & H. Kemshall (Eds.), *Contemporary sex offender risk management, volume I* (pp. 61–87). Palgrave Macmillan.

Thomas, T. (2016). *Policing sexual offences and sex offenders*. Palgrave Macmillan.

Thornton, D., Kelley, S. M., & Nelligan, K. E. (2017). Protective factors and mental illness in men with a history of sexual offending. *Aggression and Violent Behavior, 32*, 29–36. https://doi.org/10.1016/j.avb.2016.12.003

Travers, R., Williams, F., & Willis, G. (2020). Recognising a trailblazer; celebrating a colleague; thanking a friend. *Journal of Sexual Aggression, 26*(2), 145–150. https://doi.org/10.1080/13552600.2020.1774991

Willis, G., & Letourneau, E. (2018). Promoting accurate and respectful language to describe individuals and groups. *Sexual Abuse, 30*(5), 480–483. https://doi.org/10.1177/1079063218783799

Wilson, J. Q. (2011). Crime & public policy. In J. Q. Wilson & J. Petersilia (Eds.), *Crime & public policy* (pp. 619–630). Oxford University Press.

Wilson, J. Q., & Petersilia, J. (2011). *Crime & public policy*. Oxford University Press.

Index[1]

[1] Note: Page numbers followed by 'n' refer to notes.

© The Author(s), under exclusive license to Springer Nature Switzerland AG 2022

K. Uzieblo et al. (eds.), *Challenges in the Management of People Convicted of a Sexual Offence*, Palgrave Studies in Risk, Crime and Society,
https://doi.org/10.1007/978-3-030-80212-7

P

Lightning Source UK Ltd.
Milton Keynes UK
UKHW021128130223
416809UK00002B/51

9 783030 802110